Who are toxic parents?

The Inadequate Parents: Constantly focusing on their own problems, they turn their children into "mini-adults" who take care of them.

The Controllers: They use guilt, manipulation, and even overhelpfulness to direct their children's lives.

The Alcoholics: Mired in denial and chaotic mood swings, their addiction leaves little time or energy for the demands of parenthood.

The Verbal Abusers: Whether overtly abusive or subtly sarcastic, they demoralize their children with constant put-downs and rob them of their self-confidence.

The Physical Abusers: Incapable of controlling their own deep-seated rage, they often blame their children for their own ungovernable behavior.

The Sexual Abusers: Whether flagrantly sexual or covertly seductive, they are the ultimate betrayers, destroying the very heart of childhood—its innocence.

YOU ARE NOT TO BLAME FOR WHAT HAPPENED TO YOU AS A CHILD—BUT YOU CAN DO SOMETHING ABOUT IT NOW!

ALSO BY SUSAN FORWARD, Ph.D.

Betrayal of Innocence

Men Who Hate Women and the Women Who Love Them

Obsessive Love

Emotional Blackmail

When Your Lover Is a Liar

Toxic In-Laws

TOXIC PARENTS

OVERCOMING THEIR HURTFUL LEGACY AND RECLAIMING YOUR LIFE

SUSAN FORWARD, PH.D.

WITH CRAIG BUCK

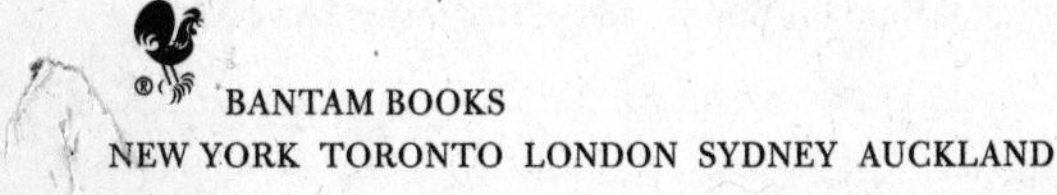

BANTAM BOOKS

NEW YORK TORONTO LONDON SYDNEY AUCKLAND

TOXIC PARENTS
A Bantam Book
Bantam hardcover edition published September 1989
Bantam mass market edition published October 1990
Bantam trade paperback / January 2002

Library of Congress Catalog Card Number: 89-6812.

For information address: Bantam Books.

ISBN 0-553-38140-7

Published simultaneously in the United States and Canada

Bantam Books are published by Bantam Books, a division of Random House, Inc. Its trademark, consisting of the words "Bantam Books" and the portrayal of a rooster, is Registered in U.S. Patent and Trademark Office and in other countries. Marca Registrada. Bantam Books, 1540 Broadway, New York, New York 10036.

PRINTED IN THE UNITED STATES OF AMERICA

BVG 20 19 18 17 16 15 14 13 12

For my children

Acknowledgments

Many people made significant contributions to this work:

Craig Buck, a dedicated and talented writer, gave form to the story I wanted to tell.

Nina Miller, M.F.C.C., a gifted therapist, gave unstintingly of her time, her knowledge, and her support. She is also the most loyal friend anyone could have.

Marty Farash, M.F.C.C., was tremendously generous with his expertise in family systems.

My wonderful editor, Toni Burbank, was, as always, insightful, sensitive, and understanding. I couldn't have asked for a calmer guide through my stormier creative moments.

Linda Grey, President and Publisher of Bantam Books who believed in me and my work from the beginning.

My gratitude is endless to the clients, friends, and others who trusted me with their most intimate feelings and secrets so that other people could be helped. I cannot name them, but they know who they are.

My children, Wendy and Matt, and my friends—especially Dorris Gathrid, Don Weisberg, Jeanne Phillips, Basil Anderman, Lynn Fischer, and Madeline Cain—are my personal rooting section, and I love them all dearly.

My stepfather, Ken Peterson, for his encouragement and many kindnesses to me.

And finally, I want to thank my mother, Harriet Peterson, for her love and support and for having the courage to change.

Contents

Introduction

> Sure, my father used to hit me, but he only did it to keep me in line. I don't see what that has to do with my marriage falling apart.
>
> —Gordon

Gordon, 38, a successful orthopedic surgeon, came to see me when his wife of six years left him. He was desperate to get her back, but she told him she wouldn't even consider coming home until he sought help for his uncontrollable temper. She was frightened by his sudden outbursts and worn down by his relentless criticism. Gordon knew he had a hot temper and that he could be a nag, but still he was shocked when his wife walked out.

I asked Gordon to tell me about himself and guided him with a few questions as he talked. When I asked him about his parents, he smiled and painted a glowing picture, especially of his father, a distinguished midwestern cardiologist:

> If it weren't for him, I wouldn't have become a doctor. He's the best. His patients all think he's a saint.

I asked him what his relationship with his father was like now. He laughed nervously and said:

> It was great . . . until I told him I was thinking about going into holistic medicine. You'd think I wanted to be a mass murderer. I told him about three months ago, and now every time we talk he starts ranting about how he didn't send me to medical school to become a faith healer. It really got bad yesterday. He got upset and told me I should forget I was ever a part of his family. That really hurt. I don't know. Maybe holistic medicine isn't such a good idea.

While Gordon was describing his father, who was obviously not as wonderful as Gordon would have liked me to believe, I noticed that he began to clasp and unclasp his hands in a very agitated way. When he caught himself doing this, he restrained himself by placing his fingertips together in the way that professors often do at their desks. It seemed a gesture he might have picked up from his father.

I asked Gordon whether his father had always been so tyrannical.

> No, not really. I mean, he yelled and screamed a lot, and I got spanked once in a while, like any other kid. But I wouldn't call him a tyrant.

Something about the way he said the word *spanked*, some subtle emotional change in his voice, struck me. I asked him about it. It turned out that his father had "spanked" him two or three times a week with a belt! It hadn't taken much for Gordon to incur a beating: a defiant word, a below-par report card, or a forgotten chore were all sufficiently venal "crimes." Nor was Gordon's father particular about where he beat his child; Gordon recalled being beaten on his back, his legs, his arms, his hands, and his buttocks. I asked Gordon how badly his father had physically hurt him.

GORDON: I didn't bleed or anything. I mean, I turned out okay. He just needed to keep me in line.

SUSAN: But you were scared of him, weren't you?

GORDON: I was scared to death, but isn't that the way it's supposed to be with parents?

SUSAN: Gordon, is that how you'd want your children to feel about you?

Gordon avoided my eyes. This was making him extremely uncomfortable. I pulled my chair closer and continued gently:

> Your wife is a pediatrician. If she saw a child in her office with the same marks on his body that you had on yours from one of your father's "spankings," would she be required by law to report it to the authorities?

Gordon didn't have to answer. His eyes filled with tears at the realization. He whispered:

> I'm getting a terrible knot in my stomach.

Gordon's defenses were down. Though he was in terrible emotional pain, he had uncovered, for the first time, the primary, long-hidden source of his temper. He had been containing a volcano of anger against his father since childhood, and whenever the pressure got too great, he would erupt at whoever was handy, usually his wife. I knew what we had to do: acknowledge and heal the battered little boy inside of him.

When I got home that evening, I found myself still thinking about Gordon. I kept seeing his eyes fill with tears as he realized how he had been mistreated. I thought about the thousands of adult men and women with whom I had worked whose daily lives were being influenced—even controlled—by patterns set during childhood by emotionally destructive parents. I realized there must be millions more who had no idea why their lives weren't working, yet who could be helped. That's when I decided to write this book.

Why Look Back?

Gordon's story is not unusual. I've seen thousands of patients in my eighteen years as a therapist, both in private practice and in hospital groups, and a solid majority have suffered a damaged sense of self-worth because a parent had regularly hit them, or criticized them, or "joked" about how stupid or ugly or unwanted they were, or overwhelmed them with guilt, or sexually abused them, or forced too much responsibility on them, or desperately overprotected them. Like Gordon, few of these people made the connection between their parents and their problems. This is a common emotional blind spot. People simply have trouble seeing that their relationship with their parents has a major impact on their lives.

Therapeutic trends, which used to rely heavily on the analysis of early life experiences, have moved away from the "then" and into the "here and now." The emphasis has shifted to examining and changing current behavior, relationships, and functioning. I believe this shift is due to clients' rejection of the enormous amounts of time and money required for many traditional therapies, often for minimal results.

I am a great believer in short-term therapy that focuses on changing destructive behavior patterns. But my experience has taught me that it is not enough to treat the symptoms; you must also deal with the sources of those symptoms. Therapy is most effective when it proceeds down a double track: both changing current self-defeating behavior and disconnecting from the traumas of the past.

Gordon had to learn techniques to control his anger, but in order to make permanent changes, ones that would stand up under stress, he also had to go back and deal with the pain of his childhood.

Our parents plant mental and emotional seeds in us—seeds that grow as we do. In some families, these are seeds of love, respect, and independence. But in many others, they are seeds of fear, obligation, or guilt.

If you belong to this second group, this book is for you. As you grew into adulthood, these seeds grew into invisible weeds that invaded your life in ways you never dreamed of. Their tendrils may have harmed your relationships, your career, or your family; they have certainly undermined your self-confidence and self-esteem.

I'm going to help you find those weeds and root them out.

What Is a Toxic Parent?

All parents are deficient from time to time. I made some terrible mistakes with my children, which caused them (and me) considerable pain. No parent can be emotionally available all the time. It's perfectly normal for parents to yell at their children once in a while. All parents occasionally become too controlling. And most parents spank their children, even if rarely. Do these lapses make them cruel or unsuitable parents?

Of course not. Parents are only human, and have plenty of problems of their own. And most children can deal with an occasional outburst of anger as long as they have plenty of love and understanding to counter it.

But there are many parents whose negative patterns of behavior are consistent and dominant in a child's life. These are the parents who do the harm.

As I searched for a phrase to describe the common ground that these harmful parents share, the word that kept running through my mind was *toxic*. Like a chemical toxin, the emotional damage inflicted by these parents spreads throughout a child's being, and as the child grows, so does the pain. What better word than *toxic* to describe parents who inflict ongoing trauma, abuse, and denigration on their children, and in most cases continue to do so even after their children are grown?

There are exceptions to the "ongoing" or "repetitive" aspects of this definition. Sexual or physical abuse can be so traumatic that often a single occurrence is enough to cause tremendous emotional damage.

Unfortunately, parenting, one of our most crucial skills, is still very much a seat-of-the-pants endeavor. Our parents learned it primarily from people who may not have done such a good job: their parents. Many of the time-honored techniques that have been passed down from generation to generation are, quite simply, bad advice masquerading as wisdom (remember "spare the rod and spoil the child"?).

What Do Toxic Parents Do to You?

Whether adult children of toxic parents were beaten when little or left alone too much, sexually abused or treated like fools, overprotected or overburdened by guilt, they almost all suffer surprisingly similar symptoms: damaged self-esteem, leading to self-destructive behavior. In one way or another, they almost all feel worthless, unlovable, and inadequate.

These feelings stem, to a great degree, from the fact that children of toxic parents blame themselves for their parents' abuse, sometimes consciously, sometimes not. It is easier for a defenseless, dependent child to feel guilty for having done something "bad" to deserve Daddy's rage than it is for that child to accept the frightening fact that Daddy, the protector, can't be trusted.

When these children become adults, they continue to bear these burdens of guilt and inadequacy, making it extremely difficult for them to develop a positive self-image. The resulting lack of confidence and self-worth can in turn color every aspect of their lives.

Taking Your Psychological Pulse

It's not always easy to figure out whether your parents are, or were, toxic. A lot of people have difficult relationships with their parents. That alone doesn't mean your parents are emotionally destructive. Many people find themselves struggling on the cusp, questioning whether they were mistreated or whether they're being "oversensitive."

I've designed the following questionnaire to help you take the first steps toward resolving that struggle. Some of these questions may make you feel anxious or uncomfortable. That's okay. It is always difficult to tell ourselves the truth about how much our parents may have hurt us. Although it might be painful, an emotional reaction is perfectly healthy.

For the sake of simplicity, these questions refer to parents in the plural, even though your answer may apply to only one parent.

I. Your Relationship with Your Parents When You Were a Child:

1. Did your parents tell you you were bad or worthless? Did they call you insulting names? Did they constantly criticize you?
2. Did your parents use physical pain to discipline you? Did they beat you with belts, brushes, or other objects?
3. Did your parents get drunk or use drugs? Did you feel confused, uncomfortable, frightened, hurt, or ashamed by this?
4. Were your parents severely depressed or unavailable because of emotional difficulties or mental or physical illness?
5. Did you have to take care of your parents because of their problems?
6. Did your parents do anything to you that had to be kept secret? Were you sexually molested in any way?
7. Were you frightened of your parents a great deal of the time?
8. Were you afraid to express anger at your parents?

II. Your Adult Life:

1. Do you find yourself in destructive or abusive relationships?
2. Do you believe that if you get too close to someone, they will hurt and/or abandon you?
3. Do you expect the worst from people? From life in general?
4. Do you have a hard time knowing who you are, what you feel, and what you want?
5. Are you afraid that if people knew the real you, they wouldn't like you?
6. Do you feel anxious when you're successful and frightened that someone will find out you're a fraud?
7. Do you get angry or sad for no apparent reason?
8. Are you a perfectionist?
9. Is it difficult for you to relax or have a good time?
10. Despite your best intentions, do you find yourself behaving "just like your parents"?

III. Your Relationship with Your Parents as an Adult:

1. Do your parents still treat you as if you were a child?
2. Are many of your major life decisions based upon whether your parents would approve?
3. Do you have intense emotional or physical reactions after you spend or anticipate spending time with your parents?
4. Are you afraid to disagree with your parents?
5. Do your parents manipulate you with threats or guilt?
6. Do your parents manipulate you with money?
7. Do you feel responsible for how your parents feel? If they're unhappy, do you feel it's your fault? Is it your job to make it better for them?
8. Do you believe that no matter what you do, it's never good enough for your parents?
9. Do you believe that someday, somehow, your parents are going to change for the better?

If you answered yes to even one-third of these questions, there is a great deal in this book that can help you. Even though some of the chapters may not seem relevant to your situation, it's important to remember that all toxic parents, regardless of the nature of their abuse, basically leave the same scars. For example, your parents may not have been alcoholic, but the chaos, instability, and loss of childhood that typify alcoholic homes are just as real for children of other types of toxic parents. The principles and techniques of recovery are similar for all adult children, as well, so I urge you not to miss any of the chapters.

Freeing Yourself from the Legacy of Toxic Parents

If you are an adult child of toxic parents, there are many things you can do to free yourself from their distorted legacy of guilt and self-doubt. I'll be discussing these various strategies throughout this book. And I want you to proceed with a great deal of hope. Not the deluded hope that your parents will magically change, but the realistic hope that you *can* psychologically unhook from the powerful and destructive influence of your parents. You just have to find the courage. It is within you.

I'll be guiding you through a series of steps that will help you see this influence clearly and then deal with it, regardless of whether you are currently in conflict with your parents, whether you have a civil but surface relationship, whether you haven't seen them for years, or even if one or both are dead!

Strange as it may seem, many people are still controlled by their parents after their deaths. The ghosts that haunt them may not be real in a supernatural sense, but they're very real in a psychological one. A parent's demands, expectations, and guilt trips can linger long after that parent has died.

You may already have recognized your need to free yourself from your parents' influence. Maybe you've even confronted them about it. One of my clients was fond of saying, "My parents don't have any control over my life . . . I hate them and they know it." But she came to realize that by fanning the flames of her anger, her parents were still manipulating her, and the energy she put into her anger was a drain on other parts of her life. Confrontation is an important step in exorcising the ghosts of the past and the demons of the present, but it must never be done in the heat of anger.

"Aren't I Supposed to Be Responsible for the Way I Am?"

By now you may be thinking, "Wait a minute, Susan. Almost all the other books and experts say I can't blame anybody else for my problems."

Baloney. Your parents are accountable for what they did. Of course, you are responsible for your adult life, but that life was largely shaped by experiences over which you had no control. The fact is:

You are *not* responsible for what was done to you as a defenseless child!

You *are* responsible for taking positive steps to do something about it now!

What Can This Book Do for You?

We are beginning an important journey together. It is a journey of truth and discovery. At its end you will find yourself far more in charge of your life than ever before. I'm not going to make grandiose assurances about your problems disappearing magically overnight. But if you have the courage and strength to do the work in this book, you *will* be able to reclaim from your parents much of the power due you as an adult, and most of the dignity due you as a human being.

This work *does* carry an emotional price tag. Once you peel away your defenses, you'll discover feelings of rage, anxiety, hurt, confusion, and especially grief. The destruction of your lifelong image of your parents can elicit powerful feelings of loss and abandonment. I want you to approach the material in this book at your own pace. If some of the work makes you uncomfortable, give it plenty of time. What's important here is progress, not speed.

To illustrate the concepts in this book, I've drawn heavily on case histories from my practice. Some have been directly transcribed from tape recordings, while I've reconstructed others from my notes. All the letters in this book are from my files and have been reproduced exactly as they were written. The unrecorded therapy sessions I've reconstructed are still vivid in my memory, and I've made every effort to re-create them just as they occurred. Only names and identifying circumstances have been changed for legal reasons. None of these cases has been "dramatized."

These cases may seem sensational, but in fact they are typical. I did not search my files for the most provocative or dramatic cases; rather, I chose cases that most clearly represent the types of stories I hear every day. The issues I will raise in this book are not aberrations of the human condition; they are part of it.

This book is divided into two sections. In the first, we will examine how different types of toxic parents operate. We'll explore various ways in which your parents might have hurt you and might still be hurting you. This understanding will prepare you for the second section, in which I'll give you specific behavioral techniques to enable you to reverse the balance of power in your relationships with your toxic parents.

The process of diminishing the negative power of your parents is a gradual one. But it will eventually release your inner strength, the self that's been hiding all these years, the unique and loving person you were meant to be. Together, we'll help free that person so that your life can finally be your own.

PART 1

Toxic Parents

1 | *Godlike Parents*

The Myth of the Perfect Parent

The ancient Greeks had a problem. The gods looked down from their ethereal playground atop Mount Olympus and passed judgment on everything the Greeks were up to. And if the gods weren't pleased, they were swift to punish. They didn't have to be kind; they didn't have to be just; they didn't even have to be right. In fact, they could be downright irrational. At their whim, they could turn you into an echo or make you push a boulder uphill for all eternity. Needless to say, the unpredictability of these powerful gods sowed quite a bit of fear and confusion among their mortal followers.

Not unlike many toxic parent-child relationships. An unpredictable parent is a fearsome god in the eyes of a child.

When we're very young, our godlike parents are everything to us. Without them, we would be unloved, unprotected, unhoused, and unfed, living in a constant state of terror, knowing we were unable to survive alone. They are our all-powerful providers. We need, they supply.

With nothing and no one to judge them against, we assume them to be perfect parents. As our world broadens beyond our crib, we develop a need to maintain this image of perfection as a defense against the great unknowns we increasingly encounter. As long as we believe our parents are perfect, we feel protected.

In our second and third years of life, we begin to assert our independence. We resist toilet training and revel in our "terrible twos." We embrace the word *no* because it allows us to exercise some control over our lives, whereas *yes* is simply an acquiescence. We struggle to develop a unique identity, establish our own will.

The process of separating from parents reaches its peak during puberty and adolescence, when we actively confront parental values, tastes, and authority. In a reasonably stable family, parents are able to withstand much of the anxiety that these changes create. For the most part, they will attempt to tolerate, if not exactly encourage, their child's emerging independence. The expression "it's just a phase" becomes a standard assurance for understanding parents, who remember their own teenage years and appreciate rebellion as a normal stage of emotional development.

Toxic parents aren't so understanding. From toilet training through adolescence, they tend to see rebellion or even individual differences as a personal attack. They defend themselves by reinforcing their child's dependence and helplessness. Instead of promoting healthy development, they unconsciously undermine it, often with the belief that they are acting in their child's best interest. They may use phrases such as "it builds character" or "she needs to learn right from wrong," but their arsenals of negativity really harm their child's self-esteem, sabotaging any budding independence. No matter how much these parents believe they're right, such assaults are confusing to a child, bewildering in their animosity, their vehemence, and their suddenness.

Our culture and our religions are almost unanimous in upholding the omnipotence of parental authority. It's acceptable to express anger at our husbands, wives, lovers, siblings, bosses, and friends, but it's almost taboo to assertively confront our parents.

How often have we heard the phrases "don't talk back to your mother" or "don't you dare shout at your father"? The Judeo-Christian tradition enshrines the taboo in our collective unconscious by pronouncing "God the Father" and directing us to "honor thy father and mother." The idea finds voices in our schools, our churches, our government ("a return to family values"), even in our corporations. According to the conventional wisdom, our parents are empowered to control us simply because they gave us life.

The child is at the mercy of his godlike parents and, like the ancient Greeks, never knows when the next lightning bolt will strike. But the child of toxic parents knows that the lightning *is* coming sooner or later. This fear becomes deeply ingrained and grows with the child. At the core of every formerly mistreated adult—even high achievers—is a little child who feels powerless and afraid.

The Cost of Appeasing the Gods

As a child's self-esteem is undermined, his dependence grows, and with it his need to believe that his parents are there to protect and provide. The only way emotional assaults or physical abuse can make sense to a child is if he or she accepts responsibility for the toxic parent's behavior.

No matter how toxic your parents might be, you still have a need to deify them. Even if you understand, on one level, that your father was wrong to beat you, you may still believe he was justified. Intellectual understanding is not enough to convince your emotions that you were not responsible.

As one of my clients put it: "I thought they were perfect, so when they treated me badly, I figured I was bad."

There are two central doctrines in this faith of godlike parents:

1. "I am bad and my parents are good."
2. "I am weak and my parents are strong."

These are powerful beliefs that can long outlive your physical dependence on your parents. These beliefs keep the faith alive; they allow you to avoid facing the painful truth that your godlike parents actually betrayed you when you were most vulnerable.

Your first step toward controlling your life is to face that truth for yourself. It will take courage, but if you're reading this book, you've already made a commitment to change. That took courage, too.

"They Never Let Me Forget How I Disgraced Them"

Sandy, 28, a striking brunette who seemed to "have it all," was seriously depressed when she first came to see me. She told me that she was unhappy with everything in her life. She had been a floral designer for several years at a prestigious shop. She had always dreamed of opening her own business, but she was convinced that she wasn't smart enough to succeed. She was terrified of failure.

Sandy had also been trying to get pregnant for more than two years, with no success. As we talked, I began to see that her inability to get pregnant was causing her to feel strong resentment toward her husband and inadequate in their relationship, despite the fact that he sounded genuinely understanding and loving. A recent conversation with her mother had aggravated the issue:

> This whole pregnancy has become a real obsession with me. When I had lunch with my mom I told her how disappointed I was. She said to me, "I'll bet it's that abortion you had. The Lord works in mysterious ways." I haven't been able to stop crying since. She never lets me forget.

I asked her about the abortion. After some initial hesitancy, she told me the story:

> It happened when I was in high school. My parents were very, very strict Catholics, so I went to parochial school. I developed early, and by the time I was twelve, I was five-foot-

> six, weighed one hundred thirty pounds, and wore a 36-C bra. Boys started paying attention to me, and I really liked it. It drove my dad crazy. The first time he caught me kissing a boy good night, he called me a whore so loud that the whole neighborhood heard. It was downhill from there. Every time I went out with a boy, Dad told me I was going to hell. He never let up. I figured I was damned anyway, so when I was fifteen I slept with this guy. Just my luck, I got pregnant. When my folks found out, they went nuts. Then I told them I wanted an abortion; they totally lost it. They must have screamed at me about "mortal sin" a thousand times. If I wasn't going to hell already, they were sure this would clinch it. The only way I could get them to sign a consent was to threaten to kill myself.

I asked Sandy how things went for her after the abortion. She slumped down in her chair with a dejected look that made my heart ache.

> Talk about a fall from grace. I mean, Dad made me feel horrible enough before, but now I felt like I didn't even have a right to exist. The more ashamed I felt, the harder I tried to make things right. I just wanted to turn back the clock, get back the love I had when I was little. But they never miss a chance to bring it up. They're like a broken record about what I did and how I disgraced them. I can't blame them. I should've never done what I did—I mean, they had such high moral expectations for me. Now I just want to make it up to them for hurting them so bad with my sins. So I do anything they want me to do. It drives my husband crazy. He and I get in these huge fights about it. But I can't help it. I just want them to forgive me.

As I listened to this lovely young woman, I was very touched by the suffering her parents' behavior had caused her and by how much she needed to deny their responsibility for that suffering. She seemed almost desperate to convince me that she was to blame for all that happened to her. Sandy's self-blame was compounded by her parents' unyielding religious beliefs. I knew I had my work cut out for me if Sandy was to see how genuinely cruel and emotionally abusive her parents had been to her. I decided this was not a time to be nonjudgmental.

SUSAN: You know something? I'm really angry for that young girl. I think your parents were awful to you. I think they misused your religion to punish you. I don't think you deserved any of it.

SANDY: I committed two mortal sins!

SUSAN: Look, you were just a kid. Maybe you made some mistakes, but you don't have to keep paying for them forever. Even the Church lets you atone and get on with your life. If your parents were as good as you say they are, they would have shown some compassion for you.

SANDY: They were trying to save my soul. If they didn't love me so much, they wouldn't care.

SUSAN: Let's look at this from a different perspective. What if you hadn't had that abortion? And you had a little girl. She'd be about sixteen now, right?

Sandy nodded, trying to figure out where I was headed.

SUSAN: Suppose she got pregnant? Would you treat her like your parents treated you?

SANDY: Not in a million years!

Sandy realized the implications of what she'd said.

SUSAN: You'd be more loving. And your parents should have been more loving. That's their failure, not yours.

Sandy had spent half her life constructing an elaborate wall of defense. Such defensive walls are all too common among adult children of toxic parents. They can be made of a variety of psychological building blocks, but the most common, the primary material in Sandy's wall, is a particularly obstinate brick called "denial."

The Power of Denial

Denial is both the most primitive and the most powerful of psychological defenses. It employs a make-believe reality to minimize, or even negate, the impact of certain painful life experiences. It even makes some of us forget what our parents did to us, allowing us to keep them on their pedestals.

The relief provided by denial is temporary at best, and the price for this relief is high. Denial is the lid on our emotional pressure cooker: the longer we leave it on, the more pressure we build up. Sooner or later, that pressure is bound to pop the lid, and we have an emotional crisis. When that happens, we have to face the truths we've been so desperately trying to avoid, except now we've got to face them during a period of extreme stress. If we can deal with our denial up front, we can avoid the crisis by opening the pressure valve and leting it out easily.

Unfortunately, your own denial is not the only denial you may have to contend with. Your parents have denial systems of their own. When you are struggling to reconstruct the truth of your past, especially when that truth reflects poorly on them, your parents may insist that "it wasn't so bad," "it didn't happen that way," or even that "it didn't happen at all." Such statements can frustrate your attempts to reconstruct your personal history, leading you to question your own impressions and memories. They undercut your confidence in your ability to perceive reality, making it that much harder to rebuild your self-esteem.

Sandy's denial was so strong that not only couldn't she see her own reality, she couldn't even acknowledge that there was another reality to see. I empathized with her pain, but I had to get her at least to consider the possibility that she had a false image of her parents. I tried to be as nonthreatening as possible:

> I respect the fact that you love your parents and that you believe they're good people. I'm sure they did some very good things for you when you were growing up. But there's got to be a part of you that knows or at least senses that loving parents don't assault their child's dignity and self-worth so relentlessly. I don't want to pull you away from your parents or your religion. You don't have to disown them or renounce the Church. But a big part of lifting your depression may depend on giving up the fantasy that they're perfect. They were cruel to you. They hurt you. Whatever you did, you had already done. No amount of haranguing from them was going to change that. Can't you feel how deeply they hurt the sensitive young girl inside of you? And how unnecessary it was?

Sandy's "yes" was barely audible. I asked her if it scared her to think about it. She just nodded, unable to talk about the depth of her fear. But she was brave enough to hang in there.

The Hopeless Hope

After two months in therapy, Sandy had made some progress but was still clinging to the myth of her perfect parents. Until she shattered that myth, she would continue to blame herself for all the unhappiness of her life. I asked her to invite her parents to a therapy session. I hoped that if I could get them to see how deeply their behavior had affected Sandy's life, they might admit some of their responsibility, making it easier for Sandy to begin repairing her negative self-image.

We barely had time to get acquainted before her father blurted:

> You don't know what a bad kid she was, Doctor. She went nuts over boys and kept leading them on. All of her problems today are because of that damned abortion.

I could see tears well up in Sandy's eyes. I rushed to defend her:

> That's not the reason Sandy is having problems, and I didn't ask you here to read me a laundry list of her crimes. We really won't get anywhere if that's all you're here for.

It didn't work. Throughout the session, Sandy's mother and father took turns attacking their daughter, despite my admonitions. It was a long hour. After they left, Sandy was quick to apologize for them:

> I know they really didn't come through for me today, but I hope you liked them. They're really good people, they just seemed nervous to be here. Maybe I shouldn't have asked them to come. . . . It probably upset them. They're not used to this kind of thing. But they really love me . . . just give them some time, you'll see.

This session and a few subsequent ones with Sandy's parents clearly indicated how closed-minded they were to anything that challenged their perception of Sandy's problems. At no point was either one willing to acknowledge any responsibility for those problems. And Sandy continued to idolize them.

"They Were Only Trying to Help"

For many adult children of toxic parents, denial is a simple, unconscious process of pushing certain events and feelings out of conscious awareness, pretending that those events never happened. But others, like Sandy, take a more subtle approach: rationalization.

When we rationalize, we use "good reasons" to explain away what is painful and uncomfortable.

Here are a few typical rationalizations:

- My father only screamed at me because my mother nagged him.
- My mother only drank because she was lonely. I should have stayed home with her more.
- My father beat me, but he didn't mean to hurt me, he only meant to teach me a lesson.
- My mother never paid any attention to me because she was so unhappy.
- I can't blame my father for molesting me. My mother wouldn't sleep with him, and men need sex.

All these rationalizations have one thing in common: they serve to make the unacceptable acceptable. On the surface, it may appear to work, but a part of you always knows the truth.

"He Only Did It Because . . ."

Louise, a small, auburn-haired woman in her midforties, was being divorced by her third husband. She came into therapy at the insistence of her adult daughter, who threatened to cut off her relationship with Louise if she didn't do something about her uncontrollable hostility.

When I first saw Louise, her extremely rigid posture and tight-lipped expression said it all. She was a volcano of contained anger. I asked her about her divorce and she told me that the men in her life always left her; her current husband was just the latest example:

> I'm one of those women who always picks Mr. Wrong. In the beginning of each relationship, it's terrific, but I know it can never last.

I listened intently as Louise expounded on the theme that all men are bastards. Then she began comparing the men in her life to her father:

> God, why can't I find somebody like my father? He looked like a movie star . . . everyone just adored him. I mean he had that charisma that just drew people to him. My mother was sick a lot, and my father would take me out . . . just him and me. Those were the best times in my life. After my dad, they just broke the mold.

I asked her if her father was still alive and Louise became very tense as she replied:

> I don't know. He just disappeared one day. I guess I was around ten. My mother was a real bitch to live with, and one day he just took off. No note, no phone call, no nothing. God, I missed him. For about a year after he left, I was so sure I could hear his car drive up every night. . . . I can't really blame him for what he did. He was so full of life. Who'd want to be tied down to a sick wife and a kid?

Louise was spending her life waiting for her idealized father to come back to her. Unable to face how callous and irresponsible he had been, Louise used extensive rationalization to keep him godlike in her eyes—despite the unspeakable pain his behavior had caused her.

Her rationalization also enabled her to deny her rage at him for abandoning her. Unfortunately, that rage found an outlet in her relationships with other men. Every time she started seeing a man, things would go smoothly for a while, as she got to know him. But as they grew closer, her fear of abandonment would get out of hand. The fear would invariably turn into hostility. She couldn't see a pattern in the fact that every man left her for the same reasons: the closer they got, the more hostile she became. Instead, she insisted her hostility was justified by the fact that they always left her.

Anger Where Anger Is Due

When I was in graduate school, one of my psychology books contained a series of drawings that graphically illustrated how people displace feelings—particularly anger. The first frame showed a man being bawled out by his boss. Obviously, it wasn't safe for the man to yell back, so the second frame showed him displacing his anger by yelling at his wife when he got home. The third showed her yelling at the kids. The kids kicked the dog, and the dog bit the cat. What impressed me about this series of images was that, despite its seeming simplicity, it is a surprisingly accurate portrayal of how we transfer strong feelings from the appropriate person to an easier target.

Louise's opinion of men is a perfect example: "They are such wimpy bastards . . . all of them. You can't trust them. They always turn on you. I'm sick of being used by men."

Louise's father had abandoned her. If she had acknowledged this fact, she would have had to renounce her cherished fantasies and godlike image of him. She would have had to let him go. Instead, she displaced her anger and mistrust from her father to other men.

Without being aware of it, Louise consistently chose men who treated her in ways that both disappointed and enraged her. As long as she could release her anger at men in general, she didn't have to feel her anger at her father.

Sandy, whom we met earlier in this chapter, displaced onto her husband the anger and disappointment she felt toward her parents for the way they had treated her pregnancy and abortion. She couldn't allow herself to be angry at her parents—that would have been too threatening to her deification of them.

Don't Speak Ill of the Dead

Death does not end the deification of toxic parents. In fact, it may increase it.

As hard as it is to acknowledge the harm done by a living parent, it is infinitely harder to accuse that parent once he or she is dead. There's a powerful taboo against criticizing the dead, as if we were kicking them while they're down. As a result, death imparts a sort of sainthood to even the worst abuser. The deification of dead parents is almost automatic.

Unfortunately, while the toxic parent is protected by the sanctity of the grave, the survivors are stuck with the emotional remains. "Don't speak ill of the dead" may be a treasured platitude, but it often inhibits the realistic resolution of conflicts with dead parents.

"You'll Always Be My Little Failure"

Valerie, a tall, delicate-featured musician in her late thirties, was referred to me by a mutual friend who was concerned that Valerie's lack of confidence was preventing her from pursuing opportunities in her singing career. About fifteen minutes into our first session, Valerie admitted that her career was going nowhere:

> I haven't had any kind of a singing job—not even a piano bar—for over a year. I've been working temp in an office to pay my rent. I don't know. Maybe it's an impossible dream. The other night I was having dinner with my folks, and we got into my problems, and my father said, "Don't worry. You'll always be my little failure." I'm sure he didn't realize how much it hurt, but those words really tore me apart.

I told Valerie that anyone would feel hurt under the circumstances. Her father had been cruel and insulting. She replied:

> I guess that's nothing new. It's the story of my life. I was the family garbage dump. I got blamed for everything. If he and my mom had problems, it was my fault. He was like a broken record. And yet, when I did anything to please him, he would beam with pride and brag about me to his cronies. God, it was wonderful to get his approval, but I felt like an emotional yo-yo sometimes.

Valerie and I worked very closely together over the next several weeks. She was just beginning to contact the magnitude of her anger and sadness toward her father.

Then he died of a stroke.

It was an unexpected death—shocking, sudden; the kind for which no one is prepared. Valerie was overwhelmed by guilt for all the anger she had expressed toward him in therapy.

> I sat there in church while he was being eulogized and I heard this outpouring of how wonderful he was all his life, and I felt like I was being an asshole for trying to blame him for my own problems. I just wanted to atone for the pain I'd caused him. I kept thinking about how much I loved him and what a bitch I'd always been to him. I don't want to talk about the bad stuff anymore . . . none of that matters now.

Valerie's grief got her off the track for a time, but eventually she came to see that her father's death could not change the reality of how he had treated her during childhood and as an adult.

Valerie has been in therapy for almost six months now. I've been happy to see her self-confidence improve steadily. She is still struggling to get her singing career off the ground, but it's no longer due to lack of trying.

Taking Them Down Off Their Pedestals

Godlike parents make rules, make judgments, and make pain. When you deify your parents, living or dead, you are agreeing to live by their version of reality. You are accepting painful feelings as a part of your life, perhaps even rationalizing them as being good for you. It's time to stop.

When you bring your toxic parents down to earth, when you find the courage to look at them realistically, you can begin to equalize the power in your relationship with them.

2 | "Just Because You Didn't Mean It Doesn't Mean It Didn't Hurt"

The Inadequate Parents

Children have basic inalienable rights—to be fed, clothed, sheltered, and protected. But along with these physical rights, they have the right to be nurtured emotionally, to have their feelings respected, and to be treated in ways that allow them to develop a sense of self-worth.

Children also have the right to be guided by appropriate parental limits on their behavior, to make mistakes, and to be disciplined without being physically or emotionally abused.

Finally, children have a right to *be* children. They have a right to spend their early years being playful, spontaneous, and irresponsible. Naturally, as children grow older, loving parents will nourish their maturity by giving them certain responsibilities and household duties, but never at the expense of childhood.

How We Learn to Be in the World

Children soak up both verbal and nonverbal messages like sponges—indiscriminately. They listen to their parents, they watch their parents, and they imitate their parents' behavior. Because they have little frame of reference outside the family, the things they learn at home about themselves and others become universal truths engraved deeply in their minds. Parental role models are central to a child's developing sense of identity—particularly as he or she develops gender identity. Despite dramatic changes in parental roles over the last twenty years, the same duties apply to parents today that applied to your parents:

1. They must provide for their children's physical needs.
2. They must protect their children from physical harm.
3. They must provide for their children's needs for love, attention, and affection.
4. They must protect their children from emotional harm.
5. They must provide moral and ethical guidelines for their children.

Clearly, the list could go on much longer, but these five responsibilities form the foundation of adequate parenting. The toxic parents we'll be discussing rarely get past the first item on the list. For the most part, they are (or were) significantly impaired in their own emotional stability or mental health. They are not only often unavailable to meet their children's needs, but in many cases they expect and demand that their children take care of the *parents'* needs.

When a parent forces parental responsibilities on a child, family roles become indistinct, distorted, or reversed. A child who is compelled to become his own parent, or even become a parent to his own parent, has no one to emulate, learn from, and look up to. Without a parental role model at this critical state of emotional development, a child's personal identity is set adrift in a hostile sea of confusion.

Les, 34, the owner of a sporting goods store, came to see me because he was a workaholic and it was making him miserable.

> My marriage went to hell because I never did anything but work. I was either gone or I was working at home. My wife got tired of living with a robot, and she left. Now it's happening again with the new lady in my life. I hate it. I really do. But I just don't know how to loosen up.

Les told me he had trouble expressing emotion of any kind, particularly tender, loving feelings. The word *fun*, he told me with considerable bitterness, wasn't in his vocabulary.

> I wish I knew how to make my girlfriend happy, but every time we start to talk, somehow I always steer the conversation back to work, and she gets upset. Maybe it's because work is the only thing I don't screw up.

Les continued for the better part of a half hour trying to convince me of how badly he messed up his relationships:

> The women I get involved with are always complaining that I don't give them enough time or affection. And it's true. I'm a lousy boyfriend and I was a really lousy husband.

I stopped him and said: "And you've got a lousy self-image. It sounds as if the only time you feel okay is when you're working. How come?"

> It's something I know how to do . . . and I do it well. I work about seventy-five hours a week . . . but I've always worked my tail off . . . ever since I was a kid. See, I was the oldest of

> three boys. I guess my mom had some kind of breakdown when I was eight. From then on, our house was always dark, with the shades drawn. My mother always seemed to be in her bathrobe, and she never talked much. My earliest memories of her were with a cup of coffee in one hand, a cigarette in the other, and glued to her goddamned soap operas. She never got up until long after we were off to school. So, it was my job to feed my two younger brothers, pack their lunches, and get them to the school bus. When we got home, she'd be lying in front of the tube or taking one of her three-hour naps. Half the time while my buddies were out playing ball, I was stuck in the house cooking dinner or cleaning up. I hated it, but somebody had to do it.

I asked Les where his father was in all of this.

> Dad traveled a lot on business, and he basically just gave up on my mother. Most of the time, he slept in the guest room . . . it was a pretty weird marriage. He sent her to a couple of doctors, but they didn't help, so he just threw in the towel.

I told Les that I ached for how lonely that little boy must have been. He dismissed my sympathy with the reply:

> I had too much to do to feel sorry for myself.

Robbers of Childhood

As a child, Les was often weighed down with responsibilities that rightfully belonged to his parents. Because he was forced to grow up too fast and too soon, Les was robbed of his childhood. While his friends were out playing ball, Les was home performing his parents' duties. To keep the family together, Les had to become a miniature adult. He had little opportunity to be playful or carefree. Since his own needs were virtually ignored, he learned to cope with loneliness and emotional deprivation by denying that he even had needs. He was there to take care of others. *He* didn't matter.

What makes this doubly sad is that in addition to having been the primary caretaker of his brothers, Les also became a parent to his mother:

> When Dad was in town, he would leave for work at seven and lots of times he wouldn't get home till nearly midnight. On his way out the door, he would always tell me, "Don't forget to do all your homework, and be sure to take care of your mother. Make sure she has enough to eat. Keep the other kids quiet . . . and see if you can do something to get a smile out of her." I spent a lot of time trying to figure out how to make my mother happy. I was so sure there was something that I could do and everything would be okay again . . . *she'd* be okay again. But no matter what I did, nothing changed. It still hasn't. I really feel rotten about that.

In addition to his housekeeping and childrearing responsibilities, which would have been overwhelming for any child, Les was expected to be his mother's emotional caretaker. This turned out to be a recipe for failure. Children who are caught in these confusing role reversals are constantly falling short. It's impossible for them to function as adults because they're *not* adults. But they don't understand why they fail; they just feel deficient and guilty because of it.

In Les's case, his driving need to work many hours beyond what was necessary served a dual purpose: it kept him from confronting the loneliness and deprivation of both his childhood and his adult life, and it reinforced his long-held belief that he could never do enough. Les's fantasy was that if he could put in enough hours, he could prove that he really was a worthwhile, adequate person, that he really could get the job done right. In essence, he was still trying to make his mother happy.

When Does It Ever Stop?

Les didn't see that his parents continued to wield their toxic power over him in his adult life. A few weeks later, however, the connection between his adult struggles and his childhood moved sharply into focus.

> Boy, whoever said "the more things change, the more they stay the same" really knew what he was talking about. I've been in L.A. for six years now, but as far as my folks are concerned, I'm not supposed to have a life. They call me a couple of times a week. It's gotten to the point where I'm afraid to answer the phone. First, my father starts in with: "Your mom's so depressed . . . couldn't you just take a little time off and come visit? You know how much it would mean to her!" Then she gets on and tells me I'm her whole life and she doesn't know how much longer she'll be around. What do you say to that? Half the time, I just jump on a plane . . . it beats dealing with the guilt of not going. But it's never enough. Nothing is. I might as well save the plane fare. Maybe I never should have moved away.

I told Les that it was typical for children who were forced to exchange emotional roles with their parents to carry into their adult lives tremendous guilt and an overdeveloped sense of responsibility. As adults, they often become trapped in a vicious cycle of accepting responsibility for everything, inevitably falling short, feeling guilty and inadequate, and then redoubling their efforts. This is a draining, depleting cycle that leads to an ever-increasing sense of failure.

Driven as a little boy by the expectations of his parents, Les learned early that his goodness was judged primarily by how much he did for the rest of his family. As an adult, his parents' external demands were transformed into internal demons that continued to drive him in the one area where he could feel some sense of worth—work.

Les had neither the time nor the appropriate role model from which to learn about the giving and receiving of love. He grew up without nourishment of his emotional life, so he simply turned off his emotions. Unfortunately, he found that he couldn't turn them back on again, even when he wanted to.

I assured Les that I understood how frustrated and bewildered he felt about his inability to open up to anyone emotionally, but I urged him to go easy on himself. He hadn't had anyone to teach him those things when he was young, and they're pretty tough to pick up on your own.

"It would be like expecting yourself to play a piano concerto when you didn't even know where middle-C was!" I told him. "You can learn, but you've got to give yourself time to pick up the basics, to practice, and maybe even to fail once or twice."

"If I Don't Take Care of Their Needs, Who Will?"

> Dear Abby:
> I'm in a crazy family. Can you get me out of here?
>
> —Hopeless

This was written by one of my clients, Melanie, when she was 13. Now a 42-year-old divorced tax accountant, Melanie came to see me because of severe depression. Although she was extremely thin, she would have been quite pretty if the recent months of erratic sleep hadn't taken their toll. She was open and talked easily about herself.

> I feel utterly hopeless all the time. Like my life is out of control. I just can't get on top of things. I feel like I'm digging myself deeper and deeper into a hole every day.

I asked her to be more specific. She bit her lip, then turned away from me as she replied:

> There's such an emptiness inside me . . . I don't think I've ever felt connected to anybody in my whole life. I've been married twice, and I've lived with several guys, but I just can't find the right one. I always pick either lazy bums or total bastards. Then of course it's up to me to set them straight. I always think I can fix them. I lend them money, I move them into my house, I've even found jobs for a couple of them. It never works, but I never learn. They don't love me, no matter how much I do for them. One of these guys hit me in front of my kids. Another took off with my car. My first husband played around. My second husband was a total lush. Some track record.

Without realizing it, Melanie was describing the classic behavior of a co-dependent personality. Originally, the term *co-dependent* was used specifically to describe the partner of an alcoholic or drug addict. *Co-dependent* was used interchangeably with the term *enabler*—someone whose life was out of control because he or she was taking responsibility for "saving" a chemically dependent person.

But in the past few years the definition of co-dependency has expanded to include all people who victimize themselves in the process of rescuing and being responsible for any compulsive, addicted, abusive, or excessively dependent person.

Melanie was attracted to very troubled men. She believed that if she could just be good enough—give enough, love enough, worry enough, help enough, cover up enough—and get them to see the error of their ways, they would love her. But they didn't. The kind of needy, self-centered men whom she picked were incapable of love. So, instead of finding the love she so desperately sought, she found emptiness. She felt used.

I discovered that the term *co-dependent* was not new to Melanie. She had first come across it when she attended a meeting of Al-Anon (a Twelve-Step program for family members of alcoholics) during her marriage to her alcoholic husband. She was certain that she wasn't a co-dependent but just had bad luck with men. She certainly had done everything she could to get Jim to stop drinking. She had finally left him when she learned he had spent a night with a woman he'd met in a bar.

Melanie once again had begun looking for Mr. Right. She blamed her problems on the men she'd been with, but she saw each one as a separate Mr. Wrong. She didn't see that the overall pattern stemmed from the way she chose her men. She thought she was looking for a man who could appreciate a giving, caring, loving, helpful woman. Surely there was a man out there who would love a woman like that. She thought co-dependency was noble.

Melanie had no idea that what she called "giving and helping" was wiping her out. She was giving to everyone except herself. She had no idea that she had actually perpetuated the irresponsible behavior of the men in her life by sweeping up behind them. When she talked about her childhood, it became clear that her pattern of trying to save troubled men was a compulsive repetition of her relationship with her father:

> I had a really weird family. My father was a successful architect, but he used his damn moods to control everybody. He'd come unglued by the slightest thing . . . like if somebody parked in his parking place or if I had a fight with my brother. He'd just go into his room, shut the door, throw himself on the bed, and cry. Just like a baby! Then my mother would fall apart and go soak in the bathtub, and I was the one who had to go in and deal with my dad. I'd just sit there, with him sobbing, trying to figure out what I could do to make

him feel better. But it didn't matter what I did, it was always just a matter of waiting it out.

I handed Melanie a checklist I had made up and asked her to tell me which points described her feelings and behavior. It was a list of the major characteristics of co-dependency. I've found it very useful over the years in helping clients determine whether they are co-dependent. If you think this term may apply to you, please go through the list.

Co-Dependency Checklist

I use "him" as a universal pronoun to refer to a troubled person of either gender. I realize that many men are in co-dependent relationships with deeply troubled wives or lovers.

1. Solving his problems or relieving his pain is the most important thing in my life—no matter what the emotional cost to me.
2. My good feelings depend on approval from him.
3. I protect him from the consequences of his behavior. I lie for him, cover up for him, and never let others say anything bad about him.
4. I try very hard to get him to do things my way.
5. I don't pay any attention to how I feel or what I want. I only care about how he feels and what he wants.
6. I will do anything to avoid getting rejected by him.
7. I will do anything to avoid making him angry at me.
8. I experience much more passion in a relationship that is stormy and full of drama.
9. I am a perfectionist and I blame myself for everything that goes wrong.
10. I feel angry, unappreciated, and used a great deal of the time.
11. I pretend that everything is fine when it isn't.
12. The struggle to get him to love me dominates my life.

Melanie answered "yes" to every statement! She was astounded to see how truly co-dependent she was. To help her begin to break out of these patterns, I told her it was essential that she make the connection between her co-dependency and her relationship with her father. I asked her to remember how she had felt when he cried.

> At first it really scared me because I thought Daddy was dying and then who would be my daddy? Then I started feeling ashamed to see him that way. But mostly I felt this terrible guilt—that it was my fault because I had picked a fight with my brother or whatever. Like I'd really let him down. The worst of it was that I felt so helpless because I couldn't make him happy. What's amazing is, he's been dead for four years, I'm forty-two years old, I've got two kids of my own, and I *still* feel guilty.

Melanie was forced to be her father's caretaker. Both her parents placed their adult responsibilities squarely on her young shoulders. At a time in her life when she needed a strong father to give her self-confidence, she found herself having to pamper an infantile father instead.

Melanie's first and most profound emotional relationship with a man was with her father. As a child she was overwhelmed by both her father's neediness and the guilt she felt when she couldn't satisfy his demands. She never stopped trying to make up for her inability to make him happy, even when he wasn't around. She just found substitute needy, troubled men to take care of. Her choice of men was dictated by her need to assuage her guilt, and by choosing the father substitutes that she did, she perpetuated the emotional deprivation she had experienced as a child.

I asked Melanie whether her mother had provided any of the love or attention that she never got from her father.

> My mother tried, but she was sick a lot of the time. She was always running to doctors and had to stay in bed when her

colitis acted up. They'd prescribe tranquilizers and she'd eat them like popcorn. I guess she got pretty hooked, I don't know. She was always out of it. Our housekeeper really raised us. I mean my mother was there, but she wasn't *there*. When I was about thirteen, I wrote that letter to Dear Abby. The damnedest thing was that my mother actually found it. You'd think she would've come to me and asked what I was so upset about, but I guess what I felt didn't matter to her. It was almost like I didn't exist.

The Invisible Child

Parents who focus their energies on their own physical and emotional survival send a very powerful message to their children: "Your feelings are not important. I'm the only one who counts." Many of these children, deprived of adequate time, attention, and care, begin to feel invisible—as if they don't even exist.

In order for children to develop a sense of self-worth—a sense that they do more than occupy space, that they matter and are important—they need their parents to validate their needs and feelings. But Melanie's father's emotional needs were so overwhelming that he never noticed Melanie's needs. She was there when he cried, but he did not reciprocate. Melanie knew that her mother had found her letter to Dear Abby, yet her mother never mentioned it to her. The message from both parents was loud and clear: she was a nonentity to them. Melanie learned to define herself in terms of *their* feelings instead of her own. If she made them feel good, *she* was good. If she made them feel bad, *she* was bad.

As a result, Melanie had a great deal of difficulty in her adult life defining her own identity. Because her independent thoughts, feelings, and needs had never been encouraged, she truly had no idea who she was or what she should expect from a loving relationship.

Unlike many adults with whom I have worked, Melanie was

already in touch with some of her anger at her parents when she came to me. Later, we would focus and work through much of that anger and confront her deep feelings of emotional abandonment. She would learn to set limits on how much she would give of herself to others and to respect her own rights, needs, and feelings. She would learn to become visible again.

The Vanishing Parent

So far we've been talking about emotionally absent parents. Physical absence creates its own set of problems.

I first met Ken, 22, in a hospital group for young-adult substance abusers. He was a thin, black-haired young man with piercing dark eyes. It was obvious in our first group meeting that he was enormously intelligent and articulate, but he was also very self-deprecating. He had trouble sitting still for the full ninety minutes; he was a bundle of nerves. I asked him to stay after group to tell me a little about himself. Mistrusting my motives, he played the tough, street-smart hustler, but after a few minutes he began to see that I had no ulterior motive, that I was genuinely interested in easing his pain, and he softened as he spoke to me.

> I always hated school and I didn't know what the hell else to do so I enlisted in the army when I was sixteen. That's where I got fucked up on drugs. I was always a fuck-up anyway.

I asked what his parents thought of his enlistment.

> It was just my mom and me. She wasn't thrilled with the idea, but I think she was glad to get rid of me. I was always getting into trouble and making her life miserable. She was a real pushover. She let me do what I wanted no matter what.

I asked him where his father had been during this period.

> My folks got divorced when I was eight. Mom really got bent out of shape from it. I always thought my dad was hip, you know? He always did "dad things" with me. We'd watch sports together on television, and he'd even take me to a game once in a while. Man, that was great! The day he moved out, I cried my fucking eyes out. He told me nothing was going to change, that he'd still come over and watch TV with me, and he'd see me every Sunday and we'd still be pals. I believed him; I was such a dork. For the first few months, I did see him a lot . . . but then it was once every month . . . then once every two months . . . then practically never. A couple of times I called him up, and he told me he was really busy. About a year after he left, my mom told me that he'd married some woman with three kids and moved out of state. It was hard for me to get it, that he had a new family now. I guess he liked them better, because he sure forgot about me in a hurry.

"This Time It's Going to Be Different"

Ken's tough-guy facade was crumbling fast. He was clearly uneasy about this talk of his father. I asked about the last time he'd seen his father.

> It was when I was fifteen, and it was a big mistake. I got sick of just Christmas cards, so I decided I was gonna surprise him. Man, was I excited. I hitched all the way there—fourteen hours. When I got there . . . I guess I expected some big welcome. I mean he was friendly, but it was no big deal. After a while I started to feel really shitty. It was like we were total strangers. He was falling all over himself with these little kids, and I just sat there feeling like a complete asshole. Man, did I get loaded after I left his house that night. I still think about him a lot. I sure as shit wouldn't want him to know I was here. As soon as I get out of here, I'm gonna try again.

> This time it's gonna be different . . . it's gonna be man-to-man.

When Ken's father abandoned his young son, he left a deep void in the boy's life. Ken was crushed. He tried to cope by acting out his anger both at school and at home. In a sense he was calling out to his father, as if his need for discipline might draw his father back. But Ken's father seemed unwilling to heed the call.

In the face of overwhelming evidence that his father did not want to be a part of his life anymore, Ken continued to hold on to the dream that somehow he could win back his father's love. In the past, his hope had set him up for severe disappointment, to which he'd react by turning to drugs. I told him I was concerned that this chain of events would continue to dominate his adult life unless we worked together to break the pattern.

Unconsciously, Ken was still rationalizing his father's abandonment by taking the blame. As a child, he had assumed that some deficiency in himself had caused his father to beat a hasty retreat. Having arrived at this conclusion, self-hatred was bound to follow. He became a young man without purpose or direction in his life. Despite his intelligence, he was restless and unhappy in school and looked to the army as a solution to his problems. When that didn't work he turned to drugs in a desperate attempt to both fill his inner emptiness and deaden his pain.

Ken's father may have been an adequate parent before the divorce, but afterward he was woefully deficient in providing even the minimal contact that his young son so desperately needed. By failing to do this, he significantly impaired Ken's developing sense of worth and lovability.

There is no such thing as a happy divorce. Divorce is invariably traumatic for everyone in the family, even though it may well be the healthiest course of action under the circumstances. But it is essential for parents to realize that they are divorcing a spouse, not a family. Both parents have a responsibility to maintain a connection to their children despite the disruption in their own lives. A divorce decree is not a license for an inadequate parent to abandon his or her children.

A parent's departure creates a particularly painful deprivation and emptiness within a child. Remember, children almost always conclude that if something negative happens within the family, it's their fault. Children of divorced parents are particularly prone to this belief. A parent who vanishes from his children's lives reinforces their feelings of invisibility, creating damage to their self-esteem that they'll drag into adulthood like a ball and chain.

It's What They Didn't Do That Hurts

It's easy to recognize abuse when a parent beats a child or subjects a child to continual tirades. But the toxicity of inadequate or deficient parents can be elusive, difficult to define. When a parent creates damage through omission rather than commission—through what they *don't* do rather than what they *do* do—the connections of adult problems to this sort of toxic parenting become very hard to see. Since the children of these parents are predisposed to deny these connections anyway, my job becomes especially difficult.

Compounding the problem is the fact that many of these parents are so troubled themselves that they evoke pity. Because these parents so often behave like helpless or irresponsible children, their adult children feel protective. They jump to their parents' defense, like a crime victim apologizing for the perpetrator.

Whether it's "they didn't mean to do any harm," or "they did the best they could," these apologies obscure the fact that these parents abdicated their responsibilities to their children. Through this abdication, these toxic parents robbed their children of positive role models, without which healthy emotional development is extremely difficult.

If you are the adult child of a deficient or inadequate parent, you probably grew up without realizing that there was an alternative to feeling responsible for them. Dancing at the end of their emotional string seemed a way of life, not a choice.

But you *do* have a choice. You can begin the process of understanding that you were wrongly forced to grow up too soon, that you were robbed of your rightful childhood. You can work on accepting how much of your life's energy has gone down the drain of misplaced responsibility. Take this first step and you'll find a new reserve of energy that is suddenly available to you for the first time—energy that you've exhausted on your toxic parents much of your life, but which can finally be used to help you become more loving and responsible to yourself.

3 | "Why Can't They Let Me Live My Own Life?"

The Controllers

Let's listen in on an imaginary conversation between an adult child and one of his controlling parents. I can guarantee you this conversation would never take place, but if these two people were capable of honestly expressing their deeply hidden feelings, they might say the following.

Adult Child: Why do you act the way you do? Why is everything I do wrong? Why can't you treat me like an adult? What difference does it make to Dad if I don't become a doctor? What difference does it make to you who I marry? When are you going to let me go? Why do you act as if every decision I make on my own is an attack on you?

Controlling Mother: I can't describe the pain I feel when you pull away from me. I need you to need me. I can't stand the thought of losing you. You're my whole life. I'm terrified that you're going to make some horrible mistakes. It would rip me apart to see you get hurt. I'd rather die than feel like a failure as a mother.

"It's for Your Own Good"

Control is not necessarily a dirty word. If a mother restrains her toddler instead of letting him wander into the street, we don't call her a controller, we call her prudent. She is exercising control that is in tune with reality, motivated by her child's need for protection and guidance.

Appropriate control becomes overcontrol when the mother restrains her child ten years later, long after the child is perfectly able to cross the street alone.

Children who are not encouraged to do, to try, to explore, to master, and to risk failure, often feel helpless and inadequate. Overcontrolled by anxious, fearful parents, these children often become anxious and fearful themselves. This makes it difficult for them to mature. When they develop through adolescence and adulthood, many of them never outgrow the need for ongoing parental guidance and control. As a result, their parents continue to invade, manipulate, and frequently dominate their lives.

The fear of not being needed motivates many controlling parents to perpetuate this sense of powerlessness in their children. These parents have an unhealthy fear of the "empty nest syndrome," the inevitable sense of loss that all parents experience when their children finally leave home. So much of a controlling parent's identity is tied up in the parental role that he or she feels betrayed and abandoned when the child becomes independent.

What makes a controlling parent so insidious is that the domination usually comes in the guise of concern. Phrases such as, "this is for your own good," "I'm only doing this for you," and, "only because I love you so much," all mean the same thing: "I'm doing this because I'm so afraid of losing you that I'm willing to make you miserable."

Direct Control

There's nothing fancy about direct control. It's overt, tangible, right out in the open. "Do as I say or I'll never speak to you again"; "Do as I say or I'll cut off your money"; "If you don't do as I say you'll no longer be a member of this family"; "If you go against my wishes you'll give me a heart attack." There's nothing subtle about it.

Direct control usually involves intimidation and is frequently humiliating. Your feelings and needs must be subordinated to those of your parents. You are dragged into a bottomless pit of ultimatums. Your opinion is worthless; your needs and desires are irrelevant. The imbalance of power is tremendous.

Michael, a charming, sweet-faced, 36-year-old advertising executive, provides a good example of this. He came to see me because his six-year marriage to a woman he deeply loved had become extremely shaky as a result of a tug-of-war between his wife and his parents.

> The real problems didn't start until I moved to California. I think my mother thought it was a temporary move. But when I told her I'd fallen in love and planned to get married, it hit her that I wanted to settle down here. That's when she really started turning on the pressure to bring me back home.

I asked Michael to tell me about the "pressure."

> The worst incident was about a year after the wedding. We were planning to go out to Boston for my folks' anniversary party when my wife came down with this horrible flu. She was really sick. I didn't want to just leave her, so I called my mother to cancel. Well, first off she bursts into tears. Then she tells me, "If you don't come for our anniversary, I'm going to die." So, I caved in and went to Boston. I got there the

> morning of the party, but right off the plane, they start in that I should stay the whole week. I didn't say yes or no, but I left the next morning. A day later I get a call from my father: "You're killing your mother. She was up all night crying. I'm afraid she's going to have a stroke." What the hell do they want me to do? Divorce my wife, come back to Boston, and move back into my old room?

Michael's parents could pull his strings from three thousand miles away. I asked him if his parents had ever come around to accepting his wife. Michael became visibly flushed with anger.

> No way! Whenever they call, they never ask how she is. In fact, they don't even mention her. It's like they're trying to pretend she doesn't exist.

I asked Michael if he ever confronted his parents about this, and he seemed embarrassed as he answered:

> I wish I had. Every time she'd get clobbered by my parents, I'd expect her to take it. When she'd complain, I'd ask her to be understanding. God, was I an idiot! My parents are slugging away at my wife, and I just keep letting them hurt her.

Michael's crime was that he had become independent. In response, his parents had become desperate, and lashed out with the tactics they knew best: withdrawing love and predicting catastrophe.

Like most controlling parents, Michael's were incredibly self-centered. They felt threatened by Michael's happiness, instead of seeing it as a validation of their parenting skills. Michael's interests were insignificant to them. According to them, he hadn't moved to California for a career opportunity, he had moved to punish them. He hadn't married for love, he had married to spite them. His wife hadn't gotten sick because she contracted a virus, she had gotten sick to deprive them.

Michael's parents were always forcing him to choose between themselves and his wife. And they made every choice an all-or-nothing decision. With directly controlling parents, there is no middle ground. If the adult child tries to gain some control over his own life, he pays the price in guilt, frustrated rage, and a deep sense of disloyalty.

When Michael first came to me, he thought his marriage was the major problem. It didn't take him long to realize that his marriage was merely a victim of the struggle for control that had begun when he moved away from home.

A child's marriage can be extremely threatening to controlling parents. They see the new spouse as a competitor for their child's devotion. This leads to horrendous battles between parents and spouse, with the adult child caught in a crossfire of divided loyalties.

Some parents will attack the new relationship with criticism, sarcasm, and predictions of failure. Others, as in Michael's case, will refuse to accept the new partner or even ignore the spouse's very existence. And still others will directly persecute the new partner. It is not unusual for these tactics to create such upheaval that the marriage is undermined.

"Why Do I Sell Myself Out to My Parents?"

Money has always been the primary language of power, making it a logical tool for controlling parents. Many toxic parents use money to keep their children dependent.

Kim came to see me with a variety of concerns. At 41 she was overweight, unhappy with her work, and divorced with two teenage children. She felt stuck in a rut: she wanted to lose weight, to take some risks in her career, and to find some direction in her life. She was convinced that her problems could all be solved if she could only find Mr. Right.

As our session went along, it became clear that Kim believed she was nothing without a man to take care of her. I asked her where she had gotten this idea.

> Well, certainly not from my husband. It was more like I had to take care of him. I met him when I was right out of college. He was twenty-seven, still living with his parents, and really floundering about what he was going to do for a living. But he was sensitive and romantic and I fell for him. My father totally disapproved, but I think he was secretly pleased that I picked someone who couldn't get it together. When I insisted on marrying him, my father told me he would support us for a while, and if worse came to worse, he'd give my husband a job in his company. Of course this makes my father sound like a terrific guy, but it gave him an incredible hold over us. Even though I was married, I was still Daddy's little girl. My father kept bailing us out financially, but in return for that, he got to tell us how to live our lives. I was playing house and raising babies and yet . . .

Kim broke off in midsentence. "And yet what?" I asked. She looked down at the floor as she finished:

> And yet . . . I still needed Daddy to take care of me.

I asked Kim if she could see the connection between her relationship with her father and her dependence on men to make her life okay.

> There's no question that my father was the most powerful person in my life. He was really adoring when I was little, but when I started to have a mind of my own, he couldn't handle it. He'd have these screaming fits if I dared to disagree with him. He'd call me terrible names. He was really loud and scary. When I was a teenager, he started using money to keep me in line. Sometimes he'd be incredibly generous, which made me feel really loved and safe. But other times he'd humiliate me by making me beg and cry for anything from movie money to schoolbooks. I was never sure what my crimes were. I just know I spent a lot of time trying to figure

> out how to please him. It was never the same two days in a row. He kept making it tougher.

For Kim, trying to please her father was like running a race in which he was always moving the finish line. The harder she ran, the farther he moved it. She couldn't win. He used money for both reward and punishment, without logic or consistency. He was alternately generous and stingy with money, just as he was with love and affection. His mixed messages confused her. Her dependency became entangled with his approval. This confusion continued into Kim's adult life.

> I encouraged my husband to go to work for my father. What a mistake that was! Now he really had us under his thumb. Everything had to be done his way—from choosing an apartment to toilet training the kids. He made Jim's life a living hell at work, so Jim finally quit. My father saw this as another example of Jim's worthlessness, even though Jim got another job. My father really lit into me about that and threatened to stop helping us, but then he did a complete about-face and, for Christmas, he bought me a new car. When he handed me the keys, he said, "Don't you wish your husband was rich like me?"

Kim's father used his financial power in very cruel and destructive ways while appearing to be magnanimous. He used it to make himself even more indispensable in Kim's eyes and to continually diminish Kim's husband. In this way he continued to control her long after she left the nest.

"Can't You Do Anything Right?"

Many toxic parents control their adult children by treating them as if they were helpless and inadequate, even when this is drastically out of sync with reality.

Martin, a thin, balding, 43-year-old president of a small construction supply company, came to see me in genuine panic. He said:

> I'm really scared. Something's happening to me. I'm having these fits of temper. It just gets out of control. I've always been a totally nonviolent person, but in the last few months, I'm screaming at my wife and kids, slamming doors, and three weeks ago, I got so pissed off I punched a hole in the wall. I'm really scared I'm going to hurt somebody.

I complimented him on his courage and foresight to come in for therapy before the problem got out of hand. I asked whom he would have liked to hit when he punched that wall. He laughed bitterly:

> That's easy—my old man. No matter how hard I try, he always makes me feel that whatever I'm doing is wrong. Would you believe he has the balls to put me down in front of my own employees?

When Martin saw that I looked puzzled, he explained:

> My father took me into his business eighteen years ago, and then he retired a couple of years later. So I've been running this business for fifteen years. But every goddamned week, my father comes in and starts looking through the accounts. Then he bitches about how I'm handling them. He follows me out of my office screaming about how I'm screwing up *his* company. Right in front of my employees he does it. The irony is, I've turned this business around. I've doubled our profits, just in the last three years, but he won't leave me alone. Is this man ever going to be satisfied?

Martin was constantly having to jump through hoops to prove himself. He had real evidence of achievement—his profits—but that evidence paled beside his father's disapproval. I suggested to Martin that his father might feel threatened by Martin's success. His father's ego seemed to be tied up with having built this business, but now his achievement was being overshadowed by his son's.

I asked Martin if during these episodes he was in touch with any feelings other than his understandable anger.

> You bet I am. I'm really ashamed to tell you this, but every time he walks into the office, I feel like I'm two years old. I can't even answer questions right. I start to stammer, apologize, and feel scared. He looks so powerful, even though I'm as big as he is physically, that I feel about half his size. He has this cold look in his eye and a critical tone in his voice. Why can't he treat me like an adult?

Martin's father used the business to keep Martin feeling inadequate, which in turn enabled his father to feel better about himself. When Dad pushed the right buttons, Martin became a helpless child in grown-up clothing.

It took some time, but Martin finally came to realize that he had to give up the hope that his father would change. Martin is now working hard to change the way he deals with his father.

The Tyranny of the Manipulator

There is another powerful form of control that, while more subtle and covert than direct control, is every bit as damaging: manipulation. Manipulators get what they want without ever having to ask for it, without ever having to risk rejection by being open about their desires.

All of us manipulate others to varying degrees. Few of us are confident enough to just ask for everything we want in this world, so we develop indirect ways of asking. We don't ask our spouse for a glass of wine, we ask if there's any open; we don't ask our guests to leave at the end of the evening, we yawn; we don't ask an attractive stranger for a phone number, we engage in small talk. Children manipulate parents as much as parents do children. Spouses, friends, and relatives all manipulate one another. Salesmen make a living out of manipulating. There's nothing inherently evil about it; in fact, it's a normal mode of human communication.

But when it becomes a tool for consistent control, manipulation can be exceedingly destructive, especially in a parent-child relationship. Because manipulative parents are so adept at hiding their true motives, their children live in a world of confusion. They know they're being had, but they can't figure out how.

"Why Does She Always Have to Help?"

One of the most common types of toxic manipulators is the "helper." Instead of letting go, the helper creates situations to make him- or herself "needed" in the adult child's life. This manipulation often comes packaged as well-meaning but unwanted assistance.

Lee, 32, is an outgoing, freckled-faced, former top-seeded amateur tennis player who has been doing very well as a tennis pro at a country club. Despite an active social life, professional recognition, and a good job, she was going into regular periods of deep depression. Her relationship with her mother quickly dominated our first session together:

> I've worked very hard to get where I am, but my mother doesn't think I can tie my own shoes. Her whole life is wrapped up in me, and it's gotten much worse since my dad died. She just doesn't let up. She's always bringing food over to my apartment because she doesn't think I eat well enough. Sometimes, I come back to my place and find that she's come in and cleaned it "as a favor." She's even rearranged my clothes and furniture!

I asked Lee if she'd ever simply asked her mother to stop doing these things.

> All the time. She just wells up with tears and cries, "What's wrong with a mother who helps a daughter she loves?" Last month I was invited to play a tournament in San Francisco. My mother went on and on about how far it was and how I couldn't possibly drive the whole way by myself. So she volunteered to come with me. When I told her she really didn't have to, she acted like I was trying to trick her out of a free vacation. So I said okay. I had really been looking forward to the time alone, but what could I say?

As Lee and I worked together in therapy, she began to see how much her feelings of competence had been undermined by her mother. But whenever Lee tried to express her frustration, she was overwhelmed by guilt because her mother appeared to be so loving and caring. Lee became increasingly angry at her mother, and since she couldn't let it out, she had to hold it in. Eventually, it found an outlet as depression.

Of course, her depression just fed the cycle. Her mother never missed an opportunity to say things such as, "Look how down in the mouth you look. Let me fix a little lunch, just to cheer you up."

On those rare occasions when Lee did work up the courage to tell her mother how she felt, her mother would become the tearful martyr. Lee would invariably feel guilty and try to apologize, but her mother would cut her off with, "Don't worry about me, I'll be all right."

I suggested to Lee that if her mother had been more direct in asking for what she wanted, Lee wouldn't have been so angry. Lee agreed.

> You're right. If she could only say, "I'm lonely, I miss you, I'd like you to spend more time with me," at least I'd know what

> I was dealing with. I'd have some choices. The way it is now, it's like she's taken over my life.

When Lee bemoaned her lack of choices, she was echoing what many adult children of manipulative parents believe. Manipulation paints people into a corner: to fight it, they have to hurt someone who's "just trying to be nice." For most people it seems easier to give in.

'Tis the Season to Be Melancholy

Manipulative parents have a field day on holidays, spreading guilt as if it were Christmas cheer. Holidays tend to intensify whatever family conflicts already exist. Instead of anticipating holiday pleasure, many people find themselves dreading the rise of family tensions that holidays often bring.

One of my clients, Fred, a 27-year-old grocery clerk, and the youngest of four siblings, told me a story of classic manipulation by his mother:

> My mother always made a big deal about all of us coming home for Christmas. Last year, I won a radio contest and got a free trip to Aspen over the holidays. I was really excited since I could never afford a trip like this myself. I love skiing, and it was an incredible chance for me to take my girlfriend someplace great. We'd both been working so hard, this vacation sounded like heaven. But when I broke the news to my mom, she looked like somebody just died. Her eyes glazed up and her lip started trembling, you know, like she was going to cry? Then she said, "It's okay, honey. You have a good time. Maybe we just won't have Christmas dinner this year," which really made me feel like a real turd.

I asked Fred whether he had managed to go on the trip anyway.

> Yeah, I went. But I had the worst time of my life. I was in such a horrible mood that I kept fighting with my girlfriend. I spent half the trip on the phone with my mother, and both my brothers, and my sister. . . . I was apologizing all over the place. It wasn't worth the agony.

I was frankly surprised that Fred had gone on his trip at all. I've seen people go to far more extravagant lengths to avoid feeling guilty than canceling a trip. Manipulative parents are masters of guilt, and Fred's mother was no exception.

> Of course, they had Christmas dinner without me. But my mother was so miserable she burned the turkey for the first time in forty years. I got three phone calls from my sister telling me how I'd killed the family tradition. My oldest brother told me everybody was totally bummed out because I wasn't there. And then my other brother really laid one on me. He said, "Us kids are all she's got. How many more Christmases do you think Mom has left?" Like I'm abandoning her on her deathbed or something. Is that fair, Susan? She's not even sixty, she's in perfect health. I'm sure he got that line straight from my mother's mouth. I'll never miss Christmas again, I'll tell you that.

Instead of expressing her feelings directly to Fred, Fred's mother enlisted her other children to do it for her. This is an extremely effective tactic for many manipulative parents. Remember, their primary goal is to avoid direct confrontation. Instead of accusing Fred herself, his mother played the role of martyr at Christmas dinner. She couldn't have made a more forceful condemnation of Fred if she'd taken an ad out in the paper.

I explained to Fred that his mother and siblings had made their own choices to have a miserable Christmas. Fred was not responsible. Nothing but their own choice had stopped them from toasting Fred in his absence and having a fun-filled evening.

As long as Fred continued to believe that he was a bad person because he dared to do something for himself, his mother would continue to control him through guilt. Fred eventually came to understand this and is now much more effective in dealing with his mother. Though she sees her son's new assertiveness as some form of "punishment," Fred has tipped the balance of power to the point where any concessions he makes are concessions of choice, not capitulation.

"Why Can't You Be More Like Your Sister?"

Many toxic parents compare one sibling unfavorably with another to make the target child feel that he's not doing enough to gain parental affection. This motivates the child to do whatever the parents want in order to regain their favor. This divide-and-conquer technique is often unleashed against children who become a little too independent, threatening the balance of the family system.

Whether consciously or unconsciously, these parents manipulate an otherwise normal sibling rivalry into a cruel competition that inhibits the growth of healthy sibling bonds. The effects are far-reaching. In addition to the obvious damage to the child's self-image, negative comparisons create resentments and jealousies between siblings that can color their relationship for a lifetime.

Rebel with a Cause

When toxic parents control us in intense, intimidating, guilt-producing, or emotionally crippling ways, we usually react in one of two ways: we capitulate or we rebel. Both of these reactions inhibit psychological separation, even though rebellion would seem to do just the opposite. The truth is, if we rebel in reaction to our parents, we are being controlled just as surely as if we submit.

Jonathan, 55, is a nice-looking, athletic bachelor who owns a large computer software company. In our first session together, he almost apologized for his intense feelings of panic and loneliness:

> Now, don't start feeling sorry for me. I've got a beautiful house. I collect cars. I've got all kinds of possessions. I really lead an okay life. But there are times when I get very, very lonely. I have so much, and I can't share it with anyone. Sometimes I get this terrible feeling of loss for what I might have had in terms of a loving, intimate relationship. I'm terrified that I'm going to end up dying alone.

I asked Jonathan if he had any idea why he was having such a difficult time with relationships.

> Every time I've gotten close to a woman . . . or even thought about marrying someone, I've panicked and run. I don't know why . . . I wish I did. My mother never lets me hear the end of it.

I asked Jonathan how he felt about this pressure from his mother.

> She's obsessed with my getting married. She's eighty-one, she's in good health, and she has plenty of her own friends, but I feel like she spends her whole day worrying about my love life. I really love her, but I can't stand being around her because of this. She lives for my happiness. She smothers me with her concern. It's like I can't peel this woman off of me. She's constantly trying to tell me how to live my life . . . always has. I mean, she would breathe for me if she could.

Jonathan's last statement was a wonderfully graphic description of "fusion." His mother was so enmeshed with him that she forgot where she ended and he began. She "fused" her life to his. Jonathan became an extension of her, as if his life were her life. Jonathan needed to free himself from her suffocating control, so he rebelled. He rejected whatever she wanted for him, including things he might otherwise desire, such as marriage.

I suggested to Jonathan that he may have been so intent on rebelling against his controlling mother that he was ignoring his own true desires. It had become so important to him not to give in to his mother's wishes that he deprived himself of the kind of relationship with a woman he claimed to want. By doing this, he created for himself an illusion that he was "his own man," but in reality his need to rebel overpowered his free will.

I call this "self-defeating rebellion." It is the flip side of capitulation. Healthy rebellion is an active exercise of free choice. It enhances personal growth and individuality. Self-defeating rebellion is a reaction against a controlling parent, an exercise in which the means attempt to justify an unsatisfactory end. This is rarely in our best interests.

Control from the Grave

One of my group members once said, "My parents are both dead, so they don't have any power over me." Another member spoke out: "They may be dead, honey, but they're still living in your head!" Both self-defeating rebellion and capitulation can persist long after a parent's death.

Many people believe that once the controlling parent dies they will be free, but the psychological umbilical cord reaches not only across continents but out of the grave. I've seen hundreds of adults who were unflinchingly loyal to their parents' demands and negative messages long after their parents were gone.

Eli, 60, a very successful businessman with an extraordinary intellect and a wry wit, made an unusually sophisticated assessment of his situation: "I'm a supporting player in my own life."

When I first met Eli, despite being a millionaire many times over, he was living in a one-room apartment, driving an old clunker, and living the lifestyle of a man who could barely make ends meet. He was extremely generous with his two adult daughters but an obsessive penny-pincher with himself.

I remember one day when he came to see me after work. I asked him how his day had been and he laughingly told me that he'd almost blown an $18 million deal because he'd been late for a meeting. Though usually punctual, Eli had circled the block for twenty minutes looking for a parking place on the street to avoid the cost of the building's lot. He had jeopardized $18 million for the sake of a $5 parking fee!

As we explored some of the roots of his obsession with saving money, it became apparent that his father's voice, even twelve years after his death, still resounded in Eli's head:

> My parents were poor immigrants. I grew up in total squalor. My folks, particularly my father, taught me to be afraid of everything. He would say, "It's a savage world out there, if you don't watch your step you'll get eaten alive." He made me feel that I had nothing to look forward to except danger, and he didn't stop even after I'd gotten married and made a lot of money. He'd always be giving me the third degree about what I was spending on things and what I bought. And when I made the mistake of telling him, his standard response was, "You idiot! You waste money on luxuries. You should be saving every penny. Hard times will come, they always do, and then you'll *need* that money." It got to the point that I was terrified to spend a penny. My father never thought of life as something that could be enjoyed, he just saw it as something we had to endure.

Eli's father projected the terrors and hardships of his own life on his son. When Eli went on to success, he heard his father's admonitions every time he tried to enjoy the fruits of his labor. His father's catastrophic predictions formed a never-ending tape loop in Eli's head. Even if Eli could bring himself to buy something for his own pleasure, his father's voice would prevent him from enjoying it.

His father's general mistrust of the future carried through to his thoughts on women. Like success, women would inevitably turn on you someday. He had a suspicion of women that bordered on paranoia. His son internalized these views as well:

> I've had nothing but bad luck with women. I've just never been able to trust them. My wife divorced me because I kept accusing her of extravagance. It was ridiculous. She'd buy a handbag or something, and I'd start thinking bankruptcy court.

As I worked with Eli, it became clear that money was not the only issue that came between him and his wife. He had a very hard time expressing feelings, especially tender ones, and she found this increasingly frustrating. This problem persists in his single life. As he expressed it:

> Every time that I take out a woman, I hear my father's voice saying, "Women love to trick men. They'll take you for all you've got if you're stupid enough to let them." I guess that's why I've always gone for inadequate women. I know they can't outsmart me. I always make lots of promises about taking care of them financially or setting them up in business, but I never follow through. I guess I'm trying to trick them before they trick me. Will I ever find a woman I can trust?

Here was a bright, perceptive man who allowed powerful forces from beyond the grave to control him, even though he understood intellectually what was happening. He was a prisoner of his father's fear and mistrust.

Eli worked extremely hard in therapy. He took risks and pushed himself to adopt new behaviors. He began to confront many of his internal terrors. Ultimately, he bought a luxurious condominium—a big step for him. He still felt guilty about it, but he learned to tolerate the guilt.

The voice inside his head will always be there, but he has learned to turn down the volume. Eli is still struggling with his mistrust of women, but he has learned to see this mistrust as a legacy from his father. He is working hard to trust the woman he's currently dating, using that trust as a weapon to gain control of his life.

I'll always remember the day he came in and told me that he'd fought off a wave of jealousy the night before and come away with a particularly warming sense of victory. He looked at me with tear-filled eyes and said, "You know, Susan, there is simply nothing in my current reality to justify my being as afraid as I was."

"I Feel Like I Can't Breathe"

Barbara, 39, a tall, slender composer of background music for television shows, came to see me in a devastating depression.

> I wake up at night, and there is an emptiness, almost like a death inside of me. I was a musical prodigy, played Mozart piano concertos at age five, and had a scholarship to Julliard by the time I was twelve. My career is going great, but I'm dying inside. I was hospitalized for depression six months ago. I think I'm going to lose myself. I don't know where to turn.

I asked Barbara if something specific had happened to precipitate her hospitalization, and she told me that she had lost both her parents within three months. My heart ached for her, but she was quick to try to dissuade me from empathizing:

> It's okay. We hadn't spoken in a few years, so I felt like I'd already lost them.

I asked her to tell me what had caused this separation.

When Chuck and I were planning to get married a little over four years ago, my parents insisted on coming and staying with us to help with the wedding. That was all I needed . . . for them to be breathing down my neck like they did when I was a kid. I mean they were always meddling . . . I was always getting the Spanish Inquisition about what I was doing, who I was doing it with, where I was going. . . . Anyway, I offered to put them up in a hotel since Chuck and I were under enough stress before the wedding, and they really got crazy. They told me that unless they could come and stay with me, they would never speak to me again. For the first time in my life, I stood up to them. What a mistake that was. First, they didn't come to the wedding, then they told the entire family what a bitch I was. Now none of them talk to me.

A few years after my marriage, my mother was told she had inoperable cancer. She made every member of the family swear not to tell me when she died. I didn't find out until five months later, when I ran into a family friend who expressed condolences. That's how I found out my mother had died. I went straight home and called my father. I don't know, I guess I thought we could patch things up. The first thing he said was: "You should be happy now, you've killed your mother!" I was devastated. He went on to grieve himself to death three months later. Every time I think of them I hear him accusing me and it makes me feel like a murderer. They're still strangling me with their accusations even though they're both six feet under. What does it take to get them out of my head, out of my life?

Like Eli, Barbara was being controlled from the grave. She spent several years feeling responsible for killing her parents, which devastated her mental health and almost destroyed her marriage. She became desperate to escape her sense of guilt.

> Since they died, I've been very suicidal. It seemed like the only way to stop those voices in my head that kept saying, "You killed your father. You killed your mother." I was so close to killing myself, but you know what kept me from doing it?

I shook my head. She smiled for the first time during our hour together and replied:

> I was afraid I might run into my parents again. It was bad enough that they ruined my life here on earth; I wasn't about to give them a chance to destroy whatever I might find on the other side.

Like most adult children of toxic parents, Barbara was able to acknowledge some of the pain her parents had caused her. But that wasn't enough to help her transfer her feelings of responsibility from herself to them. It took some doing, but we finally worked through it together and she came to accept her parents' full responsibility for their cruel behavior. Her parents were dead, but it took Barbara another year before she could get them to leave her alone.

No Separate Identity

Parents who feel good about themselves do not have to control their adult children. But the toxic parents we've met in this chapter operate from a deep sense of dissatisfaction with their lives and a fear of abandonment. Their child's independence is like the loss of a limb to them. As the child grows older, it becomes ever more important for the parent to pull the strings that keep the child dependent. As long as toxic parents can make their son or daughter feel like a child, they can maintain control.

As a result, adult children of controlling parents often have a very blurred sense of identity. They have trouble seeing themselves as separate beings from their parents. They can't distinguish their own needs from their parents' needs. They feel powerless.

All parents control their children until those children gain control of their own lives. In normal families, the transition occurs soon after adolescence. In toxic families, this healthy separation is delayed for years—or forever. It can only occur after you have made the changes that will enable you to gain mastery over your own life.

4 | "No One in This Family Is an Alcoholic"

The Alcoholics

Glenn, a tall, rugged-looking man who owns a small manufacturing company, came to me for help primarily because his timidity and lack of assertiveness were affecting both his personal and professional relationships. He said he felt nervous and restless a great deal of the time. He had overheard someone at work call him "whiny" and "depressing." He sensed that people were uneasy when they met him, which made it difficult for him to turn acquaintainces into friends.

Midway through our first session, Glenn started talking about another source of stress at work:

> About six years ago, I took my father into business with me, hoping it would straighten him out. I think the pressure of the job just made him worse. He's been an alcoholic for as long as I can remember. He drinks, he insults customers, and he costs me a lot of business. I've got to get him out of there,

> but I'm terrified. How the hell do you fire your own father? It would destroy him. Whenever I try to talk to him about it, all he says is: "You talk to me with respect or you don't talk to me at all." I'm going nuts.

Glenn's excessive sense of responsibility, his need to rescue his father, his personal insecurities, and his repressed anger were classic symptoms of adult children of alcoholics.

The Dinosaur in the Living Room

If Richard Nixon's White House staff had taken cover-up lessons from anyone in an alcoholic's family, "Watergate" would still be just a Washington hotel. Denial takes on gargantuan proportions for everyone living in an alcoholic household. Alcoholism is like a dinosaur in the living room. To an outsider the dinosaur is impossible to ignore, but for those within the home, the hopelessness of evicting the beast forces them to pretend it isn't there. That's the only way they can coexist. Lies, excuses, and secrets are as common as air in these homes, creating tremendous emotional chaos for children.

The emotional and psychological climate in alcoholic families is much the same as in families where parents abuse drugs, whether illegal or prescription. Though the cases I've chosen in this chapter focus on alcoholic parents, the painful experiences of children of drug abusers are quite similar.

Glenn's experience was characteristic:

> My earliest memory is of my father coming home from work and heading straight for the liquor cabinet. It was his nightly ritual. After downing a few, he'd come to dinner with a glass in his hand, and the damned thing was never empty. After dinner, he'd get down to some *serious* drinking. We all had to

> be very quiet so we wouldn't disturb him. I mean, for Christ's sake, you'd think that he was doing something really important, but the son of a bitch was just getting juiced. On lots of nights, I remember my sister, my mother, and I had to drag him to bed. My job was to take off his shoes and socks. The damnedest thing was that no one in the family ever mentioned what we were doing. I mean, we did it night after night. Until I got a little older, I honestly thought that dragging Dad to bed was a normal family activity. Something every family did.

Glenn learned early on that his father's drinking was a Big Secret. Though his mother told him not to tell people about "Daddy's problem," his shame alone would have been enough to keep his mouth shut. The family put on an "everything is fine" face to the outside world. They were united by their need to deal with their common enemy. The secret became the glue that kept the tortured family intact.

The Big Secret has three elements:

1. The alcoholic's denial of his or her alcoholism in the face of overwhelming evidence to the contrary and in the face of behavior that is both terrifying and humiliating to other family members.
2. The denial of the problem by the alcoholic's partner and frequently by other members of the family. They commonly excuse the drinker with excuses such as, "Mom just drinks to relax," "Dad tripped on the carpet," or, "Dad lost his job because he had a mean boss."
3. The charade of the "normal family," a facade that the family presents to one another and to the world.

"The charade of the normal family" is especially damaging to a child because it forces him to deny the validity of his own feelings and perceptions. It is almost impossible for a child to develop a strong sense of self-confidence if he must constantly lie about what he is thinking and feeling. His guilt makes him wonder whether people believe him. When he grows older, this sense that people doubt him can continue, causing him to shy away from revealing anything of himself or venturing an opinion. Like Glenn, many adult children of alcoholics become painfully shy.

It takes a tremendous amount of energy to keep the charade going. The child must always be on guard. He lives in constant fear that he may accidentally expose and betray the family. To avoid that, he often avoids making friends and thereby becomes isolated and lonely.

This loneliness drags him deeper into the family morass. He develops an enormous and distorted sense of loyalty to the only people who share his secret: his family co-conspirators. Intense, uncritical loyalty to his parents becomes second nature. When he grows to adulthood, his blind loyalty remains a destructive, controlling element in his life. This is what prevented Glenn from asking his father to leave the company, despite the fact that his business was suffering because of it.

The Little Boy Who Wasn't There

Because so much energy is expended on futile attempts to rescue the drinker and maintain the cover-up, there is little time or attention left for the basic needs of the alcoholic's children. Like children of deficient and inadequate parents, children of alcoholics often feel invisible. This becomes an especially painful catch-22 because the more troubled the home, the more the children need emotional support.

As Glenn and I explored the connection between his current difficulties and the emotional seesaw of his childhood, he remembered:

> My father never did any of the things that my friends' fathers did with them. We never tossed a football around or even watched games together. He would always say, "I don't have time—maybe later," but he always had time to sit around and get drunk. My mother would say, "Don't bother me all the time with your problems. Why don't you just go off with your friends." But I didn't have any friends. I was afraid to bring anybody home. My folks just ignored me and didn't seem to care what kind of trouble I got into just as long as they didn't have to deal with it.

I said to Glenn, "So you were okay as long as you weren't seen or heard. How did it feel being invisible?" Glenn's expression became pained as he remembered:

> It was awful. I felt like an orphan most of the time. I would do anything to get their attention. Once, when I was around eleven, I was over at a friend's house, and his dad had left his wallet out on a table in the hallway. So I took five dollars, hoping I'd get caught. I didn't care if my parents gave me hell, as long as they'd know I was there.

Glenn got the message early in life that his existence was more an aggravation than a blessing to his parents. His emotional invisibility was reinforced by the fact that it was his safest haven from his father's frequent violence. He recalled:

> My dad put me down whenever I spoke up. If I dared raise my voice to him, he'd slug me. It didn't take me long to learn not to cross him. If I stood up to my mom, she'd start bawling like a baby, then he'd get mad and belt somebody, and I'd feel twice as bad for the trouble I'd caused. So I learned to stay away out of the house as much as I could. I got an after-school job when I was twelve, and I would lie about what

> time I got off so I could come home as late as possible every night. Then I'd leave for school an hour early in the morning, just so I could get out before he woke up. I can still feel that loneliness, sitting by myself in the schoolyard every morning, waiting for somebody to show up. The funny thing is, I don't think my parents even noticed I was never around.

I asked Glenn if he thought the same fears that had kept him from asserting himself as a child were now controlling him as an adult. Glenn admitted sadly:

> I guess so. I can't ever say anything that offends anybody, no matter how much I want to. I swallow so many words, I think I'm going to throw up sometimes. I just can't stand up to people. Even people I couldn't care less about. If I think what I want to say is going to hurt somebody's feelings, I just can't say it. Period.

As with many adult children of alcoholics, Glenn felt responsible for everyone else's feelings, just as he took responsibility for his father's and mother's feelings when he was young. He went to heroic lengths to avoid confrontations with his parents because he didn't want to be responsible for causing anyone (including himself) pain. He could not express his emotions as a child should be able to. He had to suppress them, and he continued that pattern in his adult life. When Glenn helped put his father to bed, when he took responsibility for keeping his father from getting upset, he was acting as a parent, not a child. When a child is forced to adopt the role of parent, he loses his role models, threatening his developing identity. This destructive role reversal is common in alcoholic families.

"I Never Got to Be a Kid"

As we have seen, and will continue to see, role reversal occurs in almost all families where there are toxic parents. In the alcoholic family, the drinking parent actively usurps the child's role through his pathetic, needy, irrational behavior. He's such a handful of a child himself that he leaves no room for any other children in the family.

Glenn grew up believing that his role in the world was to take care of others and not to expect anything for himself.

> I remember how my mother would come running to me when Dad got out of control and she'd cry about how unhappy she was. She'd say, "What am I going to do? You kids need a father, and I can't go out to work." It upsets me, just talking about it. I used to dream about taking her away to an island where my father couldn't find us. I'd promise her that as soon as I could I'd take care of her. And that's what I'm doing now. I give her money all the time, even though I can't afford it. And I'm taking care of Dad, even though it's killing my business. Why can't I find somebody to take care of *me* for a change?

Glenn is still burdened with guilt over his inability both as a child and as an adult to fix his parents' lives. Despite his dream of finding a woman to take care of him, the woman he finally settled down with was needy and helpless. Glenn sensed that she wasn't right for him when he married her, but his need to play out the rescue fantasies of his childhood overwhelmed his better judgment.

The Myth of Fixing the Past

It didn't take long for Glenn to learn that he had married a secret drinker. If he had known before he married her, he probably would have married her anyway. He would simply have convinced himself that he could change her. Adult children of alcoholics frequently marry alcoholics. Many people find it bewildering that someone who grew up in the chaos of an alcoholic family would choose to relive the trauma. But the drive to repeat familiar patterns of feelings is common to all people, no matter how painful or self-defeating those feelings may be. The familiar provides a sense of comfort and structure for our lives. We know what the rules are, and we know what to expect.

More important, we reenact past conflicts because this time we hope to make it come out right—we're going to win the battle. This reenactment of old, painful experiences is called a "repetition compulsion."

"This Time I'll Get It Right"

I can't emphasize strongly enough how much this particular compulsion dominates our lives. Almost all self-defeating behaviors, particularly those involved in establishing and maintaining intimate relationships, begin to make a lot more sense when seen in the light of repetition compulsion. Glenn provides a perfect example:

> When I met Denise, I didn't even know she drank. When I found out, she gave up trying to hide it. I'd see her drunk three, four times a week. I begged her to stop. I took her to doctors. I pleaded with her to go to AA. I locked up all the liquor, but you know how drunks are . . . she'd always find a way. The only time she'd stop is when I'd threaten to leave. But after a while she'd fall off the wagon, and we'd be back to square one.

Since denial and cover-up seemed normal during his growing-up years, Glenn moved easily into an adult relationship where the same elements recurred. Only this time he thought he might succeed at rescuing his wife where he had failed, as a child, to rescue his parents. Glenn, like almost all adult children of alcoholics, had made a fervent promise to himself: he would never have another alcoholic in his life. But a deeply ingrained repetition compulsion is a lot stronger than any conscious promise can ever be.

"Why Do I Keep Going Back for More?"

Another promise that often dissolves because of the power of the past is the promise never to repeat the violence and abuse that are often an integral part of the alcoholic household.

Jody, a petite, black-haired, wide-eyed 26-year-old, came into one of my therapy groups at the suggestion of her supervisor at the private substance-abuse hospital where she worked as a rehabilitation counselor. As with many counselors on the program, Jody was herself a recovering alcoholic and drug abuser. I first met her at a small staff party celebrating her second year of sobriety.

Jody had recently ended a relationship with a violent, abusive man. Her supervisor was concerned that she might be tempted to return to that relationship and suggested that she see me.

In our first private session together, Jody was tough and belligerent and not at all convinced that she needed help. I wondered about the pain behind this facade. The first words she said were, "They told me I better get my ass into therapy or else I'll get canned. Why don't you give me a break and tell them I'm doing great and don't need to come back."

"I can see that you're really thrilled to be here," I replied. We both laughed, which helped ease the tension. I told her I knew she wasn't seeing me by choice, but since she was here anyway, she might as well try to get something out of it. She agreed to give one of my groups a try.

I began by telling her how concerned her colleagues were that she might go back to her abusive boyfriend. Jody admitted that they had reason to be concerned:

> I really miss that turkey. He's basically a terrific guy. It's just that sometimes I open my big mouth and it pisses him off. I

> know he loves me, and I keep hoping we'll be able to work it out.

I suggested that she had confused love with abuse, as if she unconsciously needed to elicit extreme anger from her lover as proof of his intensity and passion. I asked if this felt familiar to her, if it had happened to her in other relationships. She thought for a moment, then replied:

> I guess it was like that with my old man. He was a grade-A, fourteen-carat drunk who used to beat the shit out of us. He'd come home drunk maybe five out of seven nights a week. And he'd find any excuse to beat us. He'd beat my brother until he bled. My mom couldn't do anything to stop him. She was too scared to even try. I would fuckin' plead with him to stop, but he was like a crazy man. I don't want to give you the idea that he was some kind of monster, because when he wasn't drinking, he could be cool. I mean, he was my best friend. I loved it when we'd pal around together, just the two of us. I still love it.

Many children of alcoholics develop a high tolerance for accepting the unacceptable. With no idea of how a loving father behaves, Jody could only assume that if she wanted the good times with her father, she had to put up with the bad times. She formed a psychological connection between love and abuse. She came to believe that you don't get one without the other.

The Buddy System

Jody's father taught her by example that she should do whatever it took to keep a man happy so that he wouldn't beat her. To keep her father happy, she had become his drinking buddy at age ten.

> My dad started off by giving me a sip of booze maybe once a week. I hated the taste, but it always made him real happy when I had some. By the time I was eleven, he'd go into a liquor store and bring out a bottle. We'd sit in the car and share it, then we'd go for a joyride. At first it was exciting, but after a while I'd get pretty scared. I mean, I was just a kid, but I could tell he didn't have such great control of the car. I kept doing it because it was something I had with him that nobody else had. It was this special thing between us. I really got to like drinking because it made Dad like me more. It got worse and worse until I finally drank myself right off the deep end.

At least one out of four children of alcoholic parents become alcoholics themselves, and many of these adults were given their first drink at a very young age by the alcoholic parent. The drinking creates a special and often secret bond between parent and child. This particular type of conspiracy feels like camaraderie to a child. It is often as close as the child can get to something approaching love and approval.

Even if a child has not been actively recruited by the alcoholic, he or she remains especially vulnerable to eventually becoming an alcoholic. We don't know exactly why this happens—there may be a genetic predisposition to addictive behavior or a biochemical disorder. I also suspect a strong factor is that many behaviors and beliefs are formed through imitation of, and identification with, our parents. Adult children of alcoholics have been handed a legacy of rage, depression, loss of joy, suspiciousness, damaged relationships, and overdeveloped sense of responsibility. They have also been handed a method of trying to deal with this twisted legacy: drinking.

You Can't Trust Anybody

Because their first and most important relationship taught them that the people they love will hurt them and be terrifyingly unpredictable, most adult children of alcoholics are terrified of becoming close to another person. Successful adult relationships, whether between lovers or friends, require a significant degree of vulnerability, trust, and openness—the very elements that an alcoholic household destroys. As a result, many adult children of alcoholics are drawn to people who are emotionally unavailable because of deep conflicts of their own. In this way, the adult child can create an illusion of a relationship without confronting his or her terror of true intimacy.

Jody's Jekyll and Hyde boyfriend was a repeat of her father—sometimes wonderful, sometimes terrible. By picking a volatile and abusive man, Jody was both repeating the familiar experiences of her childhood and guaranteeing that she would never have to risk entering the uncharted waters of true intimacy. She clung desperately to the myth that her father was still the only man who really understood her. Her unwillingness to confront this myth contaminated her relationships not only with her friends but with me and with other members of her therapy group. In fact, the myth was so powerful that she eventually gave up on herself.

I still remember the sadness I felt the night she announced she was leaving group. I reminded her that she knew this work was going to be painful, that pain was part of the process. For a split second, she looked as if she might reconsider, but then:

> Look. I don't want to give up my dad. I don't want to get angry with him. And I don't want to keep defending him to you. My dad and I really need each other. Why should I trust you more than him? I don't think you or anybody in this group really gives a shit about me. I don't think any of you will really be there for me when I get hurt.

Jody's group was composed of other adults who had been abused as children, and they understood what she was going through. They were extremely supportive and loving with her, but she couldn't accept that. To Jody, the world was a devious place full of emotional vandals. She was convinced that if she let anyone get too close, they would hurt her and let her down. The irony is that these beliefs would have been very accurate in regard to her father.

Jody's inability to trust was a major casualty of her father's alcoholism. If you can't trust your father, whom can you trust? Trust is like the runt of our emotional litter; under harsh conditions, it's usually the first to die.

Trust is a common casualty among adult children of toxic parents. Listen to Glenn:

> I was always scared when my wife would want to do anything without me—even just going out with the girls for dinner. I was afraid she'd abandon me. I just didn't trust her. I was afraid she would find somebody better than me and leave me for him. I wanted to control her so she'd always be around and I wouldn't have to worry all the time.

Jealousy, possessiveness, and suspicion are recurrent themes in the relationships of many adult children of alcoholics. They learned early that relationships lead to betrayal and love leads to pain.

"But Yesterday You Said It Was Okay"

Carla, a tall, soft-spoken, dental hygienist, came into therapy at the recommendation of her physician, who suggested that her recurrent headaches might have a psychological basis. Since headaches are so often a symptom of repressed rage, one of the first things I asked her was, "What are you angry about?" My question took her by surprise, but after a moment she answered:

> You're right. I *am* angry. At my mother. I'm forty-seven years old and my mother's still running my life. Like last month. I was all set to go on this terrific trip to Mexico. I was really excited about it, but three days before I was supposed to leave, I got a call from Mom. Right on cue. I wasn't even surprised. I could tell she'd been drinking because her speech was real slurry, and she sounded like she'd been crying. She told me my dad had gone on a two-week fishing trip, and she was real depressed . . . and could I just stay with her for a few days. I told her I had this vacation planned and she started to cry. I tried to talk her into visiting my aunt, but she started saying how I didn't love her, and one thing led to another and before I knew it I promised to cancel Mexico and come out. I wouldn't have enjoyed myself anyway knowing she was in the pits again.

I told Carla that this sounded as if it was an old story for her. She agreed:

> Yeah, it happened all the time when I was a kid. I always had to take care of her. And she never appreciated it. She was always ragging at me. I never knew which of my mother's many faces I was going to see at any given time, and I could never figure out what would please her from day to day. I remember getting a D in history and being afraid to come home. A D was good for about four hours of being told that I was a worthless, ungrateful failure, and no man would ever want me. When I finally got home, it turned out she was in a good mood. She just signed my report card and said, "You're smart; you don't have to worry about grades." I couldn't believe it. But then she had her usual four cocktails before dinner that night. I set the table and forgot to put out the salt and pepper. When she sat down, she exploded as if I'd caused a world war or something. I couldn't understand how she could stop loving me just because I forgot the salt and pepper.

Carla's mother's behavior ranged from smotheringly loving to excruciatingly cruel, depending on her mood, her alcoholic consumption, or, as Carla put it, "the phase of the moon." Carla told me there was rarely any normal, everyday middle ground with her mother. So Carla was constantly trying to second-guess how to get her mother's approval. Unfortunately, the floor kept shifting beneath her feet; the same behavior would please her mother one day and set her off the next.

"It's All Your Fault"

All parents are inconsistent to some degree, but the "it's right one day and wrong the next" syndrome is dramatically intensified by alcohol. Because the signals and rules change so often and unexpectedly, the child always falls short. The parent uses criticism as a means of control, so no matter what the child does, the parent will find something to criticize. The child becomes an outlet for frustration, a scapegoat for all that is wrong with his parents. This is an insidious way for alcoholic parents to justify and ventilate their own inadequacies. The message becomes: "If you wouldn't do everything wrong, Mommy wouldn't have to drink." As Carla put it:

> I remember when I was about seven, my mother had been going at the bottle pretty heavy one morning, so I invited a friend over after school. I usually didn't invite people over because I never knew just how drunk she'd be, but this time I figured she'd be sleeping off breakfast by midafternoon. My friend and I were playing dress-up, wearing her shoes and putting on her lipstick and stuff, when suddenly the door banged open, and my mother lurched out. I was so scared I almost wet my pants. Her breath could've knocked us out. She went crazy when she saw us touching her things and started screaming, "I know why you brought your little friend over here . . . to spy on me! You're always spying on me.

> That's why I have to drink all the time. You could drive anyone to drink!"

Carla's mother was totally out of control. In addition to humiliating her daughter, she blamed her for her alcoholism. Carla was too young to see the holes in her mother's logic, so she accepted the blame.

Unconsciously, Carla still thinks she's responsible for her mother's drinking. That's why she's willing to go to such lengths to atone. She canceled a long-awaited vacation just to make a futile stab for her mother's approval.

The family scapegoat is an all-too-familiar role for children in alcoholic families. Some try to fulfill their negative self-image by resorting to self-destructive or delinquent behavior. Others unconsciously find ways to punish themselves with various emotional and even physical symptoms—such as Carla's headaches.

The Golden Child

While some children of alcoholics are forced to be the scapegoat, others are cast in the role of the family hero—the "golden child." This child is showered with approval from both parents and the outside world because of the enormous responsibility he or she is forced to assume. On the surface, this approbation would seem to put the heroic child in a much more positive environment than that of the family scapegoat, but in reality, the deprivation and the personal demons are very much the same. The golden child drives himself mercilessly to achieve unobtainable goals of perfection both in childhood and in adult life.

A few years ago I received a call on my radio show from a research chemist named Steve, who told me:

> I'm just immobilized. I'm forty-one years old and I'm successful in my career. But lately I can't make a decision. I'm in the middle of the biggest project of my life and I just can't

> concentrate. A lot of people are depending on me. I'm petrified. All my life I've been such a high achiever . . . you know . . . straight-A student, Phi Beta Kappa . . . I was always a self-starter. But now I feel paralyzed.

I asked him if there was anything going on in his life that might account for these changes. He said that his father had just been admitted to intensive care with severe liver damage. Taking my clue from that, I asked Steve if his father was an alcoholic. After a moment, he replied that both his parents were. Steve had grown up coping with the uproar at home by burying himself in schoolwork and becoming a superachiever.

> Everybody thought I was Superkid . . . my grandparents, my teachers, even my parents . . . when they were sober. I was the perfect son, the perfect student, and later on, the perfect scientist, husband, and father. [At this point, his voice broke.] I'm getting so tired of being perfect all the time!

As a child, Steve earned approval by assuming burdens beyond his capacity and managing them with a maturity beyond his years. Instead of building a core of self-esteem by being treated as an innately worthwhile human being, he had to prove his worth through external achievement alone. His self-esteem became dependent on accolades, awards, and grades instead of inner confidence.

His drivenness may also have involved an element of compensation. By becoming superadequate himself, Steve may have unconsciously tried to balance out his parents' inadequacy.

I told Steve that his father's illness had obviously stirred up a lot of unfinished business for him, and that while I knew he was in pain, it was also a wonderful opportunity for him to start to deal with some really crucial issues. I asked him to look at the fact that becoming the family hero was his special way of coping with a horrendous childhood. The role provided a certain amount of safety and structure to his life. Unfortunately, he never learned to go easy on himself. Now, many years later, his search for perfection in all aspects of his life was, as is common with most perfectionists, paralyzing him.

At my urging, Steve agreed to seek counseling both to help him through his current situation and to deal with the deprivation of his childhood.

"I Have to Be in Control at All Times"

Children growing up in alcoholic homes are buffeted by unpredictable and volatile circumstances and personalities. In reaction, they often grow up with an overpowering need to control everything and everyone in their lives. Glenn reacted to the helplessness he felt as a child by finding his own way, despite his timidity, to become a controller:

> Whenever I had a girlfriend, I always seemed to dump her while the relationship was going well. I guess I was afraid if I didn't dump her, she'd just wind up dumping me, so it was a way to stay in control. Today, I'm always telling my wife and kids how to do everything. I can't help it, I have to be in control. I run my business the same way. I mean, I still can't yell at anybody, but my employees always know when I'm unhappy. They say I put out vibes. It drives them crazy. But it's my business, right?

Glenn believed that by taking control of all aspects of his life, he could avoid reexperiencing the topsy-turvy craziness of his childhood. Of course, having problems with assertiveness forced him to find other means of control, so he fell back on manipulative techniques such as sulking or nagging, which he learned to use quite effectively.

Unfortunately, his manipulative behavior created distance and resentment between himself and the people he cared about. Like many adult children of alcoholics, Glenn's need to control people resulted in what he feared the most—rejection. It's ironic that the defenses he developed against loneliness as a child were the very things that brought him loneliness as an adult.

"How Dare You Call Your Mother a Drunk!"

If you are the adult child of an alcoholic family, chances are—unlike Steve, with two alcoholic parents—your family drama involved one parent who was a problem drinker and one who was not. In recent years we have begun to learn more about the role of the nondrinking partner in these relationships. As we discussed in chapter 2, this partner is called "the enabler" or "co-dependent."

This is the partner who, despite the suffering that the alcoholic inflicts, unconsciously supports the alcoholic's drinking. Through acceptance, co-dependents communicate that they will always be there to deal with the damage of their partner's destructive behavior. While co-dependents may nag, whine, plead, complain, threaten, and give ultimatums, they are rarely willing to take a strong enough stand to force any significant change.

Carla and I began to make valuable progress in therapy. I wanted to see her interact with her parents firsthand, so I asked her to invite them to a session. When they arrived, I could see that Carla's mother was already upset. The very fact that Carla had asked her to come seemed to unleash her guilt. When I began to discuss the painful realities of Carla's childhood, her mother broke into tears:

> I'm so ashamed. I know I wasn't a good mother to her. Carla, I'm so sorry, I really mean it. I'm really going to try to stop drinking. I'll even go into therapy if you want me to.

I told Carla's mother that psychotherapy is notoriously ineffective for treating alcoholism or any other addictive behavior unless it is used in conjunction with one of the Twelve Step programs such as Alcoholics Anonymous. Carla's mother pleaded:

> Please, Susan, don't make me go to AA. I'll do anything for Carla but that.

At this point, Carla's father interrupted angrily:

> Dammit, my wife is not an alcoholic! She is a wonderful woman who takes a couple of drinks to relax. There are millions of people just like her who have a drink now and then.

I confronted him with how truly destructive Carla's mother's behavior, combined with his lack of involvement, had been for their daughter. He exploded:

> I'm a very successful man and have a beautiful home! Why do you have to drag me and my wife into this? Just concentrate on my daughter's problems and leave us out of it. My daughter's paying for you to take care of *her*—not us. My wife and I don't need this kind of aggravation. Okay, so maybe my wife drinks a little more than most people. But she can handle it. As a matter of fact, when she has a few drinks, she's a helluva lot easier to be with!

Carla's father refused to come to any more sessions, but her mother finally agreed both to enroll in AA and to see one of my colleagues for counseling. What followed was a fascinating but not unexpected sequence of events. As Carla's mother stopped drinking, her husband developed severe gastrointestinal problems, for which—as Carla told me—his doctor couldn't find an explanation.

Clearly, I had disturbed the family's equilibrium. It became apparent that Carla's father could live and function only in a state of total denial. Alcoholic families operate in a precarious balance, with everyone acting out their assigned roles. Once Carla and her mother both started actively working on their own problems, it drastically rocked the family boat. Carla's father was admired in the community as a model of devotion and loyalty. Carla remembers more than one family member saying that her father should be a candidate for sainthood because he was so forgiving and tolerant. In reality, he was a classic co-dependent who, through his denial, gave his wife permission to remain a pitiful alcoholic. He, in turn, gained power by this. As she disappeared into a drunken haze, he was free to run the family as he saw fit.

I continued to see Carla and her mother together for family therapy. Carla's mother began to see how her husband's self-esteem depended on his having single-handed control of the family. His wife's alcoholism and his daughter's physical and emotional problems made him appear to be the only adequate member of the household. Despite the powerful facade he put on for the outside world, Carla's father—like many co-dependents—was terribly insecure. As most of us do, he picked a partner who mirrored his true feelings about himself. Choosing an inadequate partner allowed him to feel superior by comparison.

Carla's mother is now a recovering alcoholic and is making some very positive changes in her relationship with her daughter and her husband. Predictably, her husband's gastrointestinal problems continue.

Unlike Carla's father, Glenn's mother was a co-dependent who fully acknowledged the horrors of her husband's alcoholism and the child abuse that went along with it. Nevertheless, she was no more able or willing to initiate an effective course of action. As Glenn told me:

> My mother's in her late sixties, and I'm still trying to figure out why she let my father terrorize us the way he did. Why did she let her kids get smacked around? There must've been somebody she could've gone to for help. But she's like a broken record . . . all she keeps saying is: "You don't know what it was like for women then. You were supposed to stand by your man no matter what. Nobody was talking about these things out in the open like they are now. Where was I supposed to go? What was I supposed to do?"

Glenn's mother was simply overwhelmed by the family turmoil. Her helplessness, combined with her distorted sense of loyalty, gave her husband permission to continue his outrageous behavior. Glenn's mother, like many co-dependents, in essence became a child herself, leaving the real children unprotected. To this day, Glenn is caught between his need to rescue his childlike mother and his resentment of her failure to mother him.

No Fairy Tale Endings

Fairy tale endings are rare for families of alcoholics. In the best of all possible worlds, your parents would take full responsibility for their drinking, enter a treatment program, and become sober. They would validate and acknowledge the horrors of your childhood and would make an attempt to become responsible, loving parents.

Unfortunately, the reality usually falls far short of the ideal. The drinking, the denial, and the distortion of reality often continue until one or both parents die. Many adult children of alcoholics cling to the hope that their family life will magically evolve into "Ozzie and Harriet," but holding on to this hope can only set you up for a tremendous fall. Glenn found this out in a particularly poignant way:

> About a year ago, my dad told me for the first time that he loved me. I gave him a hug and thanked him, but somehow it just didn't make up for all the years that he told me I was rotten. It was ironic because I'd dreamed of that day all my life.

Glenn finally got his long-sought-after "I love you," but it wasn't enough. It left him with a sense of emptiness. It was all talk and no action. His father was still drinking. Glenn's mistake was that he was waiting for his father to change.

If you're the adult child of an alcoholic, the key to taking control of your life is to remember that *you* can change without changing your parents. Your well-being does *not* have to be dependent on your parents. You can overcome the traumas of your childhood and their power over your adult life, even if your parents stay exactly the way they've always been. You just have to commit yourself to doing the work.

I suggest to all my clients who came from homes where alcohol or drugs were abused that our work together could be greatly accelerated by their joining Adult Children of Alcoholics or a similar organization. These groups provide excellent support, and through the exchange of experiences and feelings, children of alcoholics and drug abusers come to realize that they are not alone. They can face up to the dinosaur in the living room, which is the first step toward driving it out.

5 | *The Bruises Are All on the Inside*

The Verbal Abusers

Remember the old saying, "Sticks and stones may break my bones, but words can never hurt me"? It's not true. Insulting names, degrading comments, and belittling criticism can give children extremely negative messages about themselves, messages that can have dramatic effects on their future well-being. As one caller to my radio show put it:

> If I had to choose between physical and verbal abuse, I'd take a beating anytime. You can see the marks, so at least people feel sorry for you. With the verbal stuff, it just makes you crazy. The wounds are invisible. Nobody cares. Real bruises heal a hell of a lot faster than insults.

As a society, we have traditionally considered the discipline of children a private matter, to be handled within the family, usually at the father's discretion. Today, many civic authorities have come to recognize the need for new procedures to deal with widespread physical and sexual child abuse. But even the most concerned authorities can do nothing for the verbally abused child. He is all alone.

The Power of Cruel Words

Most parents will occasionally say something derogatory to their children. This is not necessarily verbal abuse. But it *is* abusive to launch frequent verbal attacks on a child's appearance, intelligence, competence, or value as a human being.

Like controlling parents, verbal abusers have two distinct styles. There are those who attack directly, openly, viciously degrading their children. They may call their children stupid, worthless, or ugly. They may say that they wish their child had never been born. They are oblivious to their child's feelings and to the long-term effects of their constant assaults on their child's developing self-image.

Other verbal abusers are more indirect, assailing the child with a constant barrage of teasing, sarcasm, insulting nicknames, and subtle put-downs. These parents often hide their abuse behind the facade of humor. They make little jokes like, "The last time I saw a nose that big was on Mount Rushmore," or, "That's a good-looking jacket—for a clown," or, "You must have been home sick the day they passed out brains."

If the child, or any other family member, complains, the abuser invariably accuses him or her of lacking a sense of humor. "She knows I'm only kidding," he'll say, as if the victim of his abuse were a co-conspirator.

Phil, 48, had the outward appearance of a confident man. He was a tall, rugged-looking dentist with a taste for stylish clothes. But when he spoke, his voice was so quiet that I had trouble hearing him. I had to ask him several times to repeat himself. He explained that he was seeking help for his painful shyness.

> I just can't go on this way. I'm practically fifty and I'm supersensitive to almost everything that anybody says to me. I can't take anything at face value. I always think someone's making fun of me. I think my wife's making fun of me . . . I think my patients make fun of me. I lie awake at night thinking about what people said to me during the day . . . and I keep reading bad things into everything. Sometimes I think I'm going crazy.

Phil talked openly about his current life, but he closed up when I asked him about his early years. With some gentle probing, he told me that what he remembered most vividly about his childhood was his father's constant teasing. The jokes were always at Phil's expense and he often felt humiliated. When the rest of the family laughed, he felt all the more isolated.

> It was bad enough being teased, but sometimes he really scared me when he'd say things like: "This boy can't be a son of ours, look at that face. I'll bet they switched babies on us in the hospital. Why don't we take him back and swap him for the right one." I was only six, and I really thought I was going to get dropped off at the hospital. One day, I finally said to him, "Dad, why are you always picking on me?" He said, "I'm not picking on you. I'm just joking around. Can't you see that?"

Phil, like any young child, couldn't distinguish the truth from a joke, a threat from a tease. Positive humor is one of our most valuable tools for strengthening family bonds. But humor that belittles can be extremely damaging within the family. Children take sarcasm and humorous exaggeration at face value. They are not worldly enough to understand that a parent is joking when he says something like, "We're going to have to send you to preschool in China." Instead, the child may have nightmares about being abandoned in some frightening, distant land.

We have all been guilty of making jokes at someone else's expense. Most of the time, such jokes can be relatively harmless. But, as in other forms of toxic parenting, it is the frequency, the cruelty, and the source of these jokes that make them abusive. Children believe and internalize what their parents say about them. It is sadistic and destructive for a parent to make repetitive jokes at the expense of a vulnerable child.

Phil was constantly being humiliated and picked on. When he made an attempt to confront his father's behavior, he was accused of being inadequate because he "couldn't take a joke." Phil had nowhere to go with all these feelings.

As Phil described his feelings, I could see that he was still embarrassed—as if he believed that his complaints were silly. I reassured him by saying, "I understand how humiliating your father's jokes were. They hurt you terribly, yet no one took your pain seriously. But we're here to get to the bottom of your pain, not to discount it. You're safe here, Phil. No one's going to put you down."

He took a few moments to let this sink in. He was on the verge of tears, but he made an enormous effort to hide them as he said:

> I hate him. He was such a coward. I mean I was just a little kid. He didn't have to pick on me that way. He still makes jokes at my expense. He never misses a chance. If I let my guard down for one second, I get zapped! And then he comes off looking like the good guy. God, I hate that!

When Phil first came in for treatment, he made absolutely no connection between his hypersensitivity and his father's taunting. As a little boy, Phil was unprotected because his father's behavior was never recognized as abuse. Phil was in a typical "lose-lose" situation: "My dad's jokes hurt me and I'm weak because I can't take it."

Little Phil was the butt of his father's jokes and struggled to hide his feelings of inadequacy. Adult Phil was no different, but he moved in a much larger world, so he transferred his fears and negative expectations to other people. Phil went through life with his nerve ends exposed, expecting to be hurt, to be humiliated. His hypersensitivity, his shyness, and his distrust of others was an inevitable but ineffective way of attempting to protect himself against further hurt.

"I'M ONLY SAYING THIS FOR YOUR OWN GOOD"

Many parents dish out their verbal abuse under the guise of guidance. To justify cruel and denigrating remarks, they use rationalizations such as, "I'm trying to help you become a better person," or, "It's a tough world and we're teaching you to take it." Because this abuse wears the protective mask of education, it is especially difficult for the adult child to acknowledge its destructiveness.

Vicki was 34 when she came in for therapy. She was an attractive woman who worked as an account manager in a large marketing corporation, but her self-confidence was so low that it threatened her professional advancement:

> I've been working for this big company for six years, and I've done pretty well. I've been slowly moving up, you know, from secretary to office manager to account manager . . . moving through the ranks. But last week the most incredible thing just happened. My boss told me he thought I could really go places with an M.B.A., and he offered to pay for me to get one! I couldn't believe it! You'd think I'd be thrilled, but all I can feel is panic. I haven't been in school in ten years. I don't know if I can do it. And I don't know if I'm up to an M.B.A. anyway. Even people close to me say that I'm getting in over my head.

I remarked that whoever was giving her that assessment wasn't much of a friend because real friends are supportive. This embarrassed her. I asked her why she seemed uneasy. She replied that by "people close to me," she was referring to her mother.

> When I called my mother to ask her if she thought I ought to do it, she brought up some very good points. You know . . . what happens to my job if I don't make it. And had I thought about the fact that with an M.B.A., I'm going to scare away a lot of eligible men. And besides, I *am* happy with what I'm doing.

"But one reason you're happy is that you're proud that you worked your way up," I said. "Don't you want to keep going?" She agreed that she did. I suggested that the advances she'd made at work and the opportunity her boss had offered her were testaments to her worth. The evidence didn't seem to jibe with her mother's doubts. I asked if her mother had always been so negative about Vicki's abilities.

> My mom always wanted me to be the perfect little lady. She wanted me to be graceful and elegant, and to speak well . . . when I'd blow it, she'd try to shame me into doing it right. She meant well, she really did. She'd imitate me if I mispronounced a word. She'd make fun of how I looked . . . ballet recitals were the worst. Mom had dreams of being a dancer herself, but she got married instead. So I guess I was supposed to live out her dream for her, but I never danced as well as she could, at least that's what she always told me. I'll never forget one recital when I was about twelve. I thought I'd done pretty well, but my mom came backstage and said—in front of the whole class—"You danced like a hippo." I just wanted to sink through the floor. When I sulked all the way home, she told me I should learn to take a little criticism because that's the only way I was going to learn. Then she patted my arm, and I thought she was going to say something nice, but you know what she said? "Let's face it, dear, you don't do anything very well, do you?"

"Be a Success—But I Know You'll Fail"

Vicki's mother seems to have been strongly invested in making her young daughter feel inadequate. She did so through a series of confusing double messages. On one hand, she urged her daughter to excel, while on the other hand she told her how terrible she was. Vicki always felt off balance, never sure whether she was doing anything right. When she thought she'd done well, her mother deflated her; when she thought she'd done poorly, her mother told her she couldn't do any better. At a time when Vicki should have been building self-confidence, her mother was knocking it down. All in the name of making Vicki a better person.

But what was this abusive parent really doing? Vicki's mother was fighting her own feelings of inadequacy. Her own dance career was thwarted, perhaps by marriage. But perhaps she used marriage as an excuse because she didn't have the confidence to pursue a career. By establishing her superiority over her daughter, Vicki's mother could deny her feelings of inadequacy. Any occasion became fair game, even if it involved humiliating her daughter in front of her peers. It is particularly scarring for a budding adolescent to be embarrassed in this way, but the toxic parent's needs always come first.

The Competitive Parent

The need to make someone feel inadequate in order to feel adequate oneself rapidly evolves into out-and-out competition. Clearly, Vicki's mother came to see her young daughter as a threat because as Vicki grew older and became more beautiful, more mature, and more competent, her mother had more trouble feeling superior. She had to keep up the pressure, keep on demeaning her daughter, to defend against this threat.

Healthy parents experience their children's growing competence with excitement and joy. Competitive parents, on the other hand, often feel deprived, anxious, even scared. Most competitive parents are not aware of the reasons for these feelings, but they know that the child stirs them up.

During adolescence, little girls start to become women and little boys start to become men. The child's adolescence is an especially threatening time for the insecure parent. Women feel frightened that they're growing old and losing their beauty. They may see their daughters as competitors and feel the need to belittle them, especially in front of their husbands. Men may feel a threat to their virility and power. There's room for only one man in the house, so they use ridicule and humiliation to keep their sons feeling little and helpless. Many adolescents exacerbate the situation by being openly competitive as a means of testing the waters of adulthood.

Competitive parents have often been victims of deprivation in their own childhoods, whether from shortages of food, clothing, or love. No matter how much they have, they still live in fear of not having enough. Many of these parents reenact with their children the competition they experienced with their own parents or siblings. This unfair competition puts enormous pressure on a child.

Vicki simply gave up trying to accomplish anything:

> For so many years, I didn't do a lot of things, even things I really liked, because I was afraid of being humiliated. After I grew up, I kept hearing her voice, just putting me down. She didn't swear at me, she never called me dirty names. But the way she was always comparing herself to me, she made me feel like such a loser. It hurt so bad.

Despite what competitive parents may claim to want for their children, their hidden agenda is to ensure that their children can't outdo them. The unconscious messages are powerful: "You cannot be more successful than I am," "You cannot be more attractive than I am," or, "You cannot be happier than I am." In other words, "We all have our limits, and I am yours."

Because these messages are so deeply entrenched, if the adult children of competitive parents *do* manage to excel in something, they often experience tremendous guilt. The more they succeed, the more miserable they become. This often leads them to sabotage their success. For these adult children of toxic parents, underachievement is the price of peace of mind. They control their guilt by unconsciously limiting themselves so they don't outperform their parents. In a sense, they fulfill their parents' negative prophecies.

Branded by Insults

Some verbally abusive parents don't bother to hide behind rationalizations. Instead, they bombard their children with cruel insults, harangues, denunciations, and derogatory names. These parents are extraordinarily insensitive to both the pain they are inflicting and the lasting damage they are doing. Such blatant verbal abuse can sear into a child's self-worth like a cattle brand, leaving deep psychological scars.

Carol, 52, is an extremely beautiful model-turned-interior-designer. In our first session, she told me about her latest divorce—her third. The divorce had become final about a year before Carol came to see me. It had been a painful experience, and Carol was left feeling frightened about her future. At the same time, she was going through menopause and seemed on the verge of panic over losing her looks. She felt undesirable. She told me that these fears had been intensified by a recent Thanksgiving visit with her parents.

> It always ends up the same way. Every time I see my parents, I get hurt and disappointed all over again. The hardest thing is that I keep thinking maybe if I come home this time and tell them that I'm unhappy, that something's gone wrong in my life, maybe just this one time they'll say, "Gee, honey, we're really sorry," instead of, "It's your own fault." As long as I can remember, it's always been, "It's your own fault."

I told Carol that it sounded as if her parents were still exercising tremendous power over her. I asked her if she was willing to explore the roots of that power with me so that we could begin to change the patterns of dominance and control. Carol nodded and began to tell me about her childhood in a wealthy midwestern family. Her father was a prominent physician and her mother was an Olympic-level swimmer who retired from competitive athletics to raise her five children. Carol was the eldest.

> I remember feeling sad and lonely a lot of the time when I was little. My father always teased me, but when I was around eleven he started saying really horrible things.

"Like what?" I asked. She told me it didn't matter. She started biting her cuticles nervously. I knew she was trying to protect an emotional nerve. "Carol," I said, "I can see how painful this is for you. But we have to get this stuff out in the air where we can deal with it." She started slowly:

> For some reason, my father decided . . . God, this is hard . . . he decided I . . . I smelled bad. He just never let up. I mean, other people used to tell me how pretty I was, but all he could ever say was . . .

Carol stopped again and looked away. "Come on, Carol," I said, "I'm on your side."

> He used to say, "Your breasts smell bad . . . your back stinks. If people only knew how filthy and smelly your body is, they'd be disgusted." Honest to God, I'd shower three times a day. I'd change clothes all the time. I'd use tons of deodorant and perfume, but it wouldn't make any difference. One of his favorites was, "If someone turned you inside out, they'd see stink come out every pore in your body." Remember, this is coming from a respected physician. And my mother never

> said a word. She never even told me it wasn't true. I kept wondering how I could be better . . . how I could keep him from telling me how awful and smelly I was. When I went to the bathroom, I always thought if I could flush the toilet faster, maybe he wouldn't think I was so awful.

I told Carol that it sounded as if her father had reacted irrationally to her burgeoning womanhood because he couldn't deal with his preoccupation with it. It is very common for fathers to react to their daughters' blossoming sexuality with discomfort and often hostility. Even a father who is kind and loving when his daughter is small may create conflict during her adolescence in order to distance himself from sexual attractions he finds unacceptable.

To a toxic father like Carol's, a daughter's sexual development can trigger extreme feelings of anxiety, which, in his mind, justify his persecution of her. By projecting his guilt and discomfort on to her, he could deny any responsibility for his feelings. It is as if he were saying, "You are a bad and wicked person because you make me feel bad and wicked things for you."

I asked Carol whether any of this rang true for her.

> Now that I think about it, it *was* a sexual thing. I always felt his eyes on me. And he was always bugging me for details about what I was doing with my boyfriends, which was practically nothing. But he was convinced I was going to bed with everyone I went out with. He'd say things like, "Just tell me the truth and I won't punish you." He really wanted to hear me talk about sex.

During the emotional maelstrom of adolescence, Carol desperately needed a loving and supportive father to give her confidence. Instead, he subjected her to relentless denigration. Her father's verbal abuse, combined with her mother's passivity, severely damaged Carol's ability to believe in herself as a valuable and lovable person. When people told her how pretty she was, all she could think about was whether they could smell her. No amount of external validation could compete with her father's devastating messages.

> I started modeling when I was seventeen. Of course, the more successful I was, the worse my father got. I really had to get out of that house. So, I got married at nineteen to the first guy who asked me. A real doll: he hit me when I was pregnant and he left me when the baby was born. Naturally, I blamed myself. I figured I must have done something wrong. Maybe I smelled bad, I didn't know. About a year later, I married a guy who didn't beat me, but he hardly ever talked to me. I stuck that one out for ten years because I couldn't face my parents with another failed marriage. But I finally left him. Thank God I had my modeling, so I was able to support my son and myself. I even swore off men for a few years. Then I met Glen. I thought this was it; I'd somehow found the perfect guy. The first five years of our marriage was the happiest time of my life. Then I found out he'd been cheating on me almost from the day we got married. I did a lot of forgiving over the next ten years because I just didn't want to lose another marriage. Last year he left me for a woman half my age. Why can't I do anything right?

I reminded Carol that she had done a lot right: she'd been a loving and available mother; she'd raised a son who was doing well in his own life; she had *two* successful careers. But none of my assurances carried much weight. Carol had internalized her father's image of herself as a worthless, repulsive human being. As a result, most of her adult life was propelled by a self-defeating quest for the love she had craved from her father as a young girl. She chose cruel, abusive, or distant men—like her father—and tried to get them to love her the way her father never had.

I explained to Carol that by asking her father, or the men she chose to replace him, to make her feel okay about herself, she was putting her self-esteem in their hands. It didn't take a genius to see how destructive those hands had been. She had to take back control of her self-esteem by confronting the self-defeating beliefs that her father had planted in her childhood. Over the next few months she gradually came to realize that her self-esteem was not lost—she was just looking for it in the wrong place.

Perfectionist Parents

The impossible expectation that children be perfect is another common trigger for severe verbal attacks. Many verbally abusive parents are themselves high achievers, but all too often their homes become dumping grounds for career stress. (Alcoholic parents may also make impossible demands on their children, then use their children's failure to justify drinking.)

Perfectionist parents seem to operate under the illusion that if they can just get their children to be perfect, they will be a perfect family. They put the burden of stability on the child to avoid facing the fact that they, as parents, cannot provide it. The child fails and becomes the scapegoat for family problems. Once again, the child is saddled with the blame.

Children need to make mistakes and discover that it's not the end of the world. That's how they gain the confidence to try new things in life. Toxic parents impose unobtainable goals, impossible expectations, and ever-changing rules on their children. They expect their children to respond with a degree of maturity that can come only from life experiences that are inaccessible to a child. Children are not miniature adults, but toxic parents expect them to act as if they are.

Paul, 33, a dark-haired blue-eyed lab technician, came to me because of troubles at work. He was noticeably shy, self-conscious, and unsure of himself, but still he managed repeatedly to get into heated arguments with his immediate superiors. This, along with increasing concentration problems, was jeopardizing his job.

As Paul and I talked about his work, I could see that he had difficulties in dealing with authority figures. I asked him about his parents and discovered that Paul, like Carol, had been branded by insults. As he described:

> I was nine when my mother remarried. The guy must've studied with Hitler. The first thing he did when he moved in was lay down the law: democracy stopped at the front door. If he told us to jump off a cliff, we had to jump. No questions. I got it a lot worse than my sister did. He was on my case all the time, mostly about my room. He would do this god-damned inspection every day like it was some kind of army barracks. When you're nine or ten, things are always a little messy, but he didn't care. Everything had to be perfect, nothing could be out-of-place. If I left a book on the desk, he'd start screaming about how I was a disgusting pig. He'd call me a fucking little asshole or a little son of a bitch or a snot-nosed bastard. It was like his favorite sport to keep pounding me with those lousy names. He never hit me, but the god-damned names hurt just as bad.

I had a hunch that there was something about Paul that had stirred up strong feelings in his stepfather. It didn't take long to figure it out. Paul had been a shy, sensitive, withdrawn child, small for his age.

> When my stepfather was young, he was the smallest kid in the school. Everybody picked on him. By the time my mother met him, he was husky because he'd gotten into working out. You could tell he'd put it all on, though. Somehow, all that muscle always looked like it ought to be on somebody else.

Somewhere inside Paul's stepfather, a small, frightened, inadequate boy was still alive. And since Paul had so many similar characteristics, he became a symbol of his stepfather's own painful childhood. Because his stepfather had never accepted himself as a child, he felt immediate rage at the young boy who reminded him of himself. He used Paul as a scapegoat for the inadequacies he couldn't face in himself. By tyrannizing Paul with impossible demands for perfection, and then verbally abusing him when the boy fell short, his stepfather could convince himself that he was powerful and strong. The damage he was doing to Paul probably never even crossed his mind. He thought he was helping the boy to be perfect.

"I Can't Be Perfect So I Might as Well Give Up"

Paul's mother divorced her second husband when Paul was eighteen, but by that time Paul's spirit was already seriously battered. Paul knew he could never be "perfect" enough for his stepfather, so he just gave up:

> When I was fourteen, I got into drugs real bad. It was about the only time I ever felt accepted. I wasn't going to make it as a jock, and I sure wasn't the life of the party, so what else was there? Just before I graduated high school, I bought some really bad shit and nearly OD'd. Well, that did it for me . . . no way was I ever gonna go through that again.

Paul attended a junior college for a year, but quit despite both a yearning and an aptitude for a career as a scientist. He just couldn't concentrate. His IQ was extremely high, but he would buckle in the face of a challenge. He'd gotten into the habit of giving up.

When he entered the job market he found himself falling into antagonistic patterns with his bosses, again replaying his childhood. He went from job to job until he finally found one he liked. Then he came to me to try to keep it. I told him I thought I could help.

The Three P's of Perfectionism

Even though Paul's stepfather was out of his life, he still maintained a strong hold over Paul because the demeaning messages continued to play in Paul's head. As a result, Paul stayed entangled in what I call "The Three P's": Perfectionism, Procrastination, and Paralysis.

> I really like this new lab where I'm working, but I'm always terrified that I'm not going to do a perfect job. So, I put off a lot of what I have to do until way after my deadlines, or I'll rush them through at the last minute and screw up. The more I screw up, the more I keep expecting to get fired. Anytime my supervisor makes a comment, I take it personally and overreact. I'm always expecting that the world is going to come to an end because I've screwed up. Lately, I've gotten so far behind that I've been calling in sick. I just can't face it.

Paul's stepfather had implanted in Paul the need to be perfect—Perfectionism. Paul's fear of failing to do things perfectly led him to postpone doing them—Procrastination. But the more Paul put things off, the more they overwhelmed him, and his snowballing fears eventually prevented him from doing anything at all—Paralysis.

I helped Paul think through a strategy to approach his employers openly, tell them he was having personal problems that were interfering with his work, and ask for a leave of absence. They were impressed by his honesty and his concern for the quality of his work, and they granted him two months. That wasn't enough time for Paul to explore all of his problems, but it was long enough for us to get him out of the hole he'd dug for himself. By the time he returned to his job, he had been able to take the first steps toward facing what his stepfather had done to him, which made him better able to differentiate between real conflicts with his superiors and conflicts arising from his internal wounds. Even though he was to remain in therapy for another eight months, everyone at work told him that he seemed like a new man.

The "S" Word

Adult children of perfectionist parents have usually taken one of two paths. They've either driven themselves relentlessly to win parental love and approval, or they've rebelled to the point where they develop a fear of success.

There are those who behave as if someone is always keeping score. The house can never be clean enough. They can never experience pleasure in an accomplishment because they're convinced that they could have done it better. They feel genuine panic if they make the slightest mistake.

Then there are those who, like Paul, live a life of failure because they cannot deal with "the 'S' word"—Success. To Paul, being successful would have meant capitulating to his stepfather's demands. Paul probably would have continued to fail at job after job if we had not silenced his stepfather's voice within him.

The Cruelest Words: "I Wish You'd Never Been Born"

One of the most extreme examples of the havoc created by verbal abuse was Jason, 42, a handsome police officer in one of my hospital groups several years ago. The Los Angeles Police Department had insisted that he be hospitalized because the police psychologist had concluded that Jason was a suicide risk. At the hospital staff conference, I learned that Jason was consistently putting himself into unnecessarily life-threatening situations. For example, he had recently tried to make a drug bust by himself, without calling for the appropriate backup. He came very close to being killed. On the surface this appeared to be a heroic act, but it was actually reckless, irresponsible behavior. The word was out in the department: Jason was trying to kill himself in the line of duty.

It took several group sessions for me to gain Jason's confidence.

But once I did, we established a good working relationship. I still recall vividly the session in which he told about his bizarre relationship with his mother:

> My dad skipped out when I was two years old because my mother was impossible to live with. She got even worse after he left. She had this really violent temper, and she never let up on me, especially since I happened to be the spitting image of my old man. I don't remember a day when she didn't tell me she wished I'd never been born. On a good day, she'd say, "You look just like your goddamned father and you're just as rotten." On her bad days, she'd say stuff like, "I wish you were dead just like I wish your father was dead, rotting in some shallow grave."

I told Jason that his mother sounded crazy.

> I thought so too, but who's going to listen to a kid. One of our neighbors knew about it. She tried to get me into a foster home because she was convinced my mother was going to kill me. But nobody listened to her, either.

He paused for a moment and shook his head.

> Jesus, I didn't think this crap bothered me anymore, but my insides turn to ice every time I remember how much she hated me.

Jason's mother had sent him a clear message: she did not want him. When his father left and made no attempt to be a part of his son's life, he reinforced the point: Jason's existence was worthless.

Through his actions on the police force, Jason was unconsciously trying to be a dutiful, obedient son. In essence, Jason was trying to wipe out his existence, to commit suicide indirectly in order to please his mother. He knew exactly what it would take to please her because she'd told him very explicitly: "I wish you were dead."

In addition to inflicting enormous hurt and bewilderment, this form of verbal abuse can become a self-fulfilling prophecy. Jason's suicidal tendencies are relatively common among the children of such parents. For these adult children, facing and dealing with their toxic connections to the past can literally be a matter of life or death.

When "You Are" Becomes "I Am"

While there is no question that children can be damaged by put-downs from friends, teachers, siblings, and other family members, children are the most vulnerable to their parents. After all, parents are the center of a young child's universe. And if your all-knowing parents think bad things about you, they must be true. If Mother is always saying, "You're stupid," then you're stupid. If Father is always saying, "You're worthless," then you are. A child has no perspective from which to cast doubt on these assessments.

When you take these negative opinions out of other people's mouths and put them into your unconscious, you are "internalizing" them. Internalization of negative opinions—changing "you are" to "I am"—forms the foundation of low self-esteem. Besides significantly impairing your sense of yourself as a lovable, valuable, competent person, verbal abuse can create self-fulfilling negative expectations about how you will get along in the world. In the second part of this book, I'll show you how to defeat those crippling expectations by making the internal external again.

6 | *Sometimes the Bruises Are on the Outside, Too*

The Physical Abusers

> I find I get angry at myself all the time, and sometimes I cry for no reason at all. It's probably my frustration at myself. I keep thinking how my parents hurt and humiliated me. I don't keep friends for very long. I have a pattern of cutting off whole groups of friends at a time. I guess I don't want them to find out how bad I am.

Kate, 40, a blond, stern-faced quality-control manager for a large corporation, came to see me at the recommendation of her family physician. She had been having panic attacks in her car and in the elevator of the building where she worked. Her physician had prescribed tranquilizers but was concerned about Kate's aversion to leaving her apartment except to go to work. He urged her to seek psychological help.

The first thing I noticed about Kate was that her severe,

unhappy expression seemed molded onto her face—as if she had never learned to smile. It didn't take me long to discover why:

> I was raised in an upper-class suburb outside St. Louis. We had everything money could buy. From the outside we looked like this perfect family. But from the inside . . . my father would go into these crazy rages. They usually came after he had a fight with my mother. He would just turn on whichever of us was closest. He would take off his belt and start strapping me or my sister . . . across our legs . . . on our heads . . . anywhere he could hit us. When he'd start in, I'd always have this fear that he wouldn't stop.

Kate's depression and fear were the legacy of a battered child.

The All-American Crime

Inside millions of American households, ranging across all social, economic, and educational lines, a terrible crime is being committed every day—the physical abuse of children.

There is a great deal of controversy and confusion over the definition of physical abuse. Many people still believe that parents have not only the right but the responsibility to use corporal punishment on their children. The most common parenting motto in the English language is still, "Spare the rod and spoil the child." Until recently, children had virtually no legal rights. They were widely viewed as chattel, pieces of property that were "owned" by their parents. For hundreds of years, parental rights were considered inviolate—in the name of discipline, parents could do just about anything to their children, short of killing them.

Today our norms have narrowed. The problem of physical child abuse has become so widespread that public recognition has forced our legal system to set limits on physical discipline. In an attempt to clarify what constitutes physical abuse, Congress enacted the

Federal Child Abuse Prevention and Treatment Act of 1974. This act defined physical abuse as: "the infliction of physical injuries such as bruises, burns, welts, cuts, bone and skull fractures; these are caused by kicking, punching, biting, beating, knifing, strapping, paddling, etc." How this definition translates into law is often a matter of interpretation. Every state has its own child-abuse laws, and most embody definitions similar to the federal one, which is somewhat vague in its scope. A child with a broken bone has clearly been abused, but most prosecutors would be reluctant to press charges against a parent who had bruised a child during a spanking.

I'm not a lawyer and I'm not a cop, but for more than twenty years I've seen the suffering that "legal" corporal punishment can create. I have my own definition of physical abuse: any behavior that inflicts significant physical pain on a child, regardless of whether it leaves marks.

Why Do Parents Beat Their Kids?

Most of us who have children have felt the urge to strike them at one time or another. These feelings can be especially strong when a child won't stop crying, nagging, or defying us. Sometimes it has less to do with a child's behavior than with our own exhaustion, stress level, anxiety, or unhappiness. A lot of us manage to resist the impulse to hit our children. Unfortunately, many parents are not so restrained.

We can only speculate why, but physically abusive parents seem to share certain characteristics. First, they have an appalling lack of impulse control. Physically abusive parents will assault their children whenever they have strong negative feelings that they need to discharge. These parents seem to have little, if any, awareness of the consequences of what they are doing to their children. It is almost an automatic reaction to stress. The impulse and the action are one and the same.

Physical abusers themselves often come from families in which abuse was the norm. Much of their adult behavior is a direct repetition of what they experienced and learned in their youth. Their role model was an abuser. Violence was the only tool they learned to use in dealing with problems and feelings—especially feelings of anger.

Many physically abusive parents enter adulthood with tremendous emotional deficits and unmet needs. Emotionally, they are still children. They often look upon their own children as surrogate parents, to fulfill the emotional needs that their real parents never fulfilled. The abuser becomes enraged when his child can't meet his needs. He lashes out. At that moment, the child is more of a surrogate parent than ever, because it is the abuser's parent at whom the abuser is truly enraged.

Many of these parents also have problems with alcohol or drugs. Substance abuse is a frequent contributor to the breakdown of impulse control, though by no means is it the only one.

There are many types of physical abusers, but at the darkest end of the spectrum are those who have children seemingly for the sole purpose of brutalizing them. Many of these people look, talk, and act just like human beings, but they are monsters—totally devoid of the feelings and characteristics that give most of us our humanity. These people defy comprehension; there is no logic to their behavior.

The Private Holocaust—There's No Escape

Kate's father was a well-respected banker, a churchgoer, a family man—hardly the type most people would imagine when they hear the phrase *child abuser*. But Kate didn't live in an imagined reality, she lived in a real nightmare.

> My sister and I started locking our door at night because we were so scared. I'll never forget this one time when I was eleven . . . she was nine. We were hiding under our beds and he kept banging on the door. I've never been so scared in my

> life. Then, all of a sudden he came crashing through the door like in the movies. It was terrifying. The door just flew into the room. We tried to run, but he grabbed us both and threw us in the corner and started beating at us with his belt. He kept shouting, "I'll kill you if you ever lock me out again!" I thought he was going to kill us right then and there.

The climate of terror that Kate described permeates the homes of physically abused children. Even in quiet moments, these children live in fear that the volcano of rage will erupt at any moment. And when it does, anything the victim does to fend off the blows only outrages the abuser more. Kate's desperate attempts to protect herself by hiding under her bed and locking the door only intensified her father's irrational behavior. There is no safe place to hide, no escape from the abuser, no protector to run to.

You Never Know When It's Going to Happen

I first met Joe, 27, at a seminar I was conducting at a graduate school of psychology where he was studying for his master's degree. I mentioned in my presentation that I was writing a book on toxic parents. Joe sought me out at the lunch break and volunteered to be a case study for my book. I had more than enough material from my practice, but something in this young man's voice told me he needed to talk to someone. We met the following day and talked for several hours. I was impressed not only by his openness and candor but by the sincerity of his desire to use his painful experiences to help others.

> I was always getting knocked around in my bedroom, I don't even remember what for. I could be doing anything and my father would burst in and start screaming and yelling at the top of his lungs. The next thing I knew, he'd start punching me until he'd have me up against the wall. He'd keep

> pounding me so hard that I'd be dazed and didn't know what the hell was going on anymore. The scariest part of it was not ever knowing what would provoke his outbursts!

Joe spent much of his childhood waiting for the tidal wave of his father's rage and knowing there was no way to avoid it. The experience generated powerful, lifelong fears of being hurt and betrayed. Two marriages ended in divorce because he couldn't learn to trust.

> It just doesn't go away because you move out or get married. I'm always afraid of something, and I hate myself for it. But if your father, who is supposed to love you and take care of you, treated you this way, then what the hell is going to happen to you in the real world. I've screwed up a lot of relationships because I can't let anyone get too close. I'm so ashamed of myself for that, and I'm so ashamed of myself for being so damn frightened all the time. But life just scares the hell out of me. I'm really working hard in my own therapy to get on top of this stuff because I know I'm not going to be of much use to myself or anybody else until I do. But, holy Christ, it's a struggle.

It is tremendously difficult to regain feelings of trust and safety once they have been trampled by parents. All of us develop our expectations about how people will treat us based on our relationships with our parents. If those relationships are, for the most part, emotionally nourishing, respectful of our rights and feelings, we'll grow up expecting others to treat us in much the same way. These positive expectations allow us to be relatively vulnerable and open in our adult relationships. But if, as in Joe's case, childhood is a time of unrelenting anxiety, tension, and pain, then we develop negative expectations and rigid defenses.

Joe expected the worst of others. He expected to be hurt and mistreated as he was in his childhood. So he encased himself in a suit of emotional armor. He wouldn't let anyone get close to him.

Unfortunately, that suit of armor proved to be more of an emotional prison than a protection.

"I've Got So Many Problems—No Wonder I Let You Have It"

Joe never understood what set his father off. Other abusers have a need to be understood. They beat their children, then beg them to understand, even ask for their forgiveness. That's how it was for Kate:

> I remember one particularly terrible evening after dinner when my mother was out shopping. My father was really giving it to me with that damned belt. I was screaming so loud that one of our neighbors called the police, but my father managed to convince them that everything was fine. He told the cops that the noise was coming from the TV, and they bought it. I'm standing there with tears streaming down my face and welts on my arms, but they still bought it. Why shouldn't they? My father was one of the most powerful men in the city. But at least they calmed him down. After they left, he told me he'd been under a lot of stress lately. I didn't even know what *stress* meant, but he really wanted me to understand what he was going through. He told me that my mother wasn't nice to him anymore . . . that she wouldn't sleep with him and it wasn't right for a wife not to sleep with her husband. That was why he was so upset all the time.

Kate's father revealed inappropriate, intimate information to a child who was too young to understand. Yet, he expected her to nurture him emotionally. This role reversal confused and bewildered Kate, but it is common among abusive parents. They want their children to give them both relief and absolution; they batter them, then they blame their behavior on someone else.

Instead of dealing directly with his marital problems, Kate's father displaced his fury and sexual frustration onto his daughters, then rationalized his violence by blaming his wife. Physical violence against children is often a reaction to stress at work, conflict with another family member or friend, or general tension over an unsatisfying life. Children are easy targets: they can't fight back, and they can be intimidated into silence. Unfortunately for both the abuser and the victim, displacing anger gives the abuser only temporary relief. The true source of his rage remains, unchanged and destined to build up again. And, sadly, the helpless target of his rage remains as well, destined to soak up that rage and carry it into adulthood.

"I'M DOING THIS FOR YOUR OWN GOOD"

Other abusers, instead of blaming someone else for their behavior, will try to justify it as being in the child's best interests. Many parents still believe that physical punishment is the only effective way to drive home a moral or behavioral point. Many of these "lessons" are delivered in the name of religion. Never has a book been as sorely misused as the Bible to justify beatings.

I was appalled by a letter that appeared in Ann Landers's syndicated column:

> Dear Ann Landers,
> I was disappointed in your response to the girl whose mother used to strap her. The gym teacher noticed the bruises on her legs and backside and called it "child abuse." Why are you against strapping a child when the Bible tells us in plain language that this is what parents should do? Proverbs 23:13 says: "Withhold not correction from the child for if thou beatest him with the rod, he shall not die." Proverbs 23:14 says: "Thou shalt beat him with the rod and shalt deliver his soul from death."

These same parents often believe in the inherent malevolence of children. They believe that a harsh beating will keep a child from going bad. They say things such as: "I was raised with the hickory switch; a licking now and then didn't do me any harm," or, "I need to put the fear of God in him," or, "She's got to know who's boss," or, "He's got to know what he's in for so he'll toe the line."

Other parents excuse beatings as necessary rites of passage, ordeals to make a child tougher, braver, or stronger. That was what Joe was led to believe:

> My dad's mother died when my dad was fourteen. He never got over it. He's still not over it, and he's going on sixty-four. He recently told me that he was tough on me because he didn't want me to feel. Sick as it was, he theorized that if you don't feel, you won't have to go through the pain of life. I honest-to-God believe he thought he was protecting me from being hurt. He didn't want me to experience the kind of pain he'd gone through with his mother's death.

Instead of making Joe tougher or less vulnerable, the beatings left him fearful and mistrustful, far less equipped to make it in the world. It's absurd to believe that severe physical punishment will have any positive effects on a child.

In fact, research indicates that physical discipline is not particularly effective as a punishment even for specific undesirable behaviors. Beatings have proved to be only temporary deterrents, and they create in children strong feelings of rage, revenge fantasies, and self-hatred. It's quite clear that the mental, emotional, and often bodily harm caused by physical abuse far outweighs any momentary advantages.

The Passive Abuser

So far I have focused almost entirely on the actively abusive parent. But there's another player in the family drama who must share some of the responsibility. This is the parent who permits the abuse to happen out of his or her own fears, dependency, or need to maintain the family's status quo. This parent is the passive abuser.

I asked Joe what his mother was doing while he was being battered.

> She wasn't doing much of anything. Sometimes she'd lock herself in the bathroom. I always wondered why she didn't stop this crazy bastard from knocking the hell out of me all the time. But I guess she was just too scared herself. It just wasn't in her nature to confront him. See, my dad is Christian, and my mom is Jewish. She was raised in a very poor, orthodox family, and where she came from, women don't tell their men what to do. I guess she was thankful that she had a roof over her head and that her husband made a nice living.

Joe's mother did not beat her children herself, but because she did not protect them from her husband's brutality she became a partner in their abuse. Instead of taking steps to defend her children, she became a frightened child herself, helpless and passive in the face of her husband's violence. In effect, she abandoned her son.

In addition to feeling isolated and unprotected, Joe found himself saddled with an overwhelming responsibility:

> I remember when I was about ten years old, and my dad had beaten the hell out of my mother one night. I got up real early the next morning and I was waiting in the kitchen when he came down in his bathrobe. He asked me what I was doing up so early. I was scared shitless, but I said, "If you ever beat up on Mom again, I'm going to come after you with a baseball bat." He just looked at me and laughed. Then he went upstairs to take a shower and go to work.

Joe had made a classic abused-child role reversal, assuming responsibility for protecting his mother as if he were the parent and she were the child.

By allowing herself (or himself) to be overwhelmed by helplessness, the inactive parent can more easily deny her silent complicity in the abuse. And by becoming protective, or by rationalizing the silent parent's inactivity, the abused child can more easily deny the fact that *both* parents have failed him.

Kate is a case in point:

> When my father first started beating us, my sister and I would always scream for Mom to help. But she never came. She just sat downstairs and listened to us screaming for her. It didn't take us long to realize she wasn't coming. She never stood up to my father. I guess she couldn't help it.

No matter how many times I hear statements like, "I guess she couldn't help it," they still upset me. Kate's mother *could* have helped it. I told Kate that it was important for her to start looking at her mother's role realistically. Her mother should have stood up to Kate's father, or, if she was afraid of him, she should have called the police. There is *no* excuse for a parent to stand by and allow his or her children to be brutalized.

In both Kate's and Joe's cases, the father was the active abuser and the mother was the silent partner. However, this is by no means the only family scenario. In some families, the mother is the active abuser and the father is the passive one. The sexes may change, but the dynamics of passive abuse remain the same. I have had clients where *both* parents were abusive, but the abusive/passive parent combination is far more common.

Many adult children excuse the passive parent because they see that parent as a co-victim. In Joe's case, this view was intensified because he was in a role reversal in which he felt protective of his passive mother.

For Terry, a 43-year-old marketing rep, the situation was further confused when his passive parent became the sympathetic comforter. Terry, who had been physically abused by his mother through most of his childhood, idolized his ineffectual father.

> I was a very sensitive kid, more into art and music than sports. My mother always called me a sissy. She got angry with me a lot and would beat me with anything she could find. It seems like I spent most of my childhood hiding in closets. I was never sure why she beat me so much, but everything I did seemed to piss her off. I feel like she wiped out my whole childhood.

I asked Terry what his father was doing while his mother was terrorizing him.

> Lots of times, my dad would hold me while I was sobbing, and he'd tell me how sorry he was about my mother's fits. He always said there was nothing he could do about it, and that if I tried harder, things might go better for me. My dad was really a nice guy. He worked very hard so his family could live well. He gave me the only real consistent love I got when I was little.

I asked Terry if, since he has become an adult, he has talked to his father about his childhood.

> I've tried a couple times, but he always says "let bygones be bygones." Anyway, what's the point of upsetting him? My problems are with my mother, not with him.

Terry denied his father's complicity because he wanted to protect the only good childhood memories he had—those loving moments with his father. Just as he clung to his father's tenderness as a frightened child, so was he clinging to it today as a frightened adult. In trading a dark closet for a false reality, he had done nothing to face the truth.

Terry was aware of how much his mother's abuse had colored his life but far less aware of how much repressed rage he carried toward his father. Terry had spent years denying that his father had failed him. To make matters worse, his father had put much of the responsibility on Terry's head by suggesting that if Terry "tried harder," he could avoid the beatings.

Learning to Hate Yourself: "It's All My Fault"

As difficult as it may be to believe, battered children accept the blame for the crimes perpetrated against them just as surely as verbally abused children do. Joe recalled:

> My father always told me that I wasn't worth shit. If there was some way he could hook my name to a swear word while he was beating me, he would do it. By the time he got through, I honestly believed that I was the worst thing that ever lived. And that I was only getting knocked around because I deserved it.

The seeds of self-blame were planted early in Joe. How could a small child withstand this powerful propaganda about his worth? Like all abused children, Joe believed two lies: that he was bad, and that he was getting beaten only *because* he was bad.

Since these lies came from his powerful, all-knowing father, they had to be true. These lies remain unchallenged for most adults who were battered as children, including Joe. As he describes it:

> I'm so down on myself . . . I can't seem to have a good relationship with anybody. It's hard for me to believe that anybody could really care for me.

Kate expressed a similar theme when she didn't want people to find out how "bad" she was. These pervasive feelings of low self-esteem evolve into self-loathing and create life patterns of damaged relationships, loss of confidence, feelings of inadequacy, paralyzing fears, and unfocused rage.

Kate summed it up:

> All my life, it's been going through my mind that I don't deserve to be happy. I think that's why I never got married . . . never had a good relationship . . . never allowed myself any real success.

When Kate grew up, the physical abuse ended. But through self-loathing, the emotional abuse continued. Except that now, she had become her own abuser.

Abuse and Love—A Bewildering Combination

Abused children are often exposed to a bizarre mixture of pleasure and pain. Joe described intermittent terror coexisting with tender moments:

> At times my father could be funny, and sometimes, I swear, he was even gentle. Like this one time I was signed up for this big skiing competition and he got really into it. So he drove me all the way to Jackson, Wyoming, which took ten hours, just so I could practice on good snow. On the way home, Dad told me I was really special. Of course, while he's saying it, I'm thinking, "If I'm so special, why do I feel so lousy about myself?" But he said it. That's what counts. I'm still trying to recapture with him what we had that day.

The mixed messages only added to Joe's confusion, and they made it more difficult for him to face the truth about his father. I explained to Joe that an incredibly strong, perverse parent/child fusion occurs when a parent holds out a promise of love while at the same time mistreating that child. A child's world is very narrow, and no matter how abusive, the parents still represent the only available source of love and comfort. The battered child spends his entire childhood searching for the Holy Grail of parental love. That search continues into adulthood.

Kate, too, remembered:

> When I was a baby, my father would hold me, love me, and rock me. And when I was a little older, he was always there taking me to dance classes on the weekend or to the movies. He really loved me at one point in his life. I guess my greatest wish is for him to love me again the way he used to.

The Keeper of the Family Secret

Her father's sporadic benevolence kept Kate yearning for his love, hoping for a turnaround. This hope kept her bonded to him long after she reached adulthood. As part of that bonding, she believed she had to keep secret the truth of her father's behavior. A "good" girl would never betray her family.

The "family secret" is a further burden for abused children. By not talking about the abuse, the battered child cuts off any hope of emotional help. Here's Kate:

> All my life I felt like I've been living a lie. It's horrible not being able to talk freely about something that affected my life so strongly. How do you get over the pain of something if you can't talk about it? Sure, I can talk about it in therapy, but I still can't talk about it to the people who held all this power over me all those years. The only person I could ever talk about it with was the maid. I felt she was the only person in the world I could trust. Once, after my dad beat me, she said, "Honey, your dad's very sick." I never understood why he didn't go to the hospital if he was so sick.

I asked Kate what she thought would happen if she confronted her father and mother about her childhood. She stared at me for a few moments before replying:

> As for my father, I'm sure he'd fall apart . . . and then we'd be in big trouble. My mother would probably get hysterical. And my sister would be furious with me for dredging up the past. She won't even talk to *me* about it!

Kate's allegiance to the "family secret" was the glue that was holding the family together. If she broke the bond of silence, the family would fall apart.

> All of this is just welling up inside me. Every time I'm with them . . . I mean nothing ever changes. My father still gets very nasty with me. I feel like exploding and telling them how angry I am, but I sit there and bite my lip. When my father gets mad at me today, my mother pretends she doesn't hear what's going on. I was at my high school reunion a few years ago and I felt so hypocritical. My classmates all thought I had such a great family. I thought, "If they only knew." I wish I could tell my parents how they ruined my high school years. I want to scream at them that they hurt me so much I can't love anyone. I can't have a loving relationship with a man. They've paralyzed me emotionally. They still do. But I'm too scared to say anything to them.

The adult in Kate was crying out to confront her parents with the truth, but the battered, frightened child in Kate was too terrified of the consequences. She was convinced that everyone would hate her for letting the cat out of the bag. She believed the entire fabric of her family would unravel. As a result, her relationship with her parents had become a charade. Everyone pretended that nothing bad had ever happened.

Keeping the Myth Alive

I was not surprised when Kate told me that her high school classmates thought she had a great family. Many abusive families are able to present a very "normal" facade to the rest of the world. This apparent respectability is in direct opposition to the family's reality. It forms the basis of a "family myth." Joe's family myth was typical:

> It's such a goddamned farce whenever I get together with my family. Nothing's changed. My father still drinks, and I'm sure he's still hitting my mother. But from the way we all act and talk, you'd think we were *Leave It to Beaver*. Am I the only one who remembers what it was like? Am I the only one who knows the truth? It doesn't really matter because I never say anything anyway. I'm just as phony as the rest of them. I guess I can't let go of the hope that maybe someday things will be different. Maybe if we pretend hard enough, we *will* be a normal family.

Joe was caught in the same terrible conflict between wanting to confront his parents and fearing that he'd rip the family apart. When he was in high school he had written letters about how he really felt:

> I really poured my heart out in those letters, stuff about being beaten and ignored. Then I'd leave them out on my dresser, hoping my folks would read them. But I never knew if anyone did. No one ever said a word about them. I tried a diary for a while when I was in my late teens. I left that lying around, too. To this day, I don't know if my folks ever read any of it, and honest to God, I'm still too terrified to ask them.

It was not fear of another beating that prevented Joe from asking his parents about the diary or the letters. By high school, he was too grown-up for that. But if they had read his pleas and hadn't responded emotionally, he would had to have given up his fantasy that some miracle might someday give him the key to their love. After so many years, he was still afraid to find out whether they had invalidated him yet one more time.

At an Emotional Crossroads

Abused children have a caldron of rage bubbling inside them. You can't be battered, humiliated, terrified, denigrated, and blamed for your own pain without getting angry. But a battered child has no way to release this anger. In adulthood, that anger has to find an outlet.

Holly, 41, a stocky, stern-faced housewife with short, prematurely gray hair, was referred to me after being reported to the Department of Social Services by a school counselor for abusing her 10-year-old son. Her son was living temporarily with her husband's parents. Even though her therapy was court-mandated, she proved to be a highly motivated client.

> I'm so ashamed of myself. I've slapped him in the past, but this time I really went berserk. That kid makes me so damned angry. . . . You know, I always promised myself that if I had kids, I'd never raise a hand to them. Christ, I know what that's like. It's horrible. But without even realizing it, I'm turning into that crazy mother of mine. I mean, both my folks hit me, but she was the worst. I remember one time she chased me around the kitchen with a butcher knife!

Holly had a long history of acting out—that is, translating strong emotional impulses into aggressive action. As a teenager, she was in constant trouble and several times was suspended from school. As an adult, she described herself as a walking powder keg:

> Sometimes I have to just leave the house because I'm afraid of what I'll do to my kid. I feel like I can't control myself.

Holly's anger exploded onto her young son. In other extreme cases, repressed anger can express itself as violent criminal behavior, ranging from wife beating to rape to murder. Our jails are filled with adults who were physically abused as children and never learned to express their anger appropriately.

Kate, on the other hand, turned her anger inward. It found physical ways to express itself:

> No matter what anybody says or does to me, I can't ever stand up for myself. I just never feel up to it. I get headaches. I feel lousy most of the time. Everyone walks all over me, and I don't know how to stop them. Last year, I was sure I had an ulcer. I had stomachaches all the time.

Kate learned to be a victim early in her life and never stopped. She had no idea how to protect herself from being used or victimized by others. In this way she perpetuated the pain she had experienced as a child. Not unexpectedly, her enormous accumulated rage had to find a way out, but since she was afraid to express it directly, her body and her moods expressed it for her: in the form of headaches, a knotted-up stomach, and depression.

Like Father, Like Son?

In some cases, the abused child unconsciously identifies with his abusive parent. After all, the abuser looks powerful and invulnerable. Victimized children fantasize that if they possessed these qualities, they would be able to protect themselves. So, as an unconscious defense, they develop some of the very personality traits that they most hate in their toxic parent. Despite fervent promises to themselves to be different, under stress they may behave exactly like their abusers. But this syndrome is not as widespread as most people assume.

For many years it was commonly believed that almost all battered children became battering parents. After all, this was the only role model they'd had. But current studies challenge these assumptions. In fact, not only have a good many formerly abused children grown into nonabusing adults, but a number of these parents have great difficulty with even modest, nonphysical methods of disciplining their children. In rebellion against the pain of their own childhoods, these parents shy away both from setting limits and from enforcing them. This, too, can have a negative impact on a child's development, because children need the security of boundaries. But the harm done by overpermissiveness is usually far less significant than the damage done by a batterer.

The good news is that the adult victims of abusive parents *can* overcome their self-loathing, fusion to their parents, unresolved anger, overwhelming fears, and inability to trust or to feel safe.

7 | The Ultimate Betrayal
The Sexual Abusers

Incest is perhaps the cruelest, most baffling of human experiences. It is a betrayal of the most basic trust between child and parent. It is emotionally devastating. The young victims are totally dependent on their aggressors, so they have nowhere to run, no one to run to. Protectors become persecutors, and reality becomes a prison of dirty secrets. Incest betrays the very heart of childhood—its innocence.

In the last two chapters, we have looked into some of the darker realities of toxic families. We have met parents who have an extraordinary lack of empathy and compassion for their children. They batter their children with every weapon from degrading criticism to leather belts, and they still rationalize their abuses as acts of discipline or education. But now we enter a realm of behavior so perverse that it defies rationalization. This is where I must leave behind strictly psychological theories: I believe that sexual violation of children is a genuinely evil act.

What Is Incest?

Incest is difficult to define because the legal and psychological definitions are worlds apart. The legal definition is extremely narrow, usually defining incest as sexual intercourse between blood relations. As a result, millions of people did not realize they were incest victims because they had not been penetrated. From a psychological point of view, incest covers a much wider range of behaviors and relationships. These include physical contact with a child's mouth, breasts, genitals, anus, or any other body part, that is done for the purpose of sexually arousing the aggressor. That aggressor does *not* have to be a blood relative. He or she can be anyone whom the child perceives as a family member, such as a stepparent or an in-law.

There are other types of incestuous behaviors that are extremely damaging even though they may not involve any physical contact with the child's body. For example, if an aggressor exposes himself or masturbates in front of the child, or even persuades the child to pose for sexually suggestive photographs, he is committing a form of incest.

We must add to our definition of incest that the behavior has to be kept secret. A father who affectionately hugs and kisses his child is doing nothing that needs to be kept secret. In fact, such touching is essential to a child's emotional well-being. But if that father strokes the child's genitals—or makes the child stroke his—that is an act that must be kept secret. That is an act of incest.

There are also a number of far more subtle behaviors that I call psychological incest. Victims of psychological incest may not have been actually touched or assaulted sexually, but they have experienced an invasion of their sense of privacy or safety. I'm talking about invasive acts like spying on a child who is dressing or bathing, or repeatedly making seductive or sexually explicit comments to a child. While none of these behaviors fits the literal definition of incest, the victims often feel violated and suffer many of the same psychological symptoms as actual incest victims do.

The Incest Myths

When I first began my efforts to raise public awareness about the epidemic proportions of incest, I met with tremendous resistance. There is something particularly ugly and repellent about incest that keeps people from wanting even to acknowledge that it exists. In the last ten years, denial has begun to give way in the face of overwhelming evidence, and incest has become an acceptable—if still uncomfortable—topic for public discussion. But another obstacle still remains: the incest myths. They have long been articles of faith in our mass consciousness, beyond challenge. But they are not true, and they never were.

MYTH: *Incest is a rare occurrence.*

REALITY: All responsible studies and data, including those from the U.S. Department of Human Services, show that at least one out of every ten children is molested by a trusted family member before the age of 18. Only as recently as the early 1980s did we begin to realize just how epidemic incest is. Prior to that time, most people believed that incest occurred in no more than one out of a hundred thousand families.

MYTH: *Incest happens only in poor or uneducated families or in isolated, backward communities.*

REALITY: Incest is ruthlessly democratic. It cuts across all socioeconomic levels. Incest can occur as easily in your family as in the back hills of Appalachia.

MYTH: *Incest aggressors are social and sexual deviants.*

REALITY: The typical incest aggressor can be anybody. There is no common denominator or profile. They are often hardworking, respectable, churchgoing, seemingly average men and women. I've seen aggressors who were police officers, schoolteachers, captains of industry, society matrons, bricklayers, doctors, alcoholics, and clergymen. The traits they possess in common are psychological rather than social, cultural, racial, or economic.

MYTH: *Incest is a reaction to sexual deprivation.*

REALITY: Most aggressors have active sex lives within marriage, and often through extramarital affairs as well. They turn to children either for feelings of power and control or for the unconditional, nonthreatening love that only children can provide. Although these needs and drives become sexualized, sexual deprivation is rarely the trigger.

MYTH: *Children—especially teenage girls—are seductive and at least partially responsible for being molested.*

REALITY: Most children try out their sexual feelings and impulses in innocent and exploratory ways with people to whom they are bonded. Little girls flirt with their fathers and little boys with their mothers. Some teenagers are openly provocative. However, it is always 100 percent the adult's responsibility to exercise appropriate control in these situations and not to act out their own impulses.

MYTH: *Most incest stories are not true. They are actually fantasies derived from the child's own sexual yearnings.*

REALITY: This myth was created by Sigmund Freud and has permeated psychiatric teaching and practice since the beginning of the century. In his psychoanalytic practice, Freud was getting so many reports of incest from the daughters of respected, middle-class Viennese families that he groundlessly decided they couldn't all be true. To explain their frequency, he concluded that the events occurred primarily in his patients' imaginations. The legacy of Freud's error is that thousands, perhaps millions, of incest victims have been, and in some cases continue to be, denied the validation and support they need, even when they are able to muster the courage to seek professional help.

MYTH: *Children are molested more often by strangers than by someone they know.*

REALITY: The majority of sexual crimes committed against children are perpetrated by trusted members of the family.

Such a Nice Family

As with physical abusers, most incest families look normal to the rest of the world. The parents may even be community or religious leaders, with reputations for high moral standards. It's amazing how people can change behind closed doors.

Tracy, 38, is a slender, brown-haired, brown-eyed woman who owns a small bookshop in a suburb of Los Angeles. She came from one of these "normal families."

> We looked like everybody else. My father was an insurance salesman and my mother was an executive secretary. We went to church every Sunday, and we went on family vacations every summer. Real Normal Rockwell stuff . . . except, when I was about ten, my father started pushing his body up against mine. About a year later, I caught him watching me get dressed through a hole he had drilled in the wall of my bedroom. As I started developing, he would come up behind me and grab my breasts. Then, he'd offer me money to lie on the floor with my clothes off . . . so he could look at me. I felt really dirty, but I was afraid to say no. I didn't want to embarrass him. Then one day he took my hand and put it on his penis. I was so scared. . . . When he started to fondle my genitals, I didn't know what to do, so I just did what he wanted.

To the outside world, Tracy's father was a typical middle-class family man, an image that added to Tracy's confusion. Most incest families maintain this facade of normalcy for many years, sometimes forever.

Liz, an athletic-looking, blue-eyed blond videotape editor,

provides a particularly dramatic example of the split between outward appearance and reality:

> Everything was so unreal. My stepfather was this popular minister with a real big congregation. The people who came to church on Sunday just loved him. I remember sitting in church and listening to him sermonize about mortal sin. I just wanted to scream out that this man is a hypocrite. I wanted to stand up and testify in front of the whole church that this wonderful man of God is screwing his thirteen-year-old stepdaughter!

Liz, like Tracy, came from a seemingly model family. Her neighbors would have been astounded to discover what their minister was doing. But there was nothing unusual about the fact that he held a position of moral leadership, authority, and trust. A prestigious career or a graduate degree does nothing to curb incestuous impulses.

How Could This Ever Happen?

Controversial theories abound about the family climate and the role that other family members play. In my experience, however, one factor always holds true: incest simply doesn't happen in open, loving, communicative families.

Instead, incest occurs in families where there is a great deal of emotional isolation, secrecy, neediness, stress, and lack of respect. In many ways incest can be viewed as part of a total family breakdown. But it is the aggressor and the aggressor alone who commits the sexual violence. Tracy described what it was like in her house:

> We never talked about how we felt. If something bothered me, I just pushed it down. I do remember my mom cuddling me when I was little. But I never saw any affection between my mother and father. We did things together as a family, but

> there was no real closeness. I think that was what my father was looking for. Sometimes he would ask me if he could kiss me and I would say I didn't want to. Then he'd beg me and say he wouldn't hurt me, he just wanted to be close to me.

It had not occurred to Tracy that if her father was lonely and frustrated, he had alternatives to molesting his daughter. Like many aggressors, Tracy's father looked within the family, to his daughter, in an attempt to make up for whatever deprivation he experienced. This distorted use of a child to take care of an adult's emotional needs can easily become sexualized if that adult cannot control his impulses.

The Many Faces of Coercion

There is a tremendous amount of psychological coercion inherent in the parent-child relationship. Tracy's father didn't need to force his daughter into a sexual relationship.

> I would've done anything to make him happy. I was always terrified when he was doing that stuff to me, but at least he never got violent with me.

Victims like Tracy, who have not been physically coerced, often underestimate the damage they've suffered because they don't realize that emotional violence is every bit as destructive as physical violence. Children are by nature loving and trusting, easy marks for a needy, irresponsible adult. A child's emotional vulnerability is usually the only leverage some incest aggressors need.

Other aggressors reinforce their psychological advantage with threats of bodily harm, public humiliation, or abandonment. One of my clients was 7 when her father told her he would put her up for adoption if she didn't give in to his sexual demands. To a little girl, the threat that she would never see her family or friends again was terrifying enough to persuade her to do anything.

Incest aggressors will also use threats to guarantee their victims' silence. Among the most common:

- If you tell, I'll kill you.
- If you tell, I'll beat you up.
- If you tell, Mommy will get sick.
- If you tell, people will think you're crazy.
- If you tell, nobody's going to believe you.
- If you tell, Mommy will get mad at both of us.
- If you tell, I'll hate you for as long as you live.
- If you tell, they'll send me to jail and there won't be anyone to support the family.

These sorts of threats constitute emotional blackmail, preying on the naïve victim's fears and vulnerabilities.

In addition to psychological coercions, many aggressors resort to *physical* violence to force their children to submit to incest. Incest victims are rarely favored children, even apart from the sexual abuse. A few may receive money or gifts or special treatment as part of the coercion, but the majority are abused emotionally and often physically.

Liz remembers what happened when she tried to resist her minister stepfather:

> When I was almost out of junior high, I got real brave and told him that I'd decided he had to stop coming into my room at night. He got furious and started choking me. And then he started screaming that God didn't want me to make my own decisions. The Lord wanted him to decide for me. Like God really wanted him to have sex with me or something. By the time he got through choking me I could hardly breathe. I was so scared that I let him do it to me right then and there.

Why Children Don't Tell

Ninety percent of all incest victims never tell anyone what has happened, or what is happening, to them. They remain silent not only because they are afraid of getting hurt themselves, but to a great extent because they are afraid of breaking up the family by getting a parent into trouble. Incest may be frightening, but the thought of being responsible for the destruction of the family is even worse. Family loyalty is an incredibly powerful force in most children's lives, no matter how corrupt that family may be.

Connie, 36, a dynamic redhead who is a loan officer for a large bank, was the classic loyal child. Her fear of hurting her father and losing his love was more powerful than any desire to get help for herself:

> Looking back, I realize that he had me right where he wanted me. He told me that it would be the end of the family if I said anything to anybody about what we were doing, that my mother would send him away and I wouldn't have a daddy anymore, that they'd send me away to a foster home, and that everyone in the family would hate me.

In those rare instances where incest is discovered, the family unit very often *is* shattered. Whether by divorce, other legal proceedings, removal of the child from the home, or the intense stress of public disgrace, many families cannot survive the exposure of incest. Even though the breakup of the family may well be in the child's best interests, the child invariably feels responsible for that breakup. This adds greatly to his or her already overwhelming emotional burden.

The Credibility Gap

Sexually abused children realize early that their credibility is nothing compared to their aggressors'. It doesn't matter if the parent is alcoholic, chronically unemployed, or prone to violence; in our society, an adult is almost always more believable than a child. If the parent has attained a certain measure of success in life, the credibility gap becomes a chasm.

Dan, 45, an aerospace engineer, was sexually abused by his father from the time he was 5 until he went away to college:

> Even when I was little, I knew I could never tell anybody about what my father was doing to me. My mother was totally dominated by him, and I knew she'd never believe me in a million years. He was a big-deal businessman, he knew everybody worth knowing. Can you imagine me trying to get people to believe that this big honcho was making his six-year-old son give him blow jobs almost every night in the bathroom. Who'd believe me? They'd all think I was trying to get my father into trouble or something. I just couldn't win.

Dan was caught in a terrible trap. Not only was he being molested, but it was by a parent of the same sex. This compounded both his shame and his conviction that no one would believe him.

Father-son incest is far more common than most people realize. Such fathers usually appear to be heterosexual, but they are probably driven by strong homosexual impulses. Rather than admit their true feelings, they attempt to repress their homosexuality by marrying and becoming parents. With no outlet for their true sexual preference, their repressed impulses continue to grow until, eventually, they outweigh their defenses.

Dan's father's assaults began forty years ago, when incest (as well as homosexuality) was shrouded in misconceptions and myths. Like most other incest victims, Dan sensed the hopelessness of trying to seek help because it seemed preposterous that a man of his father's social status could commit such a crime. Parents, no matter how toxic, have a monopoly on power and credibility.

"I Feel So Dirty"

The shame of the incest victim is unique. Even very young victims know that incest must be kept secret. Whether or not they're told to keep silent, they sense the forbiddenness and shame in the behavior of the aggressor. They know that they are being violated, even if they are too young to understand sexuality. They feel dirty.

Just as verbally and physically abused children internalize blame, so do incest victims. However, in incest, the blame is compounded by the shame. The belief that "it's all my fault" is never more intense than with the incest victim. This belief fosters strong feelings of self-loathing and shame. In addition to having somehow to cope with the actual incest, the victim must now guard against being caught and exposed as a "dirty, disgusting" person.

Liz was terrified of being found out.

> I was only ten, but I felt like I was the worst slut there ever was. I really wanted to tell on my stepfather, but I was afraid everyone, including my mom, would hate me for it. I knew that everybody would think I was bad. I couldn't stand the thought that I would be the one coming off as evil, even though that's how I felt. So I just pushed it all down inside.

It's hard for outsiders to understand why a 10-year-old whose stepfather is forcing her to have intercourse with him would feel guilty. The answer, of course, lies in the child's unwillingness to see the trusted parent as bad. Somebody has to take the blame for these shameful, humiliating, frightening acts, and since it can't be the parent, it must be the child.

The feelings of being dirty, bad, and responsible create tremendous psychological isolation for incest victims. They feel totally alone, both within the family and in the outside world. They think no one will believe their horrible secret, yet that secret so overshadows their lives that it often prevents them from making friends. This isolation in turn can force them back to the aggressor, who is often their only source of attention, no matter how perverse.

If the victim experiences any pleasure from the incest, his or her shame is magnified. A few adults who were victims recall sexual arousal from the experience, regardless of the confusion or embarrassment they felt. It is even harder for these victims to later renounce their sense of responsibility. Tracy actually had orgasms. She explained:

> I knew it was wrong, but it did feel good. The guy was a real bastard to do it to me, but I'm as guilty as him because I liked it.

I'd heard the same story before, but it still tore at my heart. I told Tracy, as I'd told others before her:

> There's nothing wrong with liking the stimulation. Your body is biologically programmed to like those feelings. But the fact that it felt good didn't make what he was doing right and it didn't make you wrong. You were still a victim. It was *his* responsibility, as an adult, to control himself, no matter what you felt.

There is one more guilt that is unique to many incest victims: taking father away from mother. Father-daughter victims often talk about having felt like "the other woman." This, of course, made it even harder for them to seek help from the one person they might have had reason to expect it from—their mother. Instead, they felt they were betraying Mother, adding yet another layer of guilt to their inner world.

Insane Jealousy: "You Belong to Me"

Incest fuses the victim to the aggressor in a crazy and intense way. In father-daughter incest in particular, the father often becomes obsessed with his daughter and insanely jealous of her boyfriends. He may beat her or verbally abuse her to drive home the message that she belongs to only one man: Daddy.

This obsession dramatically distorts the normal developmental stages of childhood and adolescence. Instead of being able to become progressively more independent from parental control, the incest victim is increasingly bonded to the aggressor.

In Tracy's case, she knew that her father's jealousy was crazy, but she didn't see how cruel and degrading it was because she confused it with love. It is common for incest victims to mistake obsession for love. Not only does this drastically alter their ability to understand that they are being victimized, but it can wreak havoc with their expectations of love later in life.

Most parents experience some anxiety when their children begin dating and start bonding to people outside the family. But the incestuous father experiences this normal stage of development as betrayal, rejection, disloyalty, and even abandonment. Tracy's father's reaction was typical—rage, accusations, and punishment:

> He would wait up when I was out on a date, and when I got home, he'd give me the third degree. He would question me endlessly about who I was going out with, what was I doing with him, where was I letting him touch me, and did I let him put his tongue in my mouth. If he so much as caught me kissing a boy good night, he'd come out of the house screaming "tramp," and scare the guy off.

When Tracy's father called her vile and insulting names, he was doing what many incestuous fathers do: removing the badness, the evil, and the blame from himself and projecting it onto her. But other aggressors bond their victims with tenderness, making it even harder for the child to resolve the conflicting emotions of guilt and love.

"You're My Whole Life"

Doug, 46, a slight, tense man who worked as a machinist, came to me because of a wide range of sexual difficulties including recurrent impotence. He had been molested by his mother from the age of 7 to his late teens.

> She would fondle my genitals until I had an orgasm, but I always thought that because there was no intercourse it was no big deal. She made me do the same to her. She told me I was her whole life and that this was her special way of showing her love to me. But now, every time I try to get close to a woman, I feel like I'm cheating on my mother.

The enormous secret Doug shared with his mother bound him tightly to her. Her sick behavior may have confused him, but her message was clear: she was the only woman in his life. This message was in many ways as damaging as the incest itself. As a result, when he attempted to separate and have adult relationships with other women, his feelings of disloyalty and guilt took a terrible toll on his emotional well-being and sexuality.

Capping the Volcano

The only way many victims can survive their early incest traumas is to mount a psychological cover-up, pushing these memories so far beneath conscious awareness that they may not surface for many years, if ever.

Incest memories often come flooding back unexpectedly because of some particular life event. I've had clients report memories being triggered by such things as the birth of a child, marriage, death of a family member, seeing something about incest in the media, or even reliving the trauma in a dream.

It is also common for these memories to surface if the victim is in therapy working on other issues, though many victims still won't mention the incest without prodding from the therapist.

Even when these memories emerge, many victims panic and try to push them back by refusing to believe them.

One of the most dramatic, emotional experiences I've ever had as a therapist was with Julie, 46, a Ph.D. in biochemistry who was on the staff of a large research center in Los Angeles. Julie came to see me after hearing me discuss incest on one of my radio programs. She told me that she had been molested by her brother from the age of 8 until she was 15.

> I've been having these terrible fantasies about dying or going crazy and ending up in an institution. Lately, I've been spending most of my time in bed with the covers pulled up over my head. I never leave the house except to go to work, and I'm barely functioning there. Everyone's really worried about me. I know it's all connected to my brother, but I just can't talk about it. I feel like I'm drowning in this.

Julie was very fragile, apparently on the verge of a serious breakdown. She would laugh hysterically one minute and break into convulsive sobs the next. She had almost no control over the emotions that were overwhelming her.

> My brother raped me the first time when I was eight. He was fourteen and really strong for his age. After that he forced himself on me at least three or four times a week. The pain was so unbearable that I sort of went away from myself. I realize now that he must have been pretty crazy, because he'd tie

> me up and torture me with knives, scissors, razor blades, screwdrivers, anything he could find. The only way I could survive was to pretend that this was happening to someone else.

I asked Julie where her parents were while these horrors were taking place.

> I never told my parents anything about what Tommy was doing to me because he threatened to kill me if I did, and I believed him. My dad was a lawyer who put in sixteen-hour days including weekends, and my mom was a pill junkie. Neither one of them ever protected me. The few hours that Dad was home, he wanted peace and quiet, and he expected me to look after Mom. My whole childhood seems like one big blur of nothing but pain.

Julie had been badly damaged and was frightened of therapy, but she mustered the courage to enter one of my incest-victim groups. For the next several months, she worked hard on healing from her brother's torturous sexual abuse. Her emotional health improved noticeably during those months, and she no longer felt as if she was walking a tightrope between hysteria and depression. Yet, despite her improvement, my instincts told me that something was missing. There was still something dark and hidden festering inside her.

One night she came to group looking distraught. She had had a sudden memory that frightened her:

> A couple of nights ago, I had this real clear memory of my mother forcing me to perform oral sex on her. I really must be going crazy. I was probably imagining all those things about my brother, too. This could just never have happened with my mother. Sure, she was doped up all the time, but she just couldn't have done that to me. I'm really losing it, Susan. You've got to put me in the hospital.

I said, "Sweetie, if you imagined the experiences with your brother, then how come you've improved so much by working on them?" That made some sense to her. I continued, "You know, these things don't generally come out of people's imaginations. If you're remembering this incident with your mother now, it's because you're stronger than you were—you're more able to deal with it now."

I told Julie that her unconscious had been very protective of her. Had she remembered this episode when she was as fragile as when I first met her, she might have had a total emotional collapse. But, through her work in group, her emotional world was becoming more stable. Her unconscious had allowed this repressed memory to surface because she was ready to cope with it.

Few people talk about mother-daughter incest, but I have treated at least a dozen victims of it. The motivation appears to be a grotesque distortion of the need for tenderness, physical contact, and affection. Mothers who are capable of violating normal maternal bonding in this way are usually extremely disturbed and often psychotic.

It was Julie's struggle to repress her memories that brought her close to a breakdown. Yet, as painful and disturbing as those memories were, their release was the key to Julie's progressive recovery.

A Double Life

Incest victims often become very skillful child actors. In their inner world, there is so much terror, confusion, sadness, loneliness, and isolation that many develop a false self with which to relate to the outside world, to act as if things were fine and normal. Tracy talked about her "as if" self with considerable insight:

> I felt like I was two people inside one body. In front of my friends, I was very outgoing and friendly. But as soon as I was in our apartment, I became a total recluse. I'd have these crying jags that just wouldn't stop. I hated socializing with my family because I had to pretend that everything was fine. You

> have no idea how hard it was to keep playing these two roles all the time. Sometimes I felt like I didn't have an ounce of strength left.

Dan, too, deserved an Oscar. He described:

> I was feeling so guilty about what my father was doing to me at night. I really felt like an object; I hated myself. But I played the part of a happy me and nobody in the family caught on. Then, all of a sudden, I stopped dreaming. I even stopped crying. I'd pretend I was a happy kid. I was the class clown, and I was a good piano player. I loved to entertain . . . anything to get people to like me. But, inside I was aching. I was a secret drunk by the time I was thirteen.

By entertaining other people, Dan was able to feel some sense of acceptance and accomplishment. But, because the real self inside him was in such agony, he experienced very little genuine pleasure. This is the cost of living a lie.

The Silent Partner

The aggressor and the victim put on good performances to keep their secret inside the house. But what about the other parent?

When I first began working with adults who were sexually abused as children, I found that many father-daughter victims seemed angrier at their mothers than at their fathers. Many victims tortured themselves with the often unanswerable question of how much their mothers knew about the incest. Many were convinced that their mothers must have known something, because in some instances the signs of abuse were quite blatant. Others were convinced that their mothers *should* have known, should have picked up the behavioral changes in their daughters, should have sensed something was wrong, and should have been more tuned in to what was going on in the family.

Tracy, who seemed very businesslike when she described how her insurance-salesman father graduated from watching her undress to fondling her genitals, cried several times as she talked about her mother:

> I always seem to be angry with my mother. I could love her and hate her at the same time. Here's this woman who'd always see me depressed, crying hysterically in my room, and she'd never say one goddamned word. Can you believe that any mother in her right mind wouldn't find it unusual to see her own daughter in tears all the time? I couldn't just tell her what was going on, but maybe if she'd asked . . . I don't know. Maybe I couldn't have told her anyway. God, I wish she could have found out about what he was doing to me.

Tracy expressed a wish that I have heard from thousands of incest victims—that somehow, someone, especially their mother, would discover the incest without the victim's having to go through the pain of telling.

I agreed with Tracy that her mother was incredibly insensitive to her daughter's unhappiness, but that didn't necessarily mean that Tracy's mother had any knowledge of what was going on.

There are three types of mothers in incest families: those who genuinely *don't* know, those who *may* know, and those who *do* know.

Is it possible for a mother to live in an incest family and not know? Several theories contend that it is not, that every mother would somehow sense incest in her family. I disagree. I am convinced that some mothers truly don't know.

The second type of mother is the classic silent partner. She wears blinders. The incest clues are there, but she chooses to ignore them in a misguided attempt to protect herself and her family.

The final type is the most reprehensible: the mother who is told of the molestation by her children but does nothing about it. When this happens, the victim is doubly betrayed.

When Liz was 13, she made one desperate attempt to tell her mother about her stepfather's escalating sexual assaults:

> I really felt trapped. I thought if I told my mother she would at least talk to him. What a joke. She almost collapsed in tears and said . . . I'll never forget her words: "Why are you telling me this, what are you trying to do to me? I've lived with your stepfather for nine years. I know he couldn't do this. He's a minister. Everyone respects us. You must have been dreaming. Why are you trying to ruin my life? God will punish you." I couldn't believe it. It had taken so much out of me just to tell her, but she just turned on me. I ended up comforting her.

Liz began to cry. I hugged her for several minutes as she relieved the pain and the grief of her mother's all-too-typical response to the truth. Liz's mother was a classic silent partner—passive, dependent, and infantile. She was intensely preoccupied with her own survival and with keeping the family intact. As a result, she needed to deny anything that might rock the family boat.

Many silent partners were abused children themselves. They suffer from extremely low self-esteem and may be reenacting the struggles of their own childhoods. They usually become overwhelmed by any conflict that threatens the status quo because they don't want to confront their own fears and dependency. As is often the case, Liz wound up taking care of her mother emotionally, even though it was Liz who most needed support.

A few mothers actually push their daughters into incest. Debra, a member of Liz's incest group, told a particularly shocking story:

> People tell me I'm pretty—I know men are always looking—but I've spent most of my life thinking I look like the creature from *Alien*. I've always felt slimy, you know, disgusting. What my father did to me was bad enough, but what really hurt was my mother. She was the middleman. She set up the time and

> place, and sometimes she even held my head in her lap while he did it. I kept begging her not to make me do it, but she'd say, "Please, honey, do it for me. I'm not enough for him, and if you don't give him what he wants, he'll go find some other woman. Then we'll be out on the street."
>
> I try to understand why she did what she did, but I have two children of my own and it seems like the most inconceivable thing that any mother could ever do.

Many psychologists believe that silent partners transfer their wife/maternal role to their daughters. This was certainly true of Debra's mother, though it is unusual for this transfer to be done so overtly.

But in my experience, most silent partners do not so much transfer their role as abdicate their personal power. They don't usually push their daughters to replace them, but they allow themselves and their daughters to become dominated by the aggressor. Their fears and dependency needs prove more powerful than their maternal instincts, leaving their daughters unprotected.

The Legacy of Incest

Every adult who was molested as a child brings from his or her childhood pervasive feelings of being hopelessly inadequate, worthless, and genuinely bad. No matter how different their lives may appear on the surface, all adult victims of incest share a legacy of tragic feelings, The Three D's of incest: Dirty, Damaged, and Different. Connie's life was severely distorted by The Three D's. As she described:

> I used to feel like I went to school with a sign on my forehead that said "incest victim." I still think a lot of the time that people can look right inside me and see how disgusting I am. I'm just not like other people. I'm not normal.

Over the years, other victims have described themselves as feeling like "the Elephant Man," "a creature from outer space," "an escapee from the funny farm," and "lower than the lowest scum on earth."

Incest is a form of psychological cancer. It is not terminal, but treatment is necessary and sometimes painful. Connie let hers go untreated for more than twenty years. It took a terrible toll on her life, especially in the area of relationships.

"I Don't Know What a Loving Relationship Feels Like"

Connie's feelings of self-disgust led her through a series of degrading relationships with men. Because her first relationship with a man (her father) involved betrayal and exploitation, love and abuse were woven tightly together in her mind. As an adult, she was attracted to men who enabled her to reenact this familiar scenario. A healthy relationship, one involving caring and respect, would have felt unnatural, out of sync with her view of herself.

Most incest victims have an especially difficult time with adult love relationships. If by chance a victim should manage to find a loving relationship, the ghosts from the past usually contaminate it—often in the area of sexuality.

Robbed of Sexuality

Tracy's incest trauma seriously affected her marriage to a kind and caring man. She told me:

> My relationship with David is falling apart. He's a terrific guy, but how long can he put up with this? Sex is just terrible. It always has been. I don't even want to go through the motions anymore. I hate his touching me. I wish sex had never been invented.

It's quite common for a victim to feel revulsion at the thought of sex. This is a normal reaction to incest. Sex becomes an indelible reminder of the pain and betrayal. The tape starts playing in her head: "Sex is dirty, sex is bad. . . . I did terrible things when I was little . . . if I do those terrible things now, I'll feel like a bad person again."

Many victims talk about being unable to have sex without being haunted by flashbacks. They try to be intimate with someone they care about, but in their minds they are vividly reliving the original incest traumas. During sex, adults who were victims often see or hear their aggressors in the room with them. These flashbacks bring up all their negative feelings about themselves, and their sexuality fizzles like a doused fire.

Other incest victims, like Connie, use their sexuality in self-denigrating ways because they've grown to believe that sex is all they're good for. Though they may have slept with hundreds of men in exchange for a little affection, many of these victims still feel repelled by sex.

"Why Do Good Feelings Make Me Feel Bad?"

A victim who, as an adult, has managed to become sexually responsive and orgasmic (and many do) may still feel guilty about her sexual feelings, making them difficult if not impossible to enjoy. Guilt can make good feelings feel bad.

In contrast to Tracy, Liz was very responsive sexually, but the ghosts from the past were no less intrusive:

> I have lots of orgasms. I love to have sex every way possible. Where it gets really bad for me is afterwards. I get so depressed. When it's over, I don't want to be held or touched. . . . I just want the guy to get away from me. He doesn't understand it. A couple of times when sex has been especially good for me, I had fantasies about killing myself afterwards.

Even though Liz experienced sexual pleasure, she still had intense feelings of self-loathing. As a result, she needed to atone for this pleasure by punishing herself, even to the extent of visualizing suicide. It was as if by having these self-abasing feelings and fantasies, she could somehow make up for her "sinful" and "shameful" sexual arousal.

"I Can't Punish Myself Enough"

In the preceding chapter we saw victims of physical abuse turn their pain and rage against themselves—or in some cases against others. Incest victims tend to follow the same patterns, releasing their repressed rage and unresolved grief in a wide variety of ways.

Depression is an extremely common expression of suppressed incest conflicts. It may range from a general sense of sadness to nearly total immobilization.

A disproportionate number of incest victims, particularly women, allow themselves to become overweight as adults. The weight serves two important purposes for the victim: (1) she imagines it will keep men away from her, and (2) the body mass creates a false illusion of strength and power. Many victims become terrified when they first begin to lose weight because it makes them feel helpless and vulnerable once again.

Recurrent headaches are also common among incest victims. These headaches are not only a physical manifestation of repressed rage and anxiety but are also a form of self-punishment.

Many incest victims lose themselves in a haze of alcohol and drug abuse. This provides a temporary deadening of their feelings of loss and emptiness. However, this delay in confronting the real problem only prolongs the victim's suffering.

A great number of incest victims also seek punishment from the world at large. They sabotage relationships, seeking punishment from the ones they love. They sabotage themselves at work, seeking punishment from colleagues or employers. A few commit violent crimes, seeking punishment from society. Others become prostitutes, seeking punishment from pimps, from patrons—or even from God.

"This Time It's Going to Be Better"

There is a baffling paradox in the fact that no matter how painful their lives have been, a great number of incest victims remain fused to their toxic parents. The pain came from those parents, but the victims still look to them to alleviate it. It is very hard for adult incest victims to give up the myth of the happy family.

One of the most powerful legacies of incest is this never-ending search for the magic key that will unlock the treasure chest of your parents' love and approval. This search is like emotional quicksand, bogging the victim down in an impossible dream, preventing her from getting on with her life.

Liz summed it up:

> I keep thinking that someday they will reach out and say, "We think you're wonderful and we love you the way you are." Even though I know that my stepfather is a child molester, and even though my mother chose him and didn't protect me . . . it's like I need to have *them* forgive *me*.

The Healthiest Member of the Family

Many people are shocked when I say that the incest victims I've worked with are usually the healthiest members of their families. After all, the victim usually has the symptoms—self-blame, depression, destructive behaviors, sexual problems, suicide attempts, substance abuse—while the rest of the family often seems outwardly healthy.

But despite this, it is usually the victim who ultimately has the clearest vision of the truth. She was forced to sacrifice herself to cover up the craziness and the stress in the family system. All her life she was the bearer of the family secret. She lived with tremendous emotional pain in order to protect the myth of the good family. But because of all this pain and conflict, the victim is usually the first to seek help. Her parents, on the other hand, will almost always refuse to let go of their denials and defenses. They refuse to deal with reality.

With treatment, most victims are able to reclaim their dignity and their power. Recognizing a problem and seeking help is a sign not only of health but of courage.

8 | Why Do Parents Behave This Way?

The Family System

We are all forged in a crucible called family. In recent years, we have come to recognize that "family" is more than a collection of related people. It is a system, a group of interconnecting people, each of whom affects the others in profound and often hidden ways. It is a complex network of love, jealousy, pride, anxiety, joy, guilt—a constant ebb and flow of the full range of human emotions. These emotions bubble up through a murky sea of family attitudes, perceptions, and relationships. And like the sea, very little of the inner workings of a family system is visible from the surface. The deeper you dive, the more you discover.

Your family system constituted your entire reality when you were young. You made decisions as a child—about who you are and how you're supposed to interact with others—based on how your family system taught you to see the world. If you had toxic parents, you probably made decisions such as: "I can't trust anybody"; "I'm not worth caring about"; or, "I'll never amount to anything." Those decisions were self-defeating and need to be changed. You *can* change many of these early decisions, and with them your life scenario, but you must first understand how much of what you feel, how you live, and what you believe has been shaped by your family system.

Remember, your parents had parents too. A toxic family system is like a multicar pile-up on the freeway, causing damage generation after generation after generation. This system is not something that your parents invented; it is the result of the accumulated feelings, rules, interactions, and beliefs that have been handed down from your ancestors.

Beliefs: There Is Only One Truth

If you want to begin to make sense of the confusion and chaos of a toxic family system, you need to look first at family beliefs, especially those beliefs that determine how parents interact with their children and how children are supposed to behave. One family, for example, may believe that a child's feelings are important, while another may believe that a child is a second-class citizen. Such beliefs determine our attitudes, judgments, and perceptions. They are incredibly powerful. They separate good from bad and right from wrong. They define relationships, moral values, education, sexuality, career choices, ethics, and finances. They mold family behavior.

Reasonably mature and caring parents will have beliefs that take into consideration the feelings and needs of all family members. They will provide a solid basis for a child's development and subsequent independence. Such beliefs might be: "children are entitled to disagree"; "it's wrong to deliberately hurt your child"; or, "children should feel free to make mistakes."

A toxic parent's beliefs about children, on the other hand, are almost always self-centered and self-serving. They believe things like, "children should respect their parents no matter what"; "there are only two ways to do things, my way and the wrong way"; or, "children should be seen but not heard." These types of beliefs form the soil from which toxic parental behavior grows.

Toxic parents resist any external reality that challenges their beliefs. Rather than change, they develop a distorted view of reality to support the beliefs they already have. Unfortunately, children lack the sophistication to discriminate between true reality and distorted reality. As children of toxic parents grow up, they carry their parents' distorted beliefs unchallenged into their own adult lives.

There are two types of beliefs: spoken and unspoken. Spoken beliefs are expressed or communicated directly. They are out there. You can hear them. Spoken beliefs are often disguised as words of advice, expressed in terms of "shoulds," "oughts," and "supposed to's."

These overtly expressed beliefs have the advantage of giving us something tangible to wrestle with as we become adults. Although these beliefs may have become a part of us, the fact that they are stated makes them easy to examine, and perhaps to discard in favor of beliefs that are more relevant to our lives.

For example, a parental belief that divorce is wrong might keep a daughter in a loveless marriage. But the belief can be challenged. The daughter can ask herself, "What's 'wrong' with divorce?" And her answer to that question may lead her to reject her parents' belief.

It's not as easy to reject a belief that you don't even know exists. Unspoken beliefs can dictate many basic assumptions about life. They exist below the level of awareness. These are the beliefs that were implied by the way your father treated your mother, or by the way either one of them treated you. They are an important part of what we learn from our parents' behavior.

It is a very rare family that will sit down to dinner to discuss beliefs such as: "women are second-class citizens"; "children should sacrifice themselves for their parents"; "children are bad by nature"; or, "children should stay inadequate so their parents can stay needed." Even if the family knew that they held these beliefs, few would admit to them. Yet these negative unspoken beliefs dominate many families with toxic parents, disastrously affecting their children's lives.

Michael—whose mother threatened to have a heart attack when he moved away—provided a telling example of unspoken parental beliefs:

> For years I felt like a bad son because I moved to California and got married. I really believed that if you don't put your parents above everything else in life, you're a rotten kid. My folks never came out and said that, but I got the message loud and clear. No matter how terribly they treated my wife, I never defended her against them. I really believed that children are supposed to take whatever their folks dish out. I was supposed to crawl to them to make amends. I was their little sap.

Michael's parents' behavior communicated their belief that they were the only ones with rights and privileges. Without saying it, they infused in Michael the belief that only their feelings counted, and that Michael existed only to make them happy. These beliefs were strangling Michael; they almost destroyed his marriage.

Had Michael not come in for therapy, he probably would have passed these beliefs on to his own children. Instead, he learned to recognize his unspoken beliefs, which enabled him to challenge them. Michael's parents, like all toxic parents, reacted by being punitive and withdrawing their love. This was a tactic to regain control of Michael's life. Thanks to Michael's new understanding of his relationship with his parents, he didn't fall for that one either.

"Women Can't Survive Without Men to Take Care of Them"

Kim—whose volatile father controlled her with his moods and his money—also accepted many of her parents' unspoken beliefs. As she described it:

> My father and mother had a horrible marriage. She was scared to death of him, and I'm sure he hit her, even though I never actually saw him do it. Lots of times, I would go in to comfort her because she'd be sobbing in her bed, and she would tell me how miserable she was with him. I used to ask her why she didn't leave him, and she'd say, "What do you want me to do? I don't have any skills, and I couldn't stand giving all of this up. Do you kids want us to be out on the street?"

Without knowing it, Kim's mother reinforced the belief Kim had already learned from her father's behavior: women are helpless without men. This belief led Kim to remain dependent on her powerful father, but the price was her dignity and her chance for a healthy relationship.

There are as many different parental beliefs as there are parents. They form the skeleton of our intellectual perception of the world. This skeleton's flesh is made up of our feelings and behaviors; the skeleton gives them shape. When toxic parents provide us with distorted beliefs, our feelings and behaviors may become as skewed as the skeleton beneath them.

Spoken and Unspoken Rules

From parental beliefs come parental rules. Like beliefs, parental rules evolve over time. Rules are the manifestations of beliefs. They are the enforcers, the simple "do's and don'ts."

For example, a family belief that people should marry only within their religion would spawn such rules as: "don't date anyone from another religion"; "do date boys you meet at church"; and, "don't approve of friends who fall in love with someone not of their faith."

As with beliefs, there are spoken rules and unspoken rules. Spoken rules may be arbitrary, but they tend to be clear: "spend every

Christmas at home," or, "don't talk back to your parents." Because they are out in the open, we can, as adults, challenge them.

But unspoken family rules are like phantom puppeteers, pulling invisible strings and demanding blind obedience. They are unseen, covert rules that exist below the level of awareness—rules such as: "don't be more successful than your father"; "don't be happier than your mother"; "don't lead your own life"; "don't ever stop needing me"; or "don't abandon me."

Lee—the tennis teacher whose mother couldn't do enough for her—lived by a particularly damaging unspoken rule. Her mother enforced the rule every time she imposed herself under the guise of helping. When she offered to drive Lee to San Francisco, or clean up Lee's apartment, or bring over dinner, her underlying belief was: "as long as my daughter can't take care of herself, she'll need me." This belief translated into the rule: "don't be adequate." Of course, Lee's mother never said these words, and if confronted she would unquestionably deny wanting her daughter to remain helpless. But her behavior told Lee exactly how to keep her mother happy: stay dependent.

Kim's father did the same thing. He laid down rules to govern his daughter's life without ever having to verbalize them. As long as Kim picked inadequate men, as long as she kept going back to her father to bail her out, and as long as her need for his approval dominated her life, she was obeying the unspoken rule: "don't grow up, always be Daddy's little girl."

Unspoken rules have a tenacious hold on our lives. To change them, we must first understand them.

Obedience No Matter What

If beliefs are the bones and rules are the flesh of the family system, then "blind obedience" is the muscle that propels that body.

We blindly obey family rules because to disobey is to be a traitor to one's family. Allegiances to country, political ideals, or religion pale in comparison to the intensity of the allegiance to family. We all have these loyalties. They bind us to the family system, to our parents, and to their beliefs. They drive us to obey the family rules. If these rules are reasonable, they can provide some ethical and moral structure for a child's development.

But in families with toxic parents, the rules are based on family role distortions and bizarre perceptions of reality. Blind obedience to these rules leads to destructive, self-defeating behavior.

Kate—who was beaten by her father—shows how hard it is to escape the cycle of blind obedience:

> I really think I want to get well. I don't want to be depressed. I don't want to screw up relationships. I don't want to have the kind of life I'm living. I don't want to be angry and afraid. But every time I get close to taking some positive steps for myself, I blow it. It's like I'm terrified to give up the pain, it feels so familiar. Like it's the way I'm *supposed* to feel.

Kate was obeying her abusive father's rules: "accept the fact that you're the bad one"; "don't be happy"; and, "endure the pain." Anytime she came close to defying these rules, the power of her loyalty to the family system proved much stronger than her conscious wishes. She had to obey, and when she did, the familiarity of her feelings was comforting, despite the fact that they were painful. Obedience seemed the easy way out.

Glenn, too, was being loyal to his family when he took his alcoholic father into his manufacturing company and gave money that he needed to his mother. He believed that his parents would fall apart if he didn't take care of them. The family rule was: "take care of others, no matter what the cost to yourself." Glenn brought the rule with him into marriage. He obeyed it by devoting his life to rescuing his father, rescuing his mother, and rescuing his alcoholic wife.

Glenn railed against his blind obedience, but he couldn't seem to free himself.

> They never gave a damn about me when I was a kid, but somehow I have to take care of them. It makes me sore as hell. No matter what I do for them, it doesn't change anything. I hate it, but I just don't know any other way to do it.

The Obedience Trap

The kind of obedience I'm talking about is not a matter of free choice; it is rarely the result of a conscious decision. Jody—who became her father's drinking buddy when she was 10—left therapy abruptly because her growing awareness was forcing her to challenge the belief that she was the bad one. She was breaking the rules that said, "don't tell the truth"; "don't grow up and leave Daddy"; and, "don't have healthy relationships."

On paper, these rules seem ridiculous. Who would obey a rule like "don't have healthy relationships"? Unfortunately, the answer is, most adult children of toxic parents. Remember, these are mostly *unconscious* rules. No one sets out to have a bad relationship, but that doesn't stop millions of people from doing it over and over again.

When I asked Jody to examine her family beliefs, and what her obedience to the family rules was doing to her life, her anxiety caused her to leave therapy. It's as if she were saying, "My need to obey my father is more important than my need to get well."

Even if both parents are dead, their adult children continue to honor the family system. Eli—the rich man who lived like a pauper—realized after several months of therapy how his father was still controlling him from the grave:

> It's so astounding to me that all the fear and guilt I feel whenever I try to do something nice for myself is my way of not betraying my father. I'm doing well. I *don't* have to worry about my world collapsing. But I still have trouble getting that through my thick skull. My father's voice keeps coming back from the grave to tell me how my business success can't last,

> every woman I date is out to make a fool of me, every business associate is out to cheat me. And I believe him. It amazes me. It's like being miserable is my way of keeping his memory alive.

The payoff for Eli in living a narrow, unfulfilling life was the comfort of remaining loyal to the family by embracing his father's beliefs ("life is meant to be endured, not enjoyed") and obeying the family rules ("don't spend your money" and "don't trust anybody").

Blind obedience forges our behavior patterns early in life and prevents us from escaping those patterns. There is often a huge gap between our parents' expectations and demands and what we really want for ourselves. Unfortunately, our unconscious pressure to obey almost always overshadows our conscious needs and desires. We can discard destructive rules only by turning a light on the unconscious and bringing those rules to the surface. Only when we can see the rules clearly can we exercise free choice.

I Don't Know Where You End and I Begin

The single most dramatic difference between healthy and toxic family systems is the amount of freedom that exists for family members to express themselves as individuals. Healthy families encourage individuality, personal responsibility, and independence. They encourage the development of their children's sense of adequacy and self-respect.

Unhealthy families discourage individual expression. Everyone must conform to the thoughts and actions of the toxic parents. They promote fusion, a blurring of personal boundaries, a welding together of family members. On an unconscious level, it is hard for family members to know where one ends and another begins. In their efforts to be close, they often suffocate one another's individuality.

In an enmeshed family you pay for intermittent feelings of approval and safety with your selfhood. For example, you may not be able to ask yourself, "Am I too tired to see my folks tonight?" Instead, you may have to ask, "If I don't go, will Dad get angry and hit Mom? Will Mom get drunk and pass out? Will they stop talking to me for the next month?" These questions arise because you already know how responsible you'll feel if any of these events occur. Every decision you make becomes intricately interwoven with the rest of your family. Your feelings, behaviors, and decisions are no longer your own. You are not yourself, you are an appendage of your family system.

To Be Different Is to Be Bad

When Fred decided to go skiing instead of spending Christmas with his family, he was trying to be an individual, trying to free himself from his family system. Instead, all hell broke loose. His mother and his siblings treated him like the Grinch who stole Christmas, shoveling guilt by the trainload. Instead of skiing with his lover down the idyllic slopes of Aspen, Fred sat alone in his hotel room, nervously cradling his telephone, desperately seeking forgiveness for the misery his family blamed him for causing.

When Fred tried to do something healthy for himself—something that the rest of the family disapproved of—his family formed a united front against him. He became the common enemy, the threat to the system. They attacked with anger, blame, and recriminations. Because he was so tied in to the family, the guilt he felt was enough to bring him back into line.

In families like Fred's, much of a child's identity and his illusions of safety depend on feeling enmeshed. He develops a need to be a part of other people and to have them be a part of him. He can't stand the thought of being cast out. This need for enmeshment carries right into adult relationships.

Kim fought this need when she ended her marriage:

> Even though the marriage wasn't that great, at least I felt part of somebody. And when it ended and he suddenly wasn't

> there, I felt terrified. I felt like I was nothing. I felt like I didn't exist. I guess the only time I feel okay is when I'm with a man and he tells me I'm okay.

When Kim was little, her enmeshment with her powerful father created a precarious security for her. Whenever she attempted to separate from him, he found ways to stifle her independence. As an adult, she could not feel safe unless she was part of a man and a man was part of her.

Enmeshment creates almost total dependence on approval and validation from outside yourself. Lovers, bosses, friends, even strangers become the stand-ins for parents. Adults like Kim who were raised in families where there was no permission to be an individual frequently become approval junkies, constantly seeking their next fix.

The Family Balancing Act

As we saw in Michael's case, an enmeshed family can maintain an illusion of love and stability as long as no one attempts to separate and as long as everyone follows the family rules. When Michael decided to move away, to marry, to begin his own family, and to lead a life separate from his parents, he unwittingly upset the family balance.

Every family creates its own balance to achieve some sort of stability. As long as family members interact in certain familiar and predictable ways, this balance, or equilibrium, is not upset.

The word *balance* implies serenity and order. But in a toxic family system, maintaining balance is like a precarious high-wire act. In such families, chaos is a way of life, becoming the only thing they can depend on. All of the toxic behaviors we've seen so far—even battering and incest—serve to maintain this precarious family balance. In fact, toxic parents often fight the loss of equilibrium by *increasing* chaos.

Michael is a perfect example. If his mother could create enough uproar in the family, Michael's guilt would drag him back to settle things down. He would do anything to restore the balance in the family, even if he had to surrender control over his own life. The more toxic the family, the less it takes to threaten it, and the more any imbalance seems like a threat to survival. That is why toxic parents may react to even minor deviations as if their lives were at stake.

Glenn upset his family balance by telling the truth. He explained:

> One day when I was about twenty, I decided I was going to confront my father about his drinking. I was terrified to do it, but I knew something was wrong. I decided to tell my father that I didn't like the way he acted when he was drunk, and I didn't want him to do it anymore. It was amazing what happened. My mother jumped to his defense, making me feel guilty for even bringing it up. My father denied everything. I looked to my sisters for support, but they just tried to make peace. I felt terrible, like I'd done something awful. The fact is, I'd exposed a truth: that my father was an alcoholic. But I just ended up feeling crazy for even trying.

I asked Glenn whether his attempt to expose the truth had had any lasting effect on family interactions.

> It was amazing. I was like a leper. Nobody wanted to talk to me. Like, who was I to make accusations? They treated me like I didn't exist. I couldn't take being ignored by my family anymore. So I shut up about the drinking. I didn't talk about it for another twenty years . . . until now.

In Glenn's family, everyone had a role designed to perpetuate the family system. Dad's role was to drink; Mom played the codependent; and, in a reversal of roles, the children played parents.

This was predictable and familiar and therefore felt safe. When Glenn tried to challenge these roles, he threatened the balance. His punishment was exile to an emotional Siberia.

It doesn't take much to kick off a crisis in a toxic family system: Father loses his job, a relative dies, an in-law moves in, a daughter starts spending too much time with a new boyfriend, a son moves out, or Mother gets sick. As Glenn's family did when he tried to confront his father's drinking, most toxic parents respond to crisis with denial, secrecy, and, worst of all, blame. And that blame always targets the children.

How Toxic Parents Cope

In a relatively well-functioning family, parents tend to cope with life pressures by *working out* problems through openly communicating, exploring options, and not being afraid to seek outside help if they need it. Toxic parents, on the other hand, react to threats to their balance by *acting out* their fears and frustrations, with little thought for the consequences to their children. Their coping mechanisms are rigid and familiar to them. Among the most common:

1. *Denial.* As you've seen throughout this book, denial is often the first coping mechanism to which toxic parents resort to regain equilibrium. Denial has two faces: "nothing is wrong" and "something was wrong but it won't happen again." Denial minimizes, discounts, jokes away, rationalizes, or relabels destructive behavior. Relabeling—a form of denial—takes a problem and hides it behind euphemisms. An alcoholic becomes a "social drinker"; a batterer is a "strict disciplinarian."
2. *Projection.* Projection also has two faces: parents may accuse the child of the very inadequacies they suffer from, and they may blame the child for the toxic behaviors that result from their inadequacies. For example, an inadequate father who can't hold down a job will accuse his son of being lazy and shiftless; an alcoholic mother will blame her daughter for

causing the unhappiness that drives her to drink. It is not unusual for toxic parents to use both kinds of projection to avoid taking responsibility for their own behavior and their own deficiencies. They need to find a scapegoat, and it's often the most vulnerable child in the family.

3. *Sabotage.* In a family with a severely dysfunctional parent—crazy, drunk, ill, or violent—other family members will assume the roles of rescuers and caretakers. This creates a comfortable balance of weak/strong, bad/good, or sick/healthy. If the dysfunctional parent starts to get better or enters a treatment program, this can severely threaten the family balance. The rest of the family (especially the other parent) may unconsciously find ways to sabotage the dysfunctional parent's progress so that everyone can return to his or her familiar role. This can also happen if a troubled child starts to improve. I have seen toxic parents pull their child out of therapy when the child shows signs of becoming healthier.
4. *Triangling.* In a toxic family system, one parent will often enlist the child as a confidant or ally against the other parent. Children become part of an unhealthy triangle in which they are being pulled apart by the pressure to choose sides. When Mom says, "I'm miserable with your father," or Dad says, "Your mom won't sleep with me anymore," the child becomes an emotional dumping ground, allowing the parents to relieve themselves of some of their discomfort without having to face the source of their problems.
5. *Keeping secrets.* Secrets help toxic parents cope by turning their families into private little clubs to which no outsiders are admitted. This provides a bond to pull the family together, especially when the family balance is threatened. The child who hides abuse by telling her teacher that she fell down the stairs is protecting the family club from outside interference.

When you look at toxic parents from the perspective of the family system—their beliefs, their rules, and your obedience to those rules—a lot of your self-destructive behavior comes into focus. You come closer to understanding the powerful forces that drive so much of your parents' behavior and ultimately your own.

Understanding is the beginning of change. It opens new options and choices. But seeing things differently is not enough. True freedom can come only from *doing* things differently.

PART 2

Reclaiming Your Life

Using the Second Half of This Book

Now our focus will shift from what your parents did to you to what *you* can do for yourself to lessen their power over your life. I will give you specific techniques and behavioral strategies to change self-defeating life patterns and become the person you want to be.

These strategies are not intended to replace but rather to enhance work in therapy, support groups, or Twelve Step programs. Some of you may elect to do this work on your own, but if you are an adult victim of *physical* or *sexual* abuse, I believe that professional help is *essential* for you.

If you abuse drugs or alcohol to deaden your feelings, you must deal with your compulsion before attempting the work in this book. There's no way to gain control of your life if you are being controlled by an addiction. For that reason, I insist that any of my clients who are substance abusers also join a program such as

Alcoholics Anonymous or Narcotics Anonymous. The work in this book should be undertaken only after a minimum of six months of sobriety. Your emotions are extremely raw in the beginning phase of recovery, and there is always the danger that uncovering and exploring painful childhood experiences during this time may cause you to slip back into substance abuse.

It would be both unrealistic and irresponsible of me to suggest that if you follow the path I outline, all your problems will disappear overnight. But I *can* assure you that if you do this work, you'll discover exciting new ways of relating to your parents and to others. You will be able to define who you are and how you want to live your life. And you will discover a new sense of confidence and self-worth.

9 | *You Don't Have to Forgive*

At this point, you may be asking yourself, "Isn't the first step to forgive my parents?" My answer is *no*. This may shock, anger, dismay, or confuse many of you. Most of us have been led to believe exactly the opposite—that forgiveness is the first step toward healing.

In fact, it is not necessary to forgive your parents in order to feel better about yourself and to change your life!

Certainly I'm aware that this flies in the face of some of our most cherished religious, spiritual, philosophical, and psychological principles. According to the Judeo-Christian ethic, "To err is human, to forgive divine." I am also aware that there are many experts in the various helping professions who sincerely believe that forgiveness is not only the *first* step but often the *only* step necessary for inner peace. I disagree completely.

Early in my professional career I too believed that to forgive people who had injured you, especially parents, was an important part of the healing process. I often encouraged clients—many of whom had been severely mistreated—to forgive cruel or abusive parents. In addition, many of my clients entered therapy claiming to have already forgiven their toxic parents, but I discovered that, more often than not, they didn't feel any better for having forgiven. They still felt bad about themselves. They still had their symptoms. Forgiving hadn't created any significant or lasting changes for them. In fact, some of them felt even *more* inadequate. They'd say things such as: "Maybe I didn't forgive enough"; "My minister said I didn't truly forgive in my heart"; or, "Can't I do anything right?"

I took a long, hard look at the concept of forgiveness. I began to wonder if it could actually *impede* progress rather than *enhance* it.

I came to realize that there are two facets to forgiveness: giving up the need for revenge, and absolving the guilty party of responsibility. I didn't have much trouble accepting the idea that people have to let go of the need to get even. Revenge is a very normal but negative motivation. It bogs you down in obsessive fantasies about striking back to get satisfaction; it creates a lot of frustration and unhappiness; it works against your emotional well-being. Despite how sweet revenge may feel for a moment, it keeps stirring up the emotional chaos between you and your parents, wasting precious time and energy. Letting go of your need for revenge is difficult, but it is clearly a healthy step.

But the other facet of forgiveness was not as clear-cut. I felt there was something wrong with unquestioningly absolving someone of his rightful responsibility, particularly if he had severely mistreated an innocent child. Why in the world should you "pardon" a father who terrorized and battered you, who made your childhood a living hell? How are you supposed to "overlook" the fact that you had to come home to a dark house and nurse your drunken mother almost every day? And do you really have to "forgive" a father who raped you at the age of 7?

The more I thought about it, the more I realized that this absolution was really another form of denial: "If I forgive you, we can pretend that what happened wasn't so terrible." I came to realize that this aspect of forgiveness was actually preventing a lot of people from getting on with their lives.

The Forgiveness Trap

One of the most dangerous things about forgiveness is that it undercuts your ability to let go of your pent-up emotions. How can you acknowledge your anger against a parent whom you've already forgiven? Responsibility can go only one of two places: outward, onto the people who have hurt you, or inward, into yourself. Someone's got to be responsible. So you may forgive your *parents* but end up hating *yourself* all the more in exchange.

I also noticed that many clients rushed to forgiveness to avoid much of the painful work of therapy. They believed that by forgiving they could find a shortcut to feeling better. A handful of them "forgave," left therapy, and wound up sinking even deeper into depression or anxiety.

Several of these clients clung to their fantasies: "All I have to do is forgive and I will be healed, I will have wonderful mental health, everybody is going to love everybody, we'll hug a lot, and we'll finally be happy." Clients all too often discovered that the empty promise of forgiveness had merely set them up for bitter disappointment. Some of them experienced a rush of well-being, but it didn't last because nothing had really changed in the way they felt or in their family interactions.

I remember an especially touching session with a client named Stephanie, whose experience illustrates some of the typical problems of premature forgiveness. Stephanie, 27, was an extremely devout born-again Christian when I met her. At age 11, Stephanie had been raped by her stepfather. He had continued to abuse her until her mother threw him out of the house (for other reasons) a year later. Over the next four years, Stephanie had been molested by several of her mother's many boyfriends. She ran away from home at 16 and became a prostitute. Seven years later, she was almost beaten to death by a client. While recovering in the hospital Stephanie met an orderly who persuaded her to visit his church. A few years later they married and had a son. She was genuinely attempting to rebuild her life. But, despite her new family and her new religion, Stephanie was miserable. She spent two years in therapy, but still she couldn't shake her intense depression. That's when she came to me.

I put Stephanie in one of my incest-victims' groups. In her first session, Stephanie assured us that she had made her peace and had forgiven both her stepfather and her cold, inadequate mother. I told her that if she wanted to get rid of her depression she might have to "unforgive" for a while, to get in touch with her anger. She insisted that she believed deeply in forgiveness, that she didn't need to get angry to get better. A fairly intense struggle developed between us, partly because I was asking her to do something painful, but also because her religious beliefs contradicted her psychological needs.

Stephanie did her work dutifully, but she refused to tap in to her rage. Little by little, however, she began to have outbursts of anger on behalf of other people. For example, one night she embraced another group member, saying, "Your father was a monster, I hate him!"

A few weeks later, her own repressed rage finally came out. She screamed, cursed, and accused her parents of destroying her childhood and crippling her adult years. Afterward, I hugged her as she sobbed. I could feel her body relax. When she was calmer, I teasingly asked, "What kind of way is that for a nice Christian girl to behave?" I will never forget her reply:

> I guess God wants me to get better more than He wants me to forgive.

That night was the turning point for her.

People *can* forgive toxic parents, but they should do it at the conclusion—not at the beginning—of their emotional housecleaning. People need to get angry about what happened to them. They need to grieve over the fact that they never had the parental love they yearned for. They need to stop diminishing or discounting the damage that was done to them. Too often, "forgive and forget" means "pretend it didn't happen."

I also believe that forgiveness is appropriate only when parents do something to *earn* it. Toxic parents, especially the more abusive ones, need to acknowledge what happened, take responsibility, and show a willingness to make amends. If you unilaterally absolve parents who continue to treat you badly, who deny much of your reality and feelings, and who continue to project blame onto you, you may seriously impede the emotional work you need to do. If one or both parents are dead, you can still heal the damage, by forgiving *yourself* and releasing much of the hold that they had over your emotional well-being.

At this point, you may be wondering, understandably, if you will remain bitter and angry for the rest of your life if you don't forgive your parents. In fact, quite the opposite is true. What I have seen over the years is that emotional and mental peace comes as a result of releasing yourself from your toxic parents' control, without necessarily having to forgive them. And that release can come only after you've worked through your intense feelings of outrage and grief and after you've put the responsibility on *their* shoulders, where it belongs.

10 | "I'm a Grown-up. Why Don't I Feel Like One?"

Children of toxic parents have so much need for parental approval that it prevents them from living the lives they desire. It's true that most adults have at least some ongoing enmeshment with their parents. If asked, "Are you able to have your own thoughts, actions, and feelings without in any way considering your parents' hopes or expectations?" few could answer with a categorical "yes." In fact, in a healthy family, some amount of enmeshment is beneficial. It helps to create feelings of belonging, of family communion. Even in healthy families, however, that influence can go too far. And in toxic families it goes right off the scale.

Some people feel embarrassed or resentful when I suggest that they may be self-defeatingly tied to their parents. Please remember that this is a common struggle. Few people are sufficiently evolved to be completely "in charge" of their own lives and totally free of the need for parental approval. Most of us have left home physically, but very few of us have left home emotionally.

There are basically two types of enmeshment. The first involves continually giving in to your parents in order to placate them. No matter what your own needs or desires, your parents' needs and desires always come first.

The second type involves doing just the opposite. You may be just as enmeshed if you scream at, threaten, or become totally alienated from your parents. In this case, as contradictory as it may seem, your parents still have enormous control over how you feel and behave. As long as you continue to react so strongly to them, you give them the power to upset you, which allows them to control you.

To help you determine how enmeshed you still are with your parents, I have designed three checklists, one for beliefs, one for feelings, and one for behaviors. Use them as catalysts to help you uncover your self-constricting beliefs, feelings, and behaviors.

Remember, where I use the term *parents*, you may prefer to substitute *father* or *mother*. I use the plural only to simplify the list.

What Do You Believe?

As we saw in chapter 8, beliefs are deeply ingrained attitudes, perceptions, and concepts about people, relationships, and morality. Before you can begin any process of growth and change in your life, it is essential that you first become aware of the connection between erroneous beliefs, negative feelings, and self-defeating behaviors.

Here's how it works: a belief like, "I can't ever win, my parents have all the power," will probably lead you to feel helpless, afraid, frustrated, and overwhelmed. In an effort to defend against these feelings, you will automatically back down in disagreements, give in to your parents' wishes, and perhaps use drugs or alcohol in an attempt to avoid these feelings altogether. It all starts with beliefs.

This first checklist will help you identify some of the beliefs that underlie your feelings and behaviors. Put a mark next to each statement that rings true for you.

In My Relationship with My Parents, This Is What I Believe:

— It is up to me to make my parents happy.
— It is up to me to make my parents proud.
— I am my parents' whole life.
— My parents couldn't survive without me.
— I couldn't survive without my parents.
— If I told my parents the truth about (my divorce, my abortion, my being gay, my fiancée being an atheist, etc.), it would kill them.
— If I stand up to my parents, I'll lose them forever.
— If I tell them how much they hurt me, they'll cut me out of their lives.
— I shouldn't do or say anything that would hurt my parents' feelings.
— My parents' feelings are more important than mine.
— There's no point in talking to my parents because it wouldn't do any good.
— If my parents would only change, I would feel better about myself.
— I have to make it up to my parents for being such a bad person.
— If I could just get them to see how much they're hurting me, I know they'd be different.
— No matter what they did, they are my parents and I have to honor them.
— My parents don't have any control over my life. I fight with them all the time.

If four or more of these beliefs apply to you, you are still very enmeshed with your parents. As hard as it may be to accept, all of these beliefs are self-defeating. They prevent you from being a separate and independent person. They increase dependency and rob you of your adult power.

Several of these beliefs put full responsibility on your shoulders for how your parents feel. When toxic parents feel bad, they often look for others to blame, and those others are usually their children. If you were made to believe that your parents' feelings were your responsibility, you probably still believe that it's within your power to "make" them—and often everyone else—either happy or sad.

Many experts on human behavior contend that you can't "make" anyone feel anything—that each person is totally responsible for how he "chooses" to feel. I don't think that's true. I believe we *do* have an effect on the feelings of everyone we are connected to. But having an effect is not the same thing as being responsible for fixing those feelings. Just as you are responsible for finding ways to make yourself feel better when someone hurts you, your parents are responsible for finding their own ways to feel better when someone hurts them.

For example, if you do something that is neither cruel nor abusive but nevertheless makes your mother feel sad—such as marrying someone she disapproves of or taking a job out of town—it is up to your mother to find ways to feel better. It's perfectly appropriate for you to say something like, "I'm sorry you're upset," but it is not your responsibility to change your plans for the sole purpose of taking care of your mother's feelings. When you ignore your needs for the sake of your mother's feelings, you are doing a disservice not only to yourself but to your mother, as well. The anger and resentment that you will inevitably feel cannot help but affect your relationship. And if your efforts to make your mother happy fail, you will feel guilty and inadequate.

When you base the majority of your life decisions on how they will make your parents feel, you are relinquishing free choice. If their feelings *always* come first, *they* are in the driver's seat of *your* life.

Think about what other beliefs you may have that keep you from feeling like an effective adult with your parents. Add them to the list. This list will become part of a short exercise I'll ask you to do later.

False Beliefs, Painful Feelings

Self-defeating beliefs always lead to painful feelings. By examining your feelings, you can begin to understand both the beliefs that spawned them and the behaviors that result.

Most of us think our feelings are reactions to things that happen to us, things that come from outside of ourselves. But in reality, even the most extreme fear, pleasure, or pain grows out of some kind of belief.

For example, you get very brave one day and tell your alcoholic father that you are no longer willing to be with him when he's drunk. He starts screaming about how ungrateful and disrespectful you are. You feel guilty. You may think your guilt is a result of your father's behavior, but that's only half the story. Before your feelings washed through you, certain beliefs were triggered in your mind—beliefs you probably weren't aware of. In this case, these beliefs might have been: "children should never talk back to their parents," or, "my father has an illness and it's up to me to take care of him." Because you have not been true to these deep-seated beliefs, you react with guilt.

When you are faced with a situation that calls for an emotional response, family beliefs run through your mind like an unconscious patter. Understanding that these beliefs almost always precede your feelings is more than an interesting psychological exercise.

Understanding the relationship between your beliefs and your feelings is an essential step toward putting a stop to self-defeating behavior!

"But I Don't Feel Anything"

We all have strong emotional reactions to our parents. Some of us are in touch with these feelings, but others protect themselves from the intensity of their emotions by burying them.

You may have gotten strong messages in your childhood that it wasn't safe to feel. Perhaps you were punished for expressing feelings, or perhaps your feelings were so painful that you pushed them deep into your unconscious in order to survive. Perhaps you had to convince yourself that you just didn't care, or perhaps you needed to prove to your parents that they couldn't get to you.

As an adult it may be very difficult for you to turn your emotional faucets back on. The connection between powerful feelings and your past and current relationship with your parents may be especially difficult for you to see. The feelings I'm discussing throughout this book may seem foreign to you. Perhaps you describe yourself as cold or numb, or you believe that you don't have any feelings—that you don't have much to offer in the way of love or caring. If so, your childhood feelings were probably very intense, and you required a great deal of protective defenses to make it into adulthood.

If your feelings are deeply buried, you can use these checklists as a starting point to get in touch with them. You can also try to imagine what the feelings might be of someone else who has the same relationship to his parents as you have. Many people find that they simply cannot reach their feelings without therapy. Your feelings are not lost, they are just misplaced, and sometimes it takes professional help to reclaim them. But whatever it takes, you cannot do this work without connecting with your feelings.

It's important that you take it easy as you begin to allow some of your blocked feelings to surface. You may feel very upset for a period of time as your feelings come to life. Many people enter therapy expecting to feel better immediately. They are dismayed when they discover that usually they have to feel worse before they can feel better. This is emotional surgery, and as with any surgery, the wounds must be cleaned out before they heal, and it takes time for the pain to go away. But the pain is a sign that the healing process has started.

To help you bring your feelings into focus, I have divided them into four groups: guilt, fear, sadness, and anger. We are concerned here with these automatic, predictable, negative feelings—the ones that usually cause you trouble.

Check the statements in this list that most closely describe how you feel.

In My Relationship with My Parents, This Is What I Feel:

— I feel guilty when I don't live up to my parents' expectations.
— I feel guilty when I do something that upsets them.
— I feel guilty when I go against their advice.
— I feel guilty when I argue with them.
— I feel guilty when I get angry with them.
— I feel guilty when I disappoint my parents or hurt their feelings.
— I feel guilty when I don't do enough for them.
— I feel guilty when I don't do everything they ask me to do.
— I feel guilty when I say no to them.

— I feel scared when my parents yell at me.
— I feel scared when they're angry at me.
— I feel scared when I'm angry at them.
— I feel scared when I have to tell them something they may not want to hear.
— I feel scared when they threaten to withdraw their love.
— I feel scared when I disagree with them.
— I feel scared when I try to stand up to them.

— I feel sad when my parents are unhappy.
— I feel sad when I know I've let my parents down.
— I feel sad when I can't make their lives better for them.
— I feel sad when my parents tell me I've ruined their lives.
— I feel sad when I do something that I want to do and it hurts my parents.

—— I feel sad when my parents don't like my (husband, wife, lover, friends).

—— I feel angry when my parents criticize me.
—— I feel angry when my parents try to control me.
—— I feel angry when they tell me how to live my life.
—— I feel angry when they tell me how I should think, feel, or behave.
—— I feel angry when they tell me what I should or shouldn't do.
—— I feel angry when they make demands on me.
—— I feel angry when they try to live their lives through me.
—— I feel angry when they expect me to take care of them.
—— I feel angry when they reject me.

Please add any feelings you have that aren't covered. These may include physical reactions to your parents. Physical reactions are often the language through which we express painful feelings, especially when it isn't safe to say them to the people we're upset with. We often say with our bodies what we can't or won't say with our mouths. The particular physical symptoms are influenced by such things as family medical history, predispositions or vulnerabilities in certain parts of your body, and your unique personality and emotional setup. It's not unusual for adult children of toxic parents to suffer headaches, stomachaches, muscle tension, fatigue, loss of appetite or compulsion to eat, sleep problems, and nausea. These reactions should never be discounted, and if they intensify to stress-related diseases such as cardiovascular or gastrointestinal disorders, they can be lethal. Therefore, it is essential that you seek medical help for any physical condition that persists, even if you are convinced that it is emotional in origin.

If you checked more than one-third of the statements on the lists, you are still closely enmeshed with your parents and your emotional world is largely controlled by them.

SEEING THE CONNECTION

Try putting a "because" after each of the feelings that applies to you, and follow the "because" with a belief from your first list (p. 184). This piggyback technique can help you make a lot more sense out of some of your reactions. For example, "I feel guilty when I do something that upsets them *because* I shouldn't do or say anything that will hurt my parents' feelings"; "I feel sad when I know I've let my parents down *because* it's up to me to make my parents happy"; "I feel scared when I'm angry with them *because* if I stand up to my parents, I'll lose them forever."

Once you begin to make these all-important connections, you will probably be surprised at how many of your feelings have their roots in your beliefs. This exercise is tremendously important because once you understand the source of your feelings, you can start to take control of them.

What Are You Doing?

Beliefs lead to rules, feelings make you obey them, and that's what leads to behavior. If you want to change your behavior, you've got to work all the way through the equation, changing your beliefs and feelings in order to change your rules.

When you recognize that behavior is the end product of beliefs and feelings, some of your behaviors start to make more sense.

Here's a list of some behaviors that might grow out of the beliefs and feelings I have already listed. These behaviors fall into two basic categories: compliant and aggressive. Check the ones that apply to you. Again, if you identify any of your destructive behaviors that I have not listed, add them to the list.

In My Relationship with My Parents, This Is How I Behave:

Compliant Behaviors:

—— I often give in to my parents no matter how I feel.

—— I often don't tell them what I really think.

—— I often don't tell them how I really feel.

—— I often act as if everything is fine between us even when it isn't.

—— I am often phony and superficial when I'm with my parents.

—— I often do things in relation to my parents out of guilt or fear rather than out of free choice.

—— I try very hard to get them to change.

—— I try very hard to get them to see and understand my point of view.

—— I often become the peacemaker in any conflict with them.

—— I often make very painful sacrifices in my own life in order to please them.

—— I continue to be the bearer of the family secrets.

Aggressive Behaviors:

—— I am constantly arguing with my parents to show them that I'm right.

—— I constantly do things that I know they don't like to show them that I'm my own person.

—— I often scream, yell, or curse at my parents to show them they can't control me.

—— I often have to restrain myself to keep from attacking them physically.

—— I blew my stack and cut my parents out of my life.

If two or more of these behaviors fit you, then enmeshment with your parents is still a major issue in your life.

It is not difficult to see how compliant behaviors keep you from being independent. But enmeshment through aggressive behaviors is less clear. These behaviors would appear to separate you from your parents. They create the illusion that you are fighting back rather than capitulating. In reality, aggressive behaviors still indicate enmeshment because of the intensity of your feelings; the repetitiveness and predictability of your reactions; and the fact that your behavior is not determined by your free choice, but rather by your defensive need to prove how separate you are.

Compliance and aggression are merely two sides of the same behavioral coin.

Reacting to the Checklists

Carol, the model-turned-interior-designer who had been verbally abused by her father, was astounded when she added up the results of her checklists. She discovered that at age 52 she was still highly enmeshed with her parents.

> I'm so ashamed. I'm middle-aged, been married three times, have a grown son, and my parents are still pulling my strings. Can you believe . . . I checked off nearly every belief and feeling on the lists. And talk about Ms. Compliant . . . When am I going to get it through my thick skull that my parents aren't ever going to change? They've always been cruel and unsupportive, and I guess they always will be.

I told Carol that feelings of shame and embarrassment are common for someone who considers herself an adult but suddenly sees that she's still controlled by her parents. We would all like to believe that we are independent adults making our own decisions about our own lives.

Carol probably was right: her parents weren't going to change. But she was. The first step in shaking off the destructive bonds is understanding what makes them so strong.

Like many of my clients, Carol reacted angrily to the realization that she was still enmeshed. She wanted to rush right out and challenge her parents. If you have that impulse, resist it. This is not the right time. Impulsive action almost always backfires.

Avoid taking confrontative action when your emotions are at fever pitch. Your perspective and judgment will be clouded.

There is plenty of time to integrate your new awareness into your life. But first you've got to map out a plan of action.

Remember, this is the beginning of a process, not an overnight cure. The preceding lists are just the beginning of your exploration. There are some very complex and often bewildering issues ahead. You don't want to dive into the water until you've checked for rocks beneath the surface. You can't change lifelong patterns overnight no matter how self-defeating they may be. What you *can* do is start to challenge your constricting beliefs and self-defeating behaviors and eventually discard them to allow your true self to emerge. But before you can recover your true self, you've got to know who you are.

11 | The Beginnings of Self-Definition

Emotional independence doesn't mean that you have to cut yourself off from your parents. It means that you can be part of the family while at the same time being a separate individual. It means you can be who you are and let your parents be who they are.

When you feel free to have your own beliefs, feelings, and behaviors, apart from those of your parents (or others), you are "self-defined." If your parents don't like what you do or think, inevitably you will have to tolerate some discomfort. And you'll have to tolerate *their* discomfort with *you* when you don't rush in to change yourself for them. Even if some of your beliefs are identical to those of your parents, or your behavior meets with their approval, it is essential that you make your own choices and that you feel free to agree or disagree with them.

This doesn't mean I encourage you to ride roughshod over other people's feelings or to ignore the impact that your behavior may have on them. But neither can you allow them to ride roughshod over you. We all have to find a balance between taking care of ourselves and being concerned about the feelings of others.

No one can be self-defined 100 percent of the time. We are all part of a larger society. No one is totally free from the desire for approval from others. No one is completely free from emotional dependency of some kind, and very few of us would want to be. Human beings are social animals, and open relationships demand a certain amount of emotional *inter*dependence. For this reason, self-definition must be somewhat flexible. There's nothing wrong with making a compromise for your parents, as long as it is something you've chosen to do of your own free will. What I'm talking about here is maintaining your emotional integrity, being true to yourself.

It's Okay to Be Selfish Sometimes

Many people don't stand up for themselves because they confuse self-definition with selfishness. The word *selfish* pushes all of our guilt buttons. Sandy—the hairdresser whose unforgiving parents continued to punish her in adulthood for the abortion she had had when she was 15—put herself through an emotional hell to avoid being labeled selfish. She explained:

> Talk about being between a rock and a hard place. I think I may have just ruined my entire life. My folks are having their house remodeled, and my mother called me last week to tell me that the noise is driving her crazy, so she and Dad want to move in with us until the remodeling is done, which could be weeks. I really didn't want to say "yes," but what could I do? I mean they *are* my parents. When my husband found out, he just about died. See, he uses the spare room as an office and he's in the middle of a big project right now. So he made me

> call my mother back and suggest that maybe it would be better for her and Dad to go to a hotel instead. Well, she just about went through the ceiling. I got a half hour on how ungrateful and selfish I am, how this is the least I can do, considering everything they've done for me. I told her I'd have to discuss it with Bill, but I already know what he'll say. What can I do, Susan?

I suggested that Sandy use this minicrisis as an opportunity to begin the process of self-definition. It was time for her to take a look at the current uproar and see it not as an isolated incident but as the latest problem in an ongoing pattern in her relationship with her parents. This wasn't about their moving in with her, it was about her automatic reaction of placating and accommodating them. If she wanted to break that pattern, she had to focus first on what *she* wanted as opposed to what her parents were demanding of her. I asked her if she even *knew* what she wanted.

> **SANDY:** The first thing that comes to mind is I want my parents to leave me alone. I don't want them to stay with us. It'll be horrible. I mean, I feel guilty just even admitting that, because kids are supposed to be there for their parents. Maybe I'll just tell them they can stay. Then I won't feel so awful about it. It's a lot easier fighting with Bill than it is fighting with them. Why can't I make everybody happy?
>
> **SUSAN:** You answer that question.
>
> **SANDY:** I don't know the answer. That's why I'm here. I mean, I know I don't want them living with me right now, but I love them—I can't just turn my back on them.
>
> **SUSAN:** I'm not asking you to turn your back on them. I'm asking you to imagine what it would be like to say "no" to them sometimes, to set limits on how much you're willing to sacrifice for them. Be "self-defined," Sandy. Make decisions based on what *you* want and what *you* need rather than on what they want or need.

Sandy: That sounds so selfish.

Susan: It's okay to be selfish sometimes.

Sandy: I want to be a good person, Susan. I was raised to believe that good people do things for others.

Susan: Sweetie, if you were as good to you as you are to your parents, you probably wouldn't need to be here. You're a very good person—to everybody but you.

Sandy: Then how come I feel so bad?

Sandy started to cry. It was so important for her to prove to her mother that she was neither selfish nor ungrateful that she was willing to throw both her home and her marriage into near-pandemonium.

Sandy based many of her life decisions on an overdeveloped sense of obligation to her parents. She believed she had a responsibility to bury her needs beneath theirs. She rarely did what *she* wanted to do, and this had led to years of repressed anger and lack of personal fulfillment that eventually expressed themselves as depression.

Sandy, like most of us, reacted to her parents in an almost automatic, knee-jerk way. When we react, we usually act without thinking, without listening, and without exploring our options. People are usually the most reactive when they feel emotionally threatened or assaulted. This reactiveness can take place in a relationship with almost anyone in our lives—a lover, a boss, a child, or a friend—but it is almost always the most intense with our parents.

When you are reactive, you are dependent on the approval of others. You feel good about yourself only when no one disagrees with you, criticizes you, or disapproves of you. Your feelings are often far out of proportion to the events that evoked them. You'll perceive a small suggestion as a personal attack; a minor constructive criticism as a personal failure. Without the approval of others, you have a hard time maintaining even minimal emotional stability.

When you're reactive, you typically say things such as, "Every time my mother tells me how to live my life, I go crazy"; "They really know how to push my buttons, I always lose it with them"; or,

"I just have to hear my father's voice and I see red." When you allow your emotional reactions to become automatic, you're giving up control, handing your feelings to someone else on a silver platter. This gives other people enormous power over you.

Responding Versus Reacting

The opposite of being reactive is being responsive. When you're being responsive, you are thinking as well as feeling. You're aware of your feelings but you don't let them drive you to act impulsively.

Responsiveness also allows you to maintain your sense of self-worth, despite anything your parents might say about you. This is extremely rewarding. The thoughts and feelings of others no longer drag you into a pit of self-doubt. You will see all sorts of new options and choices in your dealings with other people because your perspective and your sense of reason are not being buried by emotions. Responsiveness can put back into your hands a good deal of your control over your life.

Sandy needed to become less reactive and more responsive. I cautioned her that behavioral changes are a struggle for everyone, including myself, but I assured her that she could do it if she was willing to commit to the process. She was.

The first thing I asked her to do was to recognize that most of her opinions of herself really came from things her parents had told her—from *their* definition of her. The negative parts of that definition included labeling Sandy selfish, ungrateful, and bad. It took many years for Sandy to internalize this negative self-image, so we weren't about to change it overnight. But I showed her some beginning behavioral strategies to enable her to begin the process of replacing her parents' definition of her with a more realistic view of who she really was.

I asked her to imagine that I was her mother. Through role playing, I wanted her to find a new way of answering her mother's cricitism, an alternative to her usual capitulation.

SUSAN (as Mother): You're selfish and ungrateful!

SANDY: No, I'm not! I'm always thinking of everybody else. I'm always thinking of you. I kill myself to avoid hurting you and Dad. What about all the times I was exhausted, but I still took you shopping or had you and Dad over for dinner? Nothing I ever do is enough for you.

I told Sandy that she was being defensive. She was still apologizing, arguing, and explaining. She had to stop trying to "get them to see." As long as she was still seeking her mother's approval, she was still being controlled. She needed to become nondefensive if she wanted to begin to unhook. The idea is to drain as much heat as possible out of the interaction.

To show her what I meant, I switched roles with her. Sandy would be her mother, and I would be Sandy.

SANDY (as Mother): Your father and I need a place to stay. You're being selfish and ungrateful.

SUSAN (as Sandy): Gee, Mom, it's interesting that you see it that way.

SANDY (as Mother): After everything we've done for you, I can't believe you'd even suggest that we go to a hotel.

SUSAN (as Sandy): I'm sorry you're upset.

SANDY (as Mother): Are you going to let us stay there or not?

SUSAN (as Sandy): I'm going to have to think about it.

SANDY (as Mother): I want an answer, young lady!

SUSAN (as Sandy): I know you do, Mom, but I'm going to have to think about it.

SANDY (breaking out of character): I don't know what else to say.

Sandy discovered some surprising things during this exercise. She found that nondefensive responses kept the conflict from escalating, and, equally important, she didn't have to get backed up against the wall trying to defend herself.

NONDEFENSIVENESS

None of us is taught to respond nondefensively. That's why the technique doesn't come easily. It needs to be learned and practiced. Also, most people assume that if they don't defend themselves in a conflict, their opponents will see them as weak and ride right over them. In reality the opposite is true. If you can stay calm and refuse to be stampeded, then you retain the power.

I can't stress strongly enough how essential it is to learn and use nondefensive responses, especially with toxic parents. This type of response can go a long way toward breaking the cycle of attack, retreat, defense, and escalation.

Here are some examples of nondefensive responses that you can try using in your daily interactions:

- Oh?
- Oh, I see.
- That's interesting.
- You're certainly entitled to your opinion.
- I'm sorry you don't approve.
- Let me think about that.
- Why don't we talk about this when you're not so upset.
- I'm sorry you're hurt (upset, disappointed).

It's important that you rehearse nondefensive responses by yourself before you start using them with others. To do this, imagine your parents in the room with you saying something critical or denigrating. Respond out loud to them nondefensively. Remember, the moment you argue, apologize, explain, or try to get them to change their minds, you have handed over much of your power. If you ask someone to forgive or to understand, you give them the power to withhold what you're asking for. But if you use nondefensive responses, you are asking for nothing, and when you ask for nothing, you can't be rejected.

Once you feel somewhat comfortable with nondefensive responses, try using them the next time you have a disagreement with someone other than your parents. It's a good idea to test them out on someone you're less emotionally connected to—a colleague or a casual friend. It will probably feel awkward and unnatural at first. You may find yourself lapsing back into defensive responses out of frustration. Like any new skill, you'll have to practice and be willing to make mistakes. But eventually it will become second nature.

Position Statements

There is another behavioral technique—I call it "making position statements"—that can help you become less reactive and propel you further down the road of self-definition.

Position statements define what you think and believe, what's important to you, what you are willing to do and not willing to do, what's negotiable and what's not. The issues can range in importance from your opinion of a recent film to your basic beliefs about life. Of course, before you can make a position statement, you have to determine what your position is.

When I asked Sandy what she really wanted to do about her parents' demand, she answered, "I don't know. I'm so worried about upsetting them that it's really hard for me to know just what I want myself."

Sandy's dilemma was typical of most people who have spent most of their lives feeling overly responsible for their parents. It's hard to define who you are when you've had little opportunity to do so in the past. To help Sandy make her position statement, I pointed out that there were basically only three positions she could take:

1. I'm not willing to let you stay at my house.
2. I'm willing to let you stay for a *specified*, limited time.
3. I'm willing to let you stay for as long as you want.

Sandy decided that while she really didn't want them to stay at all, it felt like too big a jump for her to tell them that. She agreed to tell them they could stay for one week. She believed that this would be a good way for her to assert her own needs while at the same time partially placating her parents.

Reframing "I Can't"

Sandy was not completely satisfied with her solution. She was still putting a burden on her husband and on their relationship, and she believed that this was due to her weakness. With a deep sigh, she said, "I guess I just can't stand up to my parents." I asked her to repeat her statement, but instead of saying, "I can't . . ." say, "*I haven't yet* stood up to my parents."

"I haven't yet" implies choice, where "don't" and "can't" imply just the opposite: finality. Lack of choice is directly connected to enmeshment. It is the key to keeping the child locked inside. Children's choices are dictated by adults. By saying, "I haven't yet," you open the door to new behavior in the future. You embrace hope.

Some people think that if they merely rephrase an unwanted behavior as a choice, instead of changing that behavior, they're admitting defeat. I disagree. I see choice as the key to self-definition. Any decision based on choice moves us away from reactiveness. There is a big difference between *choosing* to capitulate to your parents because you've considered the alternatives and decided that you're not prepared to fight, and *automatically* capitulating because you feel helpless. Making a choice means taking a step toward control; knee-jerk reacting means backsliding into being controlled. It may not feel like an enormous amount of progress, but I assure you it is.

Trying It Out on Your Parents

Some of my clients are so excited by the success they experience in trial runs with their new behaviors that they can't wait to try them out on their parents. But many others worry that their parents will become frustrated and/or infuriated at their nondefensive responses or their position statements. Toxic parents are used to pushing their children's buttons. When they don't get the reactions they expect, they get upset.

My advice to you is: go for it. The sooner the better. To delay taking this small first step, to spend weeks or months "thinking about it," will only increase your anxiety. Remember:

You are an adult and can withstand your discomfort for the purpose of becoming your own person.

The doing is rarely as bad as the anticipation. You don't need to jump in with the most emotionally charged issue between you and your parents. You can start to practice nondefensive responses when your mother doesn't like the color of your lipstick or your father criticizes your cooking.

I suggested to Sandy that she make the most of the time her parents were living with her by practicing nondefensive responses and making position statements about small things. I encouraged her to express her thoughts and opinions. Instead of saying, "You're wrong, shellfish is bad for you," she could say, "I don't happen to agree with you, I think shellfish is bad for you." In that way her position would be framed as an opinion instead of a challenge, reducing the chance of inciting an emotional reaction.

I also suggested that if she felt brave enough, she might try to tackle some of the larger problems in her relationship with her parents by setting limits, letting them know what she was and was not willing to do for them.

Although Sandy felt somewhat apprehensive about the things I was asking her to do, she knew that unless she began to try out some of this new behavior she would stay stuck in her rut. But she was pessimistic about her parents' ability to change. She asked me how she could feel good about her behavioral changes if they didn't work—if her parents didn't change as a result. I reminded her that they didn't *have* to change. If she changed her ways of responding to them, she would be single-handedly changing her relationship to them. This *could* cause them to change, but even if it didn't, Sandy would be tipping the balance of power into her own hands.

When you become self-defined—when you become responsive instead of reactive, when you make clear statements about what you feel and think, when you set limits on what you are and aren't willing to do—your relationship with your parents will have to change.

12 | Who's Really Responsible?

I wish you had a happy childhood, but I can't change the past. What I can do is help you make a major shift in your beliefs about who is responsible for the pain of your childhood. This shift is essential, because until you honestly assess who owns this responsibility, you will almost certainly go through your life shouldering the blame yourself. And as long as you're blaming *yourself*, you'll suffer shame and self-hatred, and you'll find ways to punish yourself.

Go at Your Own Pace

In the last two chapters, the work we did was primarily intellectual. I asked you to explore, to perceive, and to understand. In this chapter and the ones that follow, we'll be working on a far more emotional level. Because of this, it is especially important that you take your time. Emotional work can get pretty heavy and before you know it you may be looking for excuses to avoid it.

If you begin to feel off balance, it's okay to slow down and put the work aside for a few days. But if you find yourself continuing to put it off, set a time limit for when you're going to come back to it, and then stick to it.

You may find it useful to enlist some outside support as you begin this work. When you bring strong emotional material to the surface, a support group or therapist can be a valuable guide. A loving friend, partner, or relative can offer encouragement, but may feel intimidated by the intensity of your emotions. You may want to ask this person to read this book along with you. He or she can be much more supportive with a better understanding of what you're going through.

It Is Their Responsibility

I know I have said this many times by now, but I can't emphasize enough how important this message is and how hard it is to internalize:

You must let go of the responsibility for the painful events of your childhood and put it where it belongs.

To help you let go of the responsibility, I have designed a list of many of the things my clients have wrongly blamed themselves for. To use this list most effectively, set aside a quiet, private time for yourself to talk to the child within you. To help you visualize how little and helpless you were, you might want to use a childhood photograph. Say out loud to that child, "You were not responsible for . . ." and finish the sentence with every item on the list that applies to your life.

"You were not responsible for . . .":

1. the way they neglected or ignored you
2. the way they made you feel unloved or unlovable

3. their cruel or thoughtless teasing
4. the bad names they called you
5. their unhappiness
6. their problems
7. their choice not to do anything about their problems
8. their drinking
9. what they did when they were drinking
10. their hitting you
11. their molesting you

Add any other painful, repetitive experiences that you have always felt responsible for.

The second part of this exercise involves assigning the responsibility where it belongs—to your parents. To bring this more sharply into focus, just repeat each item on the list, but precede it now with the words, "My parents were responsible for . . ." Again, add anything that is relevant to your personal experience.

In the beginning you may understand, on an intellectual level, that it wasn't your fault, but the little child inside you may still feel responsible. It takes time for your feelings to catch up to your new awareness. You may need to repeat this exercise several times.

"I Don't Think They Meant Any Harm"

You may feel especially reluctant to assign responsibility to your parents if they were inadequate, ill, had overwhelming problems of their own, or appeared to have good intentions.

Les—who, at the age of 8, had to take care of his younger brothers following his mother's breakdown—clearly exemplifies this dilemma. I told Les that many of his struggles with women in his adult life were directly connected to the burdens of guilt and responsibility he had assumed as a child. Les remained unconvinced, despite the fact that he had gone through his responsibility list earlier in the session.

LES: But I *am* responsible. My mother was so miserable. She still is. She needs me. I just want to make things better for her.

SUSAN: How long have you been taking responsibility for her life?

LES: Since I was eight.

SUSAN: And who was responsible for you?

LES: I guess I've always felt responsible for everybody, including myself.

SUSAN: What would it mean, Les, if you began to hold your parents responsible for themselves?

LES: How can you do that with someone who is depressed, pathetic . . . who's never had a pleasurable day in her life. It wasn't her fault. She went to doctors. She tried to get better. She didn't want to be sick.

SUSAN: That still doesn't make it your responsibility. What about your father? How come he gets off the hook so easily? When is it his turn to start acting like an adult?

LES (after much thought)**:** You know something, I never thought about it that way. I guess he's just weak.

SUSAN: I recognize that with parents like yours, who weren't overtly abusive, it's a lot tougher to see how hurtful they were. But there was a lot of benevolent violence here. There was a lot of emotional neglect. No one ever cared about *your* life. You never got to have a childhood. The important thing here is not how much they were responsible for, but for you to realize that you *weren't* responsible for any of it.

Les allowed this to sink in. He worked on his new awareness for the rest of the session. From that day on, his progress was much more rapid.

You may recognize that your parents were inadequate, depressed, ill, or unavailable, but you may still sympathize with their struggles. Your parents had very limited resources, after all; most people didn't feel free to enter therapy thirty or forty years ago.

Your parents may be so passive that they seem helpless. You may be convinced that they intended no harm.

In many cases, I'm sure that no harmful intent existed, but speculating on intent is a waste of time. It's the results that count. If harm was done by inadequate parents, the intent is irrelevant. Inadequate parents are responsible both for what they did do and for what they didn't.

To help Les begin to see how true this was for him, I used an empty chair to symbolize his parents and played the role of Les myself. I wanted him to hear verbalized the things he had never been able to say for himself.

SUSAN (as Les): Mom and Dad, when I was a little kid, I felt like nobody was ever there for me. I felt scared and I felt lonely, and I didn't understand why nobody was looking out for me. I don't understand, Mom, why I had to take care of you and why Dad didn't do it. I don't understand why I didn't get to be a kid. I always thought it was because nobody loved me. I still feel that way! When are *you* going to stop draining me? When are *you* going to grow up? I'm so tired of feeling responsible for the whole family. I'm tired of being on call for you all the time. I'm tired of taking responsibility for the whole world. I'm tired of blaming myself for everything that went wrong. Mom, I'm sorry you were sick and unhappy, but it wasn't my fault!

LES: Everything you said was true. I've felt all those things. But I could *never* say those things to them.

SUSAN: Never is a long, long time, Les. Right now it's only important that you say them to yourself. Later, when we've done more work on this and you feel stronger, you might want to make a different choice.

Les began to see that his parents were adults and, as such, had certain basic responsibilities toward their children. By failing to attend to the physical and emotional needs of their children, his parents, like all inadequate parents, created a cockeyed version of the parent-child relationship.

Once Les could truly see, believe, and feel these basic truths, he could rid himself of much of the self-blame that fueled his workaholism and impaired his ability to be loving.

"He Was So Out of Control"

Adults who were severely abused as children also have difficulty putting the responsibility where it belongs. Remember, accepting blame is a survival tool for abused children. They keep the myth of the good family alive by believing that they—not their parents—are bad. This belief lies at the core of virtually all self-defeating behavior patterns in adults who were abused as children. But, it is a belief that can be reversed.

Joe—the graduate student in psychology who had been horribly battered by his violent, alcoholic father—eventually came in for therapy with me. In his first session, he offered a good example of how tenacious self-blame can be.

> **Joe:** I can look back at my childhood and know that my father had a mean streak. But I still make excuses for him because maybe he really did believe that what he did to me was for my own good. In my head, I know what he did was horrible and that no child deserves to be treated like I was treated. But in my gut, I still feel like a rotten kid who deserved what he got. And I still feel so damned guilty that I couldn't protect my mother.
>
> **Susan:** You managed to survive by taking all of the badness onto yourself. If you saw your father as bad when you were little, it would have been overwhelming and terrifying for you. But you're not a little kid anymore, Joe. You have to start telling yourself the truth. And the truth is your father was one hundred percent responsible for abusing you, for his violence, and for his drinking. He was also one hundred percent

responsible for making the choice to do nothing to resolve his problems and save his family. And while it's more comforting for you to see your mother as an innocent victim, she was one hundred percent responsible for not protecting her children and herself. She permitted the abuse to continue. You've got to start putting the responsibility where it belongs. How are you ever going to be a counselor and help other people if you refuse to deal with reality in your own life?

JOE: I hear everything you're saying, Susan, but it's just a lot of words to me.

Joe's defenses seemed rock-solid. So, instead of talking to him directly, which seemed to stir up a lot of resistance, I asked Joe to play the role of his own father.

SUSAN: I want to talk to you about some of the things that happened in Joe's childhood. Joe has told me that you were pretty violent and beat him up a lot. He also told me that you're an alcoholic.

JOE (as Father): First of all, what went on inside my family is none of your goddamned business. If I hit him, it was just to toughen him up. And my drinking is my business.

SUSAN: It may be your business, but you just about destroyed your family with it. You abused and terrified your son, and you abused and terrified your wife. Do you have any idea what that was like for Joe? Do you care how he felt?

JOE (as Father): I couldn't care less. All I care about is myself.

SUSAN: I think you're a horrible father. You've done nothing but cause a lot of people a lot of pain. I'm sure you were in pain yourself, but you were an adult, and he was a little boy. You could've done something to help yourself instead of hurting other people. You were responsible for your alcoholism then and now. I think you're a coward who can only feel powerful by beating up on women and kids. All these years, Joe has felt he was to blame, when in reality, you were.

JOE (as Father): Like hell! The little bastard used to mouth off at me all the time. He didn't do his chores . . .

SUSAN (interrupting): There was nothing Joe did or could have done to justify what you did to him.

Joe came out of character at this point.

JOE: You know, I hate to admit it, but it felt really good for you to tell my dad off. I started to feel how angry and uptight he is . . . and I just didn't want to hear anything you were saying to me. And you're right, he did almost destroy the family. What a bastard he is. But I think he's more scared than I am. At least I'm trying to deal with this stuff. He's just been running away from it all his life. He really is a coward!

As painful as it was for Joe to acknowledge these things about his father, it was also very liberating. He was beginning to put the responsibility where it belonged and was ready to start absolving himself.

Joe had told me in a previous session that he loved working with children; he often did volunteer work at a children's hospital. I asked him to visualize one of the children he worked with. Then, I asked Joe to imagine that this child was living through a childhood similar to his own. I put an empty chair in front of him and asked what he would say if that child were sitting there now.

Joe was uncomfortable with the suggestion, but after a bit of prompting he took a deep breath and began talking to the imaginary child:

> I understand that there's some bad stuff going on at your house. I'm really sorry. I hear your old man gets drunk and beats you up a lot. And he calls you bad names. And he tells you you're no good. I know how scared you must feel. See, the same thing happened to me. And I bet you feel like it's all your fault, too, but it isn't. You're really a good kid, and nobody has the right to do those things to you. Nobody! Your

> father's mean. He's sick. And he's a coward because he won't face any of his problems. I think he really enjoys beating you up; it makes me want to kill him!

Joe's whole body shook with rage. I asked him who he had really been talking to. "Myself!" he shouted. "Jesus Christ, myself!"

Joe's long-held rage was beginning to surface. He could finally start to assign responsibility to his parents for the pain and self-hatred he had borne all his life.

I asked Joe to imagine that his father was now in the chair. I reminded him that he was safe, he could say anything he wanted to. This time, Joe didn't hesitate:

> You bastard! You fucking son of a bitch! Do you have any idea what kind of misery you caused me? What kind of misery you caused the whole family? Must've made you feel like a real big man to beat up on a little kid! I've spent my whole life feeling like a worthless piece of shit, like I deserved getting my ass kicked. But I'm tired of hearing your put-downs. So, fuck you!

I wasn't surprised by the intensity of Joe's anger. Once you start putting the responsibility where it belongs, you are going to experience powerful anger at the things that were done to you and at the people who did them. But Joe was frightened by how much anger there was inside him. Like many adults who were beaten as children, he was afraid he might lose control and hurt someone, might fall apart, or might feel angry forever; he was afraid he might even go crazy.

Fear of Anger

Anger is an upsetting emotion. You may associate anger with abuse from your childhood. You may associate anger with people you saw out of control with rage. You may worry that you'll seem ugly if you get angry and that other people will reject you. You may believe that good, loving people don't get angry, or that you have no right to get angry at the parents who gave you life.

Anger is also frightening. You may be afraid that you'll destroy someone with your anger or that you'll lose control. Or, like Joe, you may be afraid that you'll never be able to turn off your anger. These fears are very real for all of us, but the fact remains:

The things we're afraid will happen if we get angry are the very things that have a good chance of happening if we don't!

When you repress your anger, you may become depressed or abrasive and other people may reject you as surely as they would if you were openly angry at them. Repressed anger is unpredictable—it can explode at any time. When it *does*, it is often uncontrollable. Anger is always destructive unless it is managed, especially if it has been allowed to fester beneath your conscious awareness.

Dealing with Anger

Adult children of toxic parents have an especially difficult time with their anger because they grew up in families where emotional expression was discouraged. Anger was something only parents had the privilege of displaying.

Most children of toxic parents develop a high tolerance for mistreatment. You may have only a vague awareness that anything out of the ordinary happened to you as a child. Chances are, you don't even know how angry you really are.

You probably deal with your anger in one of several ways: you may bury your anger and become sick or depressed; you may divert your anger into suffering and martyrdom; you may deaden it with alcohol, drugs, food, or sex; or you may blow up at every opportunity, letting your anger turn you into a tense, frustrated, suspicious, belligerent person.

Unfortunately, most of us rely on these old, reliable, ineffective methods to deal with our anger. They do nothing to help free you from the control of your parents. It is far more effective to channel your anger in ways that help you define yourself and your limits.

Let me show you some effective new ways to manage your anger:

1. Give yourself permission to *be* angry without making any judgments about your feelings. Anger is an emotion just as joy and fear are. It is neither right nor wrong—it just *is*. It belongs to you; it is a part of what makes you human. Anger is also a signal, telling you something important. It may be telling you that your rights are being trampled, that you are being insulted or used, or that your needs are not being taken care of. Anger always means that something needs to change.
2. Externalize your anger. Pound pillows, yell at photographs of the people you're angry at, or have imaginary dialogues with them in your car or alone at home. You don't have to attack or verbally assault someone to express your anger—talk to people you trust about how angry you feel. Until you get your anger out in the open, you can't deal with it.
3. Increase your physical activity. Physicalizing your anger can help release a great deal of tension from your body. If you're not able to play tennis or run or ride a bike, clean out that overflowing closet or take a dance class. Physical activity also increases the production of endorphins—brain chemicals that enhance your sense of well-being. You'll find that acknowledging your anger will increase your energy and productivity levels. Nothing is more draining than repressed anger.
4. Don't use your anger to reinforce your negative self-image. You are not bad because you're angry. Guilt over feeling angry, especially at parents, is to be expected. Say out loud: "I feel angry. I have a right to feel angry. It's okay to feel guilty about feeling angry if that's what it takes to deal with that anger. I'm not wrong or bad to feel this way."
5. Use your anger as an energy source for self-definition. Your

> anger can help you learn a great deal about what you are and are not willing to accept in your relationship with your parents. It can help you define your limits and your boundaries. It can go a long way toward freeing you from old patterns of submission, compliance, and fear of your parents' disapproval. Your anger can help you refocus your energies back to yourself and away from the impossible battle of trying to change your parents. Turn "I'm angry because my father has never let me live my own life" into "I will no longer permit my father to control me or devalue me."

Use these techniques as guidelines to help you gain some mastery over your anger. You'll have plenty of time to express your anger directly to your parents once you've done this. This mastery will be important to the success of your eventual confrontation with your parents, as we'll see in chapter 12.

Everyone has a tough time with anger, and you won't get this mastery overnight. Women especially have been socialized not to show their anger. Women are allowed to cry, to mourn openly, to get depressed, and to show tenderness, but anger is considered unbecoming to women in our society. As a result, many women are attracted to partners who can act out their anger for them. In this way, they can discharge some of their repressed anger vicariously. Unfortunately, however, many of these men who get angry easily are also controlling and abusive.

It is essential to your well-being to learn to deal with anger effectively. When you first contact your anger, you may feel shaky and guilty much of the time. Be patient and hang in there. You won't stay angry forever. The only people who do are the ones who won't admit their anger or who use it to gain power by intimidating others.

Anger is a normal human reaction to mistreatment. Adult children of toxic parents obviously have more than their share of anger. Perhaps not so obvious is the fact that they also have more than their share of grief.

GRIEF AND MOURNING

"Whaddaya mean I have to grieve?" said Joe. "Who died?"

Grief is a normal and necessary reaction to loss. It doesn't have to be loss of life. Like Joe, you've probably experienced tremendous losses in your childhood:

- loss of good feelings about yourself
- loss of feelings of safety
- loss of trust
- loss of joy and spontaneity
- loss of nurturing, respectful parents
- loss of childhood
- loss of innocence
- loss of love

You need to identify your losses in order to experience your grief. You must work through these feelings to release their hold over you.

Without realizing it, Joe began to grieve when he contacted his anger. Grief and anger are tightly intertwined. It's almost impossible for one to exist without the other.

Up until now you may not have understood how extensive your emotional losses have been. Children of toxic parents experience these losses on an almost daily basis and often ignore or repress them. These losses take a terrible toll on one's self-worth, but because grief is so painful, most people will do almost anything to avoid it.

Stepping around grief may alleviate sad feelings for a while, but delayed grief comes back to get you sooner or later—sometimes when you least expect it. Many people don't grieve at the time of a loss because they are expected to be "strong," or they believe they have to take care of everyone else. But these people invariably fall apart, sometimes years later, often over some minor event. It isn't until they finally experience their delayed grief that they are able to get back on their emotional feet. Grief has a beginning, a middle, and an end. And we all have to go through those stages. If you try to avoid grief, it will always be with you, and it will inhibit your good feelings.

The Intensity of Grief

Carol—whose verbally abusive father kept telling her she smelled bad—had been making excellent progress in therapy. She had become much more assertive in both her personal and her professional life and was on her way to becoming an expert at nondefensive communication. But when she began to contact her grief, she was astonished at how deep and intense her feelings were:

> I feel like I'm in mourning. When I think about what a good, sweet kid I was and how horribly my dad mistreated me, and how my mother just let him do it, I still can't believe it. It makes me feel so sad, even though I know it wasn't my fault. Why did he have to make me suffer so much? I'm crying one minute and I'm outraged the next.

The grieving process entails shock, rage, disbelief, and, of course, sadness. There will be times when the sadness seems never-ending. You may feel as if you'll never stop crying. You may become preoccupied with your grief. You may even feel ashamed of it.

Most men are less ashamed of getting angry than they are of expressing grief. Unlike women, men have considerably more cultural support for showing aggression and anger than for showing sadness or pain. Many men pay a terrible price in their physical and emotional well-being for the dehumanizing expectations we have about how to be a "real man."

Joe, like many men I have worked with, was far more comfortable with his anger than with the sad little boy inside, because that little boy made him feel weak and vulnerable. As a battered child, Joe learned early to keep a tight lock on his emotions. To help him begin to grieve over what he had lost in his childhood, I asked Joe to do a "burial" exercise. This is an exercise I use often, particularly with adults who were abused as children. I keep a vase of dried flowers in my office, which I placed in front of Joe to symbolize a grave. I then asked him to repeat the following:

> I hereby lay to rest my fantasy of the good family. I hereby lay to rest my hopes and expectations about my parents. I hereby lay to rest my fantasy that there was something I could have done as a child to change them. I know that I will never have the kind of parents that I wanted, and I mourn that loss. But I accept it. May these fantasies rest in peace.

As Joe ended this eulogy, tears welled up in his eyes and he said:

> God, Susan, it hurts so damn much. It really hurts! Why do I have to go through this? I feel like I'm mired in self-pity. I'm revolted by it. Aren't I just feeling sorry for myself? A lot of people had it worse than I did.

I answered:

> It's about time you felt sorry for that little boy who was hurt so badly. Who else is going to? I want you to forget everything you've heard about self-pity. Grieving the loss of a happy childhood has nothing to do with feeling sorry for yourself. People who get stuck in self-pity wait around for someone else to fix their lives for them. They avoid personal responsibility. They lack the courage to do the work I'm asking of you. Grief is active, not passive. It gets you unstuck. It allows you to heal, to do something real about your problems.

If you're like most people—like Joe—you'll go to great lengths to avoid appearing to feel sorry for yourself. You might even cheat yourself of the right to grieve the losses of your childhood. Until you absolve your inner child through feeling and expressing your anger and grief, you're just going to continue to punish yourself.

You Can't Stop Your Life

Even though working through your grief is essential for the changes you want to make, you can't stop your life while you're doing it. You still have responsibilities to yourself and others and you still need to function. Anger and grief can throw any of us off balance, so it's vitally important for you to take especially good care of yourself during this time. Do everything possible to take part in activities that you find pleasurable and interesting. You don't need to think about this stuff twenty-four hours a day. Be as nice to yourself as you would be to a friend who was having a difficult time. Reach out for all the support you can get from people who care about you.

It helps to talk about your grief, though some people may not be able to handle listening. A lot of people have not dealt with their own grief from their childhood and your grief may threaten their defenses.

Make a list of ten things you can do each week to help you pull through your grief. Think of this as a "caring contract" that you make with yourself. Your contract should include relaxing activities that give you pleasure. These may be as simple as a long bubble bath or going to a movie; or you may want to get out more often with your softball team or make the time to read an exciting novel. Whatever is on your list, it's important to *do* these things, not just think about them.

Grief Does Come to an End

Even though it may be hard to believe while you're in the midst of this work, grief *does* come to an end. It takes time to resolve grief, but it's not an indefinite process. You'll need time to integrate and accept the reality of your losses. And you'll need time to refocus your energies from the pain of the past to the rebirth of the present and the promise of the future. But eventually, the sharp stabs will become twinges. You *will* feel better when you accept the fact that you were not responsible for the losses you grieve.

Taking Personal Responsibility

Putting the responsibility where it realistically belongs—squarely on your parents—does not give you license to excuse all your self-defeating behaviors by saying, "It was all their fault." Absolving the child that you were does not in any way absolve the adult you from assuming your responsibilities.

This next list will help you focus on some of those responsibilities as they apply to your relationship with your parents. Say out loud, "As an adult, in relationship to my parents, I am responsible for . . ." and then follow it with each item on the following list:

1. becoming a separate individual from my parents
2. looking honestly at my relationship with them
3. facing the truth about my childhood
4. having the courage to acknowledge the connections between events of my childhood and my adult life
5. gaining the courage to express my real feelings to them
6. confronting and diminishing the power and control that they have over my life, whether they are alive or dead
7. changing my own behavior when it is cruel, hurtful, critical, or manipulative
8. finding the appropriate resources to help me heal my inner child
9. reclaiming my adult power and confidence

It's important to recognize that the items on this list are goals to strive toward, not things to expect yourself to do overnight. As you work toward these goals, you will have setbacks. You may fall back on old behaviors and patterns of thinking, and you may even decide to pack it all in. Don't be discouraged. In fact, you should expect to be thrown off course. This is process, not perfection. Some of these goals may be easier than others, but they are all attainable; you *can* free the child within you from perpetual punishment.

13 | Confrontation: The Road to Independence

All the work you've done in the last three chapters—the exercises, the checklists, and gaining understanding of who is really responsible—has been preparing you for confrontation. Confrontation means facing your parents thoughtfully and courageously about your painful past and your difficult present. It is the most frightening and at the same time the most empowering act that you will ever perform.

The process is simple, though not easy. When you are ready, you calmly but firmly tell your parents about the negative events you remember from your childhood. You tell them how those events affected your life and how they affect your relationship with your parents now. You clearly define the aspects of that relationship that are painful and harmful to you now. Then you lay out new ground rules.

The purpose of confrontation with your parents **is not:**

to retaliate
to punish them
to put them down
to dump your anger on them
to get something positive back from them

The purpose of confrontation with your parents **is:**

to face up to them
to overcome once and for all your fear of facing up to them
to tell your parents the truth
to determine the type of relationship you can have with them from now on

"It Won't Do Any Good"

Many people—including some prominent therapists—do not believe in confrontation. Their rationales are quite familiar: "Don't look backward, look forward"; "It will only cause more stress and anger"; or, "It doesn't heal wounds, it just reopens them." These critics simply don't understand.

It is absolutely true that confrontation may not get your parents to give you the acknowledgment, apology, recognition, or acceptance of responsibility that you seek. It is a rare toxic parent who will respond to a confrontation by saying, "It's all true, I was terrible to you," or, "Please forgive me," or, "What can I do to make it up to you now?"

In fact, just the opposite often occurs: parents deny, claim to have forgotten, project the blame back on their child, and get very angry.

If you have already attempted to confront your parents but were bitterly disappointed by the outcome, you probably gauged the success of your confrontation by whether you got a positive response from your parents. By using their response as an indicator, you set yourself up for failure. You should *expect* them to react negatively. Remember, you are doing this for yourself, not for them. You should consider your confrontation successful simply because you had the courage to do it.

Why Should I Confront My Parents?

I push people very hard to confront toxic parents. I do this for one simple reason: confrontation works. Through the years I've seen confrontations make dramatic, positive changes in the lives of thousands of people. This doesn't mean I don't appreciate how frightened people feel when they even think about confronting their parents. The emotional stakes are high. But the mere fact that you're doing it, that you're facing what are probably some of your deepest fears, is enough to begin to change the balance of power between you and your parents.

We're all afraid to face the truth about our parents. We're all afraid to acknowledge that we didn't get what we needed from them and that we're not going to get it now. But the alternative to confrontation is to live with these fears. If you avoid taking positive action on your own behalf, you're reinforcing your feelings of helplessness and inadequacy, you're undermining your self-respect.

There's one more vitally important reason for confrontation:

What you don't hand back, you pass on.

If you don't deal with your fear, your guilt, and your anger at your parents, you're going to take it out on your partner or your children.

When Should I Confront My Parents?

I urge my clients to carefully consider the timing of the confrontation. You don't want to shoot from the hip, but neither do you want to postpone the confrontation indefinitely.

When people decide to confront, they usually go through three stages:

1. I could never do that.
2. Maybe I'll do it someday, but not now.
3. When can I do it?

When I first urge clients to confront their parents, they invariably insist that it's not right for them. I can usually count on what I call the "anything but that" syndrome. Clients will agree to make any number of other changes as long as they don't have to confront their parents—anything but that!

I told Glenn—who had problems with timidity and who regretted having taken his alcoholic father into business with him—that he needed to confront his father. He needed either to set limits on his father's behavior or to get him out of the business altogether. He responded with a classic "anything but that":

> I am not going to confront my father. I know that means I'm being a wimp, but I do *not* want to cause my parents any more pain. I'm sure there are plenty of things I can do instead of confronting my father. I can find a job for him with less pressure where he won't be in front of my customers as much. I can stop letting him get to me. I can start exercising more to let off steam. I can . . .

I interrupted Glenn: " 'Anything but that,' right? Anything but the one action that can make a significant difference in your life."

I told Glenn that much of his irritability and timidity were a direct result of his repressed rage toward his father and his unwillingness to take personal responsibility for confronting his difficulties. I acknowledged that most people respond with "anything but that" early in therapy and assured him that I did not find it discouraging. He simply wasn't ready. But once we had some time to plan the confrontation and to practice it, I was sure he'd feel more confident.

Glenn had his doubts, but over time he saw several other group members make the decision to confront. All reported back with success stories. Glenn acknowledged that confrontation had worked for these people, but he was quick to add that his situation was different. Without realizing it, Glenn had moved closer to the second stage of his confrontation decision.

In the course of his therapy Glenn worked very hard to learn both nondefensive responses and position statements. He had begun to use both these techniques in business situations and with some of his friends. He was feeling good about it. But the constant stress of the day-to-day relationship with his father and the enormous weight of the unfinished business from his childhood were bogging him down.

About six weeks into group, Glenn told me that he had started thinking about confrontation. For the first time, he admitted that it was a possibility . . . for the future. He had arrived at stage 2. A few weeks later, he asked me when I thought he should do it. Stage 3.

Glenn was hoping I could conjure up some magic itinerary to tell him when his anxiety level would drop enough for him to go through with his confrontation. The truth is, quite often your anxiety level drops only *after* the confrontation. There's no way to determine a perfect time, you just have to be prepared.

There are four basic requirements you must meet before confronting your parents:

1. You must feel strong enough to handle your parents' rejection, denial, blame, anger, or any other negative consequences of confrontation.
2. You must have a sufficient support system to help you through the anticipation, the confrontation itself, and the aftermath.
3. You must have written a letter or rehearsed what you want to say, and you must have practiced nondefensive responses.
4. You must no longer feel responsible for the bad things that happened to you as a child.

This last point is especially important. If you are still carrying the responsibility of the traumas of your childhood, it is too soon to confront. You cannot confront your parents with a responsibility you are not convinced they deserve.

Once you are feeling relatively confident, and you've fulfilled the four requirements, there's no time like the present. Don't wait.

The anticipation of confrontation is always worse than confrontation itself.

I told Glenn that it was important for him to set a date for his confrontation, hopefully in this century. He needed to give himself a tangible goal to work toward. That work, I told him, would include extensive rehearsals to prepare himself for the most important performance of his life.

How Do I Confront My Parents?

Confrontation can be done either face-to-face or by letter. You will notice that I do not include the telephone as an option. While it may seem safe, confrontation by phone is almost always ineffective. It's too easy for your parents to hang up. In addition, the telephone is "artificial"; it makes true emotional expression very difficult. If your parents are in another city and it is not practical for them to come to you or for you to go to them, write to them.

Letter Writing

I am a big advocate of writing as a therapeutic technique. A letter provides a wonderful opportunity to organize what you want to say and to rework it until you're satisfied. It gives the recipient a chance to read it over more than once and to reflect on the contents. A letter is also safer if you're dealing with a potentially violent parent. Confrontation is important, but it's never worth risking physical assault.

Always write a separate letter to each parent. Even if some of the issues are the same, your relationship with and your feelings for each parent are different. Write your first letter to the parent you think is the more toxic or abusive. Those feelings will be closer to the surface, more easily tapped. Once you have opened the flood-gates by writing the first letter—assuming both your parents are alive—your feelings toward the other parent will flow more easily. In your second letter, you can confront the more benign of your parents with his or her passivity and lack of protection.

A confrontation by letter works exactly like one done in person. Both begin with the words: "I am going to say some things to you I have never said before" and both should cover four major points:

1. This is what you did to me.
2. This is how I felt about it at the time.
3. This is how it affected my life.
4. This is what I want from you now.

I have found that these four points provide a solid, focused base for all confrontations. This structure generally covers everything you need to say and will help prevent your confrontation from becoming scattered and ineffective.

Carol—whose father continually taunted her about smelling bad—decided she felt ready to confront her parents at a time when a large decorating job prevented her from going East to do it face-to-face. I assured her she could have an effective confrontation by letter. I suggested that she write the letter at home, during a quiet time, with the phone off the hook to prevent interruption.

Writing confrontation letters is always an intense emotional experience. Before sending her letter, I suggested that Carol put it aside for several days, then reread it when she was calmer. As most people do, she wound up rewriting quite a bit when she came back to her letter. You may find yourself writing several drafts before you're satisfied. Remember, you are not in an essay contest. The letter doesn't have to be a literary masterpiece—it needs only to express the truth of your feelings and experiences.

Here is a portion of the letter that Carol read to me the following week:

Dear Dad,

I'm going to say some things to you that I've never said before. First of all, I want to tell you why I haven't spent much time with you and Mother over the last several months. This may surprise and disturb you, but I haven't wanted to see you because I'm afraid of you. I'm afraid of feeling helpless and being verbally attacked by you. And I'm afraid of relying on you and then being emotionally abandoned by you again. Let me explain.

[This is what you did to me.]

When I was a very little girl, I remember this father who loved, adored, and cared for me. But, as I grew older, all of that changed. When I was about eleven, you became very cruel to me. You constantly told me I smelled bad. You blamed me for everything that went wrong. You blamed me when I lost the scholarship. You blamed me when Bob [her brother] fell and hurt himself. You blamed me when my leg got broken. You blamed me when Mom left you for a while. When Mom left, I was left without any emotional support. You told me jokes that were too dirty, talked about how sexy I looked in a sweater, and either treated me like a date or told me I looked like a whore.

I had no parenting after twelve. I am sure you were having a terrible time yourself during those years, but you hurt me very much. You may not have meant to hurt me, but that didn't make it hurt any less.

When I was fifteen, a man tried to rape me and you blamed me. I really believed it was my fault because you said so. When I was eight months pregnant with my son, my husband beat me up, and you told me I must have done something terrible to make him so angry. You constantly told me all the terrible things that Mother did. You told me that she never loved me, that I was dirty inside, and that I didn't have a brain in my head.

[How I felt about it at the time.]

I felt scared, humiliated, and confused. I wondered why you stopped loving me. I yearned to be Daddy's little girl again and wondered what I had done to lose you. I blamed myself for everything. I hated myself. I felt unlovable and disgusting.

[How it affected my life.]

I was terribly damaged as a person. Many men have been quite brutal to me and I always thought it was my fault. When Hank beat me up, I wrote him a letter of apology. I've had a deplorable lack of belief in myself, in my ability, and in my worthiness.

[This is what I want from you.]

I want you to apologize for being such a cruel, lousy father. I want you to acknowledge that the harm you did to me caused me great hurt and pain. I want you to stop the verbal attacks. The last one happened when I saw you at Bob's house and I asked for advice about my business. You yelled at me for no reason. I hated it. I submitted then, but I won't anymore. I want you to know that I won't tolerate that in the future. I would like you to acknowledge that good fathers don't leer at their daughters, that good fathers don't insult and degrade their daughters, that good fathers protect their daughters.

I'm sorry you and I didn't have the relationship we could have. I missed a lot by not being able to give my love to a father I so wanted to love. I will continue to send you cards and gifts because that makes me feel good. However, if I am going to see you, you're going to have to accept my ground rules.

I don't know you very well. I don't know what your pains were or what your fears were. I'm grateful that you were a hard worker, that you were a good provider, and that you took me on nice vacations. I remember you teaching me about trees and birds, people and politics, sports and geography, camping and skating. I remember that you laughed a lot. Also, you might like to know that I am doing much better in my life now. I don't let men beat up on me anymore. I have wonderful and supportive friends, a good profession, and a son I adore.

Please write me and acknowledge my letter. We can't change the past, but we can begin again.

—Carol

Face-to-Face

Many of my clients prefer the safety of writing letters, but many others need immediate feedback to feel that their confrontation was a success. For these clients, only a face-to-face confrontation will do.

The first step in planning a face-to-face, assuming you have already done the emotional work to prepare yourself, is to choose a place to do it. If you are in therapy, you might want to have the confrontation in your therapist's office. Your therapist can orchestrate the confrontation, make sure you get heard, help you if you get stuck, and, most important, be supportive and protective. I realize this stacks the deck against your parents, but better against them than against you, especially at such a crucial point in your work.

If you have the confrontation in your therapist's office, be sure to meet your parents *there*. No one can predict what will happen in the session. It is important for you to have your own means of getting home. Even if the confrontation ends on a positive note, you may still feel like being alone afterward, to deal with your feelings and thoughts in private.

You may prefer to do your confrontation on your own. Perhaps you don't have a therapist—or, if you do, you may feel the need to show your parents that you can assert your independence without help. Many parents simply refuse to go to a therapist's office. For whatever reason, if you decide to do it on your own, you have to decide whether to confront your parents in their home or in yours. A public place, such as a restaurant or a bar, is much too inhibiting. You need total privacy.

If you have a choice, I advise you to set the confrontation in your own home. You will feel much stronger on your own turf. If you travel to another city for your confrontation, try to get your parents to come to your hotel room.

You *can* have an effective confrontation on your parents' turf if necessary. But you will have to work hard to avoid falling victim to childhood fears, guilts, and feelings of helplessness. You should be especially wary of these childhood feelings if your parents still live in the house you grew up in.

I have no hard and fast rule about whether to confront your parents together or separately, though my preference is to do it together. Toxic parents set up family systems that rely on a great deal of secrecy, collusion, and denial to keep the family in balance. Talking to both parents at once cuts through a great deal of that.

On the other hand, if your parents have greatly differing dispositions, perspectives, or defenses, you may be better able to communicate by taking them on one at a time.

Some people are concerned about rehearsing too much and losing their spontaneity before the confrontation. Don't worry. You'll have enough anxiety to ensure plenty of deviations from what you've prepared. No matter how much you've rehearsed, the words won't come easily. In fact, it's essential that you know ahead of time that you will be very, very nervous. Your heart will pound, your stomach may knot, you may sweat, you may have a hard time catching your breath, and you may get tongue-tied and forget your lines.

Some people's minds just go blank under extreme pressure. If you're worried about this happening, you can avoid the added anxiety by writing a letter to your parents and then reading it aloud to them in your confrontation. This is an excellent way to defeat opening-night jitters and assure that you'll get your message across.

Preparing for Opening Night

No matter where you decide to have your confrontation, and no matter whether you confront your parents separately or together, you must carefully prepare what you want to say. Rehearse your lines out loud, either alone or with someone, until you know them cold. A face-to-face confrontation is like opening night on Broadway: would you go on stage without learning your lines and understanding your motivation? Before making your confrontation, you need both adequate rehearsal and a clear sense of what you wish to accomplish.

You'll want to start your confrontation by setting the rules. I suggest something like this:

> I'm going to say some things to you that I've never said before, and I want you to agree to hear me out until I'm done. This is very important to me, so please don't contradict me or interrupt me. After I've said what I need to say, you'll have all the time you want to say what you need to say. Are you willing to do that?

It is essential that your parents agree to these terms at the outset. Most parents will. If they are not willing to do even this much, it is probably better to reschedule the confrontation. It is important for you to say what you have rehearsed without getting sidetracked, interrupted, or otherwise diverted from your goals. If they refuse to hear you out, you may have to confront them by letter instead.

What to Expect

Once you get going, most toxic parents will counterattack. After all, if they had the capacity to listen, to hear, to be reasonable, to respect your feelings, and to promote your independence, they wouldn't be toxic parents. They will probably perceive your words as treacherous personal assaults. They will tend to fall back on the same tactics and defenses that they've always used, only more so.

Inadequate or deficient parents may become even more pathetic and overwhelmed. Alcoholics may deny their alcoholism more vehemently, or if they are in recovery they may use that fact to try to undercut your right to confront them. Controllers may escalate their guilt-peddling and self-righteousness. Abusive parents may become enraged and will almost certainly try to blame you for your own abuse. All of these behaviors are in the service of regaining family balance and returning you to a submissive status quo. It is a good idea to expect the worst—anything better is a bonus.

Remember, the important thing here is not their reaction but your response. If you can stand fast in the face of your parents' fury, accusations, threats, and guilt-peddling, you will experience your finest hour.

To help yourself prepare, envision the worst possible scenario. Visualize your parents' faces, furious, pitiful, tearful, whatever. Hear their angry words, their denials, their accusations. Desensitize yourself by saying out loud whatever you think your parents will say, then rehearse calm, nondefensive responses. Ask a partner or friend to play the role of one or both parents. Tell him or her to pull out all the stops and say the worst things imaginable to you. Have your substitute parent scream, yell, call you names, threaten to cut you out of the family, and accuse you of being horrible and selfish. Practice answering with such lines as:

- I'm sure you see it that way.
- Name calling and screaming won't get us anywhere.
- I'm not willing to accept your labels.
- This is a good example of why we need this meeting.
- It's not okay for you to talk to me that way.
- You agreed to hear me out.
- Let's do this some other time, when you're calmer.

Here are some typical parental reactions to confrontation, along with some key responses that you may want to study:

"It never happened." Parents who have used denial to avoid their own feelings of inadequacy or anxiety will undoubtedly use it during confrontation to promote their version of reality. They'll insist that your allegations never happened, or that you're exaggerating, or that your father could never have done such a thing. They won't remember, or they'll accuse you of lying. This reaction is especially common for alcoholics, whose denials may be reinforced by drink-induced memory lapses.

Your response: "Just because you don't remember doesn't mean it didn't happen."

"It was your fault." Toxic parents are almost never willing to accept responsibility for their destructive behavior. Instead, they'll blame you. They'll say that you were bad or that you were difficult. They'll claim they did the best they could but you always created problems for them. They'll say that you drove them crazy. They'll offer as proof the fact that everybody in the family knew what a problem you were. They'll offer up a laundry list of your alleged offenses against them.

A variation on this theme is to blame the confrontation on current difficulties in your life. "Why are you attacking us, when your real problem is that you can't hold a job, control your child, keep a husband, etc." This may even come disguised as sympathy for the turmoil you are experiencing. Anything to deflect the focus from their behavior.

Your response: "You can keep trying to make this my fault, but I'm not going to accept the responsibility for what you did to me when I was a child."

"I said I was sorry." Parents may promise to change, to become more loving, to be more supportive, but that's often just a carrot on a stick. Once the dust settles, the weight of old habits takes over and

they pull the stick back, reverting to their toxic behavior. Some parents may acknowledge a few of the things you say but be unwilling to do anything about it. The line I hear most often is, "I've said I'm sorry, what more do you want?"

Your response: "I appreciate your apology, but that's just a beginning. If you're truly sorry, you'll be available to me when I need you and you'll work through this with me to make a better relationship."

"We did the best we could." Those parents who either were inadequate or were silent partners to abuse will frequently deal with confrontation in the same passive, ineffectual ways as they've traditionally used to deal with problems. These parents will remind you of how tough they had it while you were growing up and how hard they struggled. They'll say such things as, "You'll never understand what I was going through," "You don't know how many times I tried to get him/her to stop," or, "I did the best I could." This particular style of response may stir up a lot of sympathy and compassion for your parents. This is understandable, but it makes it difficult for you to remain focused on what you need to say in your confrontation. The temptation is for you once again to put their needs ahead of your own. It's important that you acknowledge their difficulties without invalidating yours.

Your response: "I understand that you had a hard time, and I'm sure you didn't hurt me on purpose, but I need *you* to understand that the way you dealt with your problems really *did* hurt me."

"Look what we did for you." Many parents will attempt to counter your assertions by recalling the wonderful times you had as a child and the loving moments you and they shared. By focusing on the good things, they can avoid looking at the darker side of their behavior. Parents will typically remind you of gifts they gave you, places they took you, sacrifices they made for you, and thoughtful things they did. They'll say things like, "This is the thanks we get," or, "Nothing was ever enough for you."

Your response: "I appreciate those things very much, but they didn't make up for the beatings [constant criticism, violence, insults, alcoholism, etc.]."

"How can you do this to me?" Some parents act like martyrs. They'll collapse into tears, wring their hands, and express shock and disbelief at your "cruelty." They will act as if your confrontation has victimized *them*. They'll accuse you of hurting them or disappointing them. They'll complain that they don't need this, they have enough problems. They'll tell you they're not strong enough or healthy enough to take this, that the heartache will kill them. Some of their sadness will, of course, be genuine. It *is* sad for parents to face their own shortcomings, to realize they have caused their children significant pain. But their sadness can also be manipulative and controlling. It is their way of using guilt to try to make you back down.

Your response: "I'm sorry you're upset. I'm sorry you're hurt. But I'm not willing to give up on this. I've been hurting for a long time, too."

SOMETIMES IT'S REALLY IMPOSSIBLE

The typical reactions and suggested responses given above can help you avoid some emotional quicksand during confrontation. However, there are some people with whom you can't communicate no matter how hard you try.

Some parents escalate the conflict so intensely during confrontation that communication becomes impossible. No matter how reasonable, how kind, how clear, how articulate you may be, their behavior may require you to cut short the confrontation. They will twist your words and your motives, will lie, will constantly interrupt when they agreed not to, will accuse, scream, break furniture, throw dishes, and make you feel at best crazy and at worst homicidal. So, just as it is important to push past your fears and make every effort to say what you need to say to your parents, it is also important to know when that is impossible. If you have to cut short your confrontation because of their behavior, it is *their* failure, not yours.

A Quiet Confrontation

Not many confrontations get out of control, even if they get stormy. In fact, many are surprisingly calm.

Melanie—who kept trying to rescue inadequate men and who, as a child, wrote to Dear Abby because she was forced to comfort her depressed father during his frequent crying jags—opted to bring her mother, Ginny, into my office for her confrontation (her father had since died). She began with the words we had rehearsed together, and her mother agreed to hear her out.

Melanie: Mom, I need to talk to you about some things in my childhood that still hurt me. I realize how much I blamed myself when I was a little girl . . .

Ginny (interrupting): If you still feel that way, honey, then your therapy must not be doing much good.

Melanie: You agreed to hear me out and not to interrupt. We're not talking about therapy now, we're talking about my childhood. Do you remember when Daddy would get so upset with me for fighting with Neal [her brother]? Daddy would burst into tears and tell me how good Neal was to me and how awful I was to him? Do you remember all the times you would send me to Daddy's room when he was crying and tell me that I was supposed to cheer him up? Do you have any idea how much guilt you put on me to be Daddy's caretaker? I had to take care of him when I should have been being a little girl. Why didn't you take care of Daddy? Why didn't Daddy take care of himself? Why did I have to do it? You were never there even when you were there. I spent more time with the housekeepers than I spent with you. You remember when I wrote that letter to Dear Abby? You just ignored that too.

Ginny (quietly): I don't remember any of this.

Melanie: Mom, maybe you choose not to remember, but if you want to be helpful you've got to hear me out. Nobody's attacking you, I'm just trying to tell you how I feel. Okay, this is how I felt about all this stuff while it was going on. I felt totally alone, I felt like an awful person, I felt really guilty and very overwhelmed because I was trying to fix things I couldn't fix. That's how I felt. Now let me tell you how it affected my life. Up until I started working on this stuff I felt very empty. I feel better now, but I'm still scared of sensitive men. So I keep hooking up with these cold, unresponsive guys. I have a horrible time trying to figure out who I am, what I want, or what I need. I'm just beginning to figure it out. The hardest part is for me to like myself. Every time I try, I hear Daddy telling me what an awful kid I was.

Ginny (beginning to cry): I honestly don't remember those things, but I'm sure if you say that happened they must have. I guess I was so wrapped up in my own unhappiness . . .

Melanie: Oh, no. Now I'm feeling guilty because I've hurt your feelings.

Susan: Melanie, why don't you tell your mother what you want from her now?

Melanie: I want an adult-to-adult relationship. I want to be real with you. I want to be able to tell you the truth. I want you to listen to me when I talk about my experiences from the past. I want you to be willing to remember and to think and feel about what really happened. I want you to take responsibility for the fact that you didn't take care of me and you didn't protect me from Daddy's moods. I want us to start telling each other the truth.

Ginny made some genuine efforts to hear her daughter out and to validate her. She also showed some capacity for sane, rational communication. Ultimately, she agreed to try her best to comply with Melanie's requests, though it was clear that she found them somewhat overwhelming.

An Explosive Confrontation

Joe's parents were not so understanding. Joe was the graduate student in psychology whose father had beaten him. After much persuasion Joe finally got his alcoholic father and his co-dependent mother to come into my office. Joe had been eager for this confrontation for some time. It turned out to be far more volatile than Melanie's.

Joe's father, Alan, strode into my office fully expecting to take charge. He was a large, sandy-haired man who looked every one of his 60-plus years; decades of anger and alcoholism had taken a significant toll on his appearance. Joe's mother, Joanne, seemed like a gray lady—gray hair, gray complexion, gray dress, gray personality. Her eyes had that haunted look that I've seen so often in battered wives. She came in behind her husband, sat down, folded her hands, and stared at the floor.

A great deal of our first half hour was spent trying to establish some kind of atmosphere in which Joe could say what he needed to say. His father constantly interrupted, yelled, swore—anything to intimidate his son into silence. When I'd step in to protect Joe, Alan would turn and bad-mouth both me and my profession. Joe's mother barely spoke at all, and when she did it was to plead with her husband to calm down. What I saw was a microcosm of forty years of misery. Joe did surprisingly well under almost impossible circumstances. He managed with great effort to stay calm, although I could see he was seething with rage. Alan's final outburst occurred when Joe brought up his father's alcoholism.

Alan: Okay, you little shithead, that's it. Just who the fuck do you think you are? The trouble with you is that I was too easy on you. I should have made you earn everything you got. How dare you call me a drunk in front of a total stranger. You son of a bitch, you won't be happy until you tear this family apart, will you? Well I'm not going to sit here and let some miserable, ungrateful little bastard and his goddamn shrink tell me what to do.

At this point Alan stood up and headed out. He turned around at the door and asked Joanne if she was coming. Joanne pleaded with him to let her stay for the rest of the session. Alan told her that he'd be downstairs in the coffeeshop and if she wasn't there in fifteen minutes she could figure out her own way to get home. Then he stalked out.

JOANNE: I'm so sorry. I'm so ashamed. He's really not like this. It's just that he's a very proud man and can't stand to lose face. He really has a lot of wonderful qualities. . . .

JOE: Mom, stop! For God's sake stop! That's exactly what you've been doing my whole life. You lied for him, you covered up for him, you let him beat both of us, and you never did anything about it. I used to have fantasies that I was going to rescue you from all of that. Did it ever occur to you to rescue me? Do you have any idea what it felt like being a little kid in that house? Do you have any idea what kind of terror I lived with every day? Why didn't you do anything about it? Why don't you do something about it now?

JOANNE: You've got your own life. Why can't you let us be?

Joe's confrontation was explosive and frustrating, but it was actually a great success. He finally accepted the fact that his parents were beset by their own demons and overwhelmingly locked into their toxic behavior patterns. He was finally able to renounce his hopeless hope that they would change.

What to Expect After Confrontation

YOUR REACTION

Immediately after your confrontation, you may experience a sudden rush of euphoria from your newfound courage and strength. You may be flooded with relief at having finally put the confrontation behind you, even if it didn't go exactly the way you had hoped. You may feel a lot lighter for having said many of the things you were holding in for so long. But you may also feel severely off balance or disappointed. You will certainly continue to feel anxious about what's going to happen next.

Regardless of your initial reaction, it takes some time to feel the full and lasting benefits of confrontation. You'll need several weeks or even months to begin to experience the real empowerment that confrontation can give you. And you *will* experience it. Ultimately, you'll feel neither the extremes of euphoria nor disappointment. Instead, you'll enjoy a steadily increasing sense of well-being and confidence.

YOUR PARENTS' REACTIONS

The nature of your confrontation will not necessarily indicate what the ultimate outcome will be. It takes time for all parties to process the experience and to deal with it in their own ways.

For example, a confrontation that appears to end positively can turn around once your parents have time to think about it. They may experience delayed reactions. They may have been relatively calm during the confrontation, only to start in with angry recriminations later on, accusing you of creating destructive upheaval in the family.

On the other hand, I've seen confrontations that ended in anger and turmoil eventually lead to positive changes in clients' interactions with their parents. Once the initial uproar settles down, the fact that you've pried the lid off the past may result in more open, honest communication between you and your parents.

If a parent does react angrily after the confrontation, you may feel a great temptation to counterattack. Avoid inflammatory statements like, "That's just like you," or, "I can never trust anything you say." It's very important that you stick to your nondefensive guns, or you'll hand your newly won power right back to your parents. Instead, say things like the following:

- I'm willing to talk about your anger, but I'm not going to let you yell at me or insult me.
- I'll come back and talk about this when you're calmer.

If your parents express their anger by giving you the silent treatment, try something like this:

- I'm ready to talk to you whenever you're ready to stop trying to punish me with your silence.
- I've risked telling you what's on my mind. Why aren't you willing to risk the same thing?

One thing is absolutely certain: nothing will ever be the same. It's important that you pay attention to the ripple effects of your confrontation in the weeks, months, and even years afterward. You must remain clear-headed and clear-eyed as you assess your changing relationship with your parents and with other members of your family.

Your job is to hold on to *your* reality and not get pushed back into your old reactive and defensive patterns, regardless of what your parents do.

The Impact on Your Parents' Relationship with Each Other

In addition to dramatic changes in your relationship with your parents, you must expect changes in their relationship with each other.

If your confrontation involves telling the truth about a family secret that one parent has been keeping from the other, such as incest, the impact on their relationship will be profound. One parent may ally with you against the other. Their relationship may even fall apart. If your confrontation involves speaking the unspoken that everyone knew but never faced, such as alcoholism, the impact on your parents' relationship may not be as extreme, but it can still be powerful. Their relationship may become extremely shaky.

You will be tempted to blame yourself for problems your parents develop in their relationship. You will wonder if it wouldn't have been better to have left things alone.

When Carla—who gave up her trip to Mexico to visit her needy, alcoholic mother—confronted her mother's drinking and her father's co-dependency, her parents' marriage suffered a harsh blow. When her mother went into recovery, her father fell apart. His self-worth had depended largely on his playing the powerful adequate parent. With his wife no longer leaning on him, his role in the family lost its meaning. Their marriage had been built on a certain pattern of interrelating that no longer applied. They didn't know how to communicate, they had no balance, and they'd lost their common ground. Carla had mixed feelings about this.

Carla: Look what I started. I upset the whole family.

Susan: Wait a minute. You didn't start anything. *They* started it.

Carla: But if they get a divorce, I'm going to feel terrible.

Susan: There's no reason for you to feel guilty. They're reevaluating their relationship because they've got new information. You didn't invent that information, you just turned the light on.

Carla: Well, maybe that wasn't such a good idea. They had an okay marriage before.

Susan: No, they didn't.

Carla: Well, it looked okay.

Susan: No, it didn't.

Carla (after a long pause): I guess what feels so scary is that

> I've finally decided I'm not willing to sacrifice myself for them anymore. I'm going to let them be responsible for themselves for a change. And if that upsets everybody then I'll just have to deal with their unhappiness.

Carla's parents did not divorce, but neither did their marriage ever regain peace. However, though they continued their struggle with each other, it was a struggle that no longer contaminated Carla's life. By telling the truth and by not getting reenmeshed when her parents started acting out their long-smoldering conflicts with each other, she achieved a freedom for herself that she had always believed impossible.

Your Siblings' Reactions

While this book focuses primarily on your relationship with your parents, confrontation doesn't occur in a vacuum. You are part of a family system, and everyone else in that system will be affected. Just as your relationship with your parents will never be the same after confrontation, your relationship with your siblings will change as well.

Some siblings have had experiences similar to yours and will validate your memories. Others have had similar experiences but because of their own enmeshment with their parents will deny or discount even the most horrendous abuse both of you and of them. Still others may have had different experiences and will have no idea what you're talking about.

Some siblings will feel extremely threatened by your confrontation and may become enraged at you for upsetting the precarious balance of the family. This is the way Carol's brother reacted.

After Carol's father received his letter, he called and gave her some unexpected support. He told her that he didn't remember the things she had written about in her letter as she remembered them, but he apologized for any pain he had caused her. Carol was deeply touched and excited about the possibility of a new relationship with her father. Within a few weeks, however, she was devastated by a second conversation with him, in which he not only denied the experiences she had written about but denied having apologized as well. Then, to add insult to injury, Carol's younger brother called and verbally attacked her for daring to "spread disgusting lies" about their father. He told her she had a "sick mind" for accusing their father of having been abusive with her.

If your siblings react negatively to your confrontation, they may put a lot of energy into letting you know how much you've upset the family. You may receive many letters, phone calls, or visits from them. They may become your parents' emissaries, delivering messages, pleas, threats, and ultimatums. They may call you names and do all they can to convince you that you're either wrong, crazy, or both. Once again, it is essential that you use nondefensive responses and stand by your right to tell the truth.

Here are some examples of things you might say to your siblings:

- I'm willing to talk to you about this, but I won't let you insult me.
- I can understand your wanting to protect them, but what I'm saying is true.
- I'm not doing this to upset anyone, but this is something I have to do for myself.
- My relationship with you is very important to me, but I won't bury my own needs to maintain it.
- Just because it didn't happen to you doesn't mean it didn't happen to me.

Kate—whose banker father battered both her and her sister, Judy, often at the same time—was convinced that her sister would despise her for bringing up their painful past. However, Kate chose to take that risk.

> I've always felt very protective of Judy. A lot of times she got it worse than I did. The night I sent my letter to my parents, I

> called her because I wanted her to know what I was doing. She said she'd be right over, and we needed to talk. I was sure she was going to be furious. I was an absolute basket case. When I opened the door I could see she'd been crying. We threw our arms around each other and just held each other for a long time. We talked and we cried and we hugged and we laughed and we cried some more. We went over all of it. Judy remembered some things I'd totally forgotten and she was really glad to be talking about it. She told me if it weren't for me she might have kept all this inside for God knows how long. She felt so much closer to me. She didn't feel so alone with all of this garbage. She really admired my guts, and she wanted me to know she was with me all the way. When Judy said that, I just melted.

By telling the truth, both Kate and Judy were able to enrich their relationship and give each other strong support. Kate's courageous actions also inspired her sister to get some counseling to deal with the pain of her own abusive childhood.

Other Family Reactions

Confrontation affects everyone to whom you are emotionally connected, especially your partner and children, who are secondary victims of your toxic parents. After confrontation, you're going to need all the love and support you can get. Don't be afraid to ask for it. Don't be afraid to tell them that this is a very difficult time for you. But remember, they won't be experiencing the same intense emotions, and they may not fully understand why you had to do what you did. Because this may also be a difficult time for them, if they are not as supportive as you'd like, it's important that you try to show some understanding for their feelings.

Your parents may attempt to involve other family members as allies in their continuing campaign to absolve themselves and make you the villain. This may include relatives to whom you are very close, such as a grandparent or a favorite aunt. Some of these relatives may deal with the family uproar by becoming protective of your parents. Others may side with you. As with your parents and your siblings, it is important to deal with each family member on his or her own terms and remind each one that you are taking positive steps for your own well-being and that they should not feel compelled to take sides.

You may even hear from such unexpected sources as your mother's best friend or your minister. Remember, you don't owe detailed explanations to nonfamily go-betweens. If you choose not to give them, you might say something like the following:

- I appreciate your concern, but this is between my parents and me.
- I understand that you'd like to help, but I don't want to discuss this with you.
- You're making a judgment about something you don't have full information about. When things calm down, perhaps I can talk to you about it.

Sometimes a relative or close family friend simply can't understand why you had to confront your parents, and your relationship with that person may suffer as a result. This is never easy; it may be one of the more painful prices you must pay for emotional health.

The Most Dangerous Time

Far and away the most dangerous reaction you should be prepared for after confrontation is that your parents may make a last-ditch attempt to undo what you've done. They may pull out all the stops to punish you. They may harangue you about your treachery or, alternatively, stop speaking to you. They may threaten to cut you out of the family or out of their will. You have, after all, broken the family rules of silence and denial. You have destroyed the family myth. You have defined yourself as separate, striking a blow against hopeless enmeshment in the family craziness.

In essence, you have dropped an emotional atom bomb; you can expect repercussions. The angrier your parents become, the more you will be tempted to renounce your new strength and seek "peace at any price." You'll wonder whether what you've gained is really worth the uproar. All of your doubts, second thoughts, and even the yearnings to return to the status quo are common. Toxic parents will do almost anything to regain the familiar and comfortable family balance. They can be incredibly seductive when they sing their siren songs of guilt, pity, or blame.

This is when your emotional support system becomes especially important. Just as the Greek hero Ulysses had his crew lash him to the mast so that he could hear the Sirens sing without succumbing to their irresistible but fatal attraction, your friend, therapist, partner, or some combination thereof can lash you to a protective emotional mast of your own. He or she can give you the caring and validation you need to retain your faith in yourself and in the important choice you have made.

In my experience, toxic parents rarely follow through on their threats to excommunicate their children from the family. They are much too enmeshed and tend to resist drastic changes. However, there are no guarantees. I have seen parents who have cut their children out of their lives, who have made good on threats to disinherit them or stop whatever financial help they were providing. You must be emotionally and psychologically prepared for this or any other reaction.

It is not easy to hold your ground while your family adjusts around you. Facing the consequences of your new behavior is one of the bravest things you will ever ask of yourself. But it will also be one of the most rewarding.

Deciding What Kind of Relationship You Can Have with Them Now

Once the dust begins to settle and you have a chance to take a look at the effect of your confrontation on your relationship with your parents, you will discover that there are three options available to you.

First, let's say that your parents have shown some capacity for understanding your pain and have acknowledged even a small part of their responsibility for the conflicts between you. If they indicate some willingness to continue to discuss, to explore, and to share feelings and concerns with you, there is a good chance that you will be able to build, together, a less toxic relationship. You can become your parents' teacher, instructing them in the fine art of treating you as an equal and communicating without criticism or attack. You can teach them how to express their own feelings without fear. You can teach them what does and does not feel good to you in the relationship. I won't pretend that this is what happens most of the time, or even much of the time, but it *does* happen some of the time. You can't know what their resources are until you push them to the crucial test of confrontation.

Second, if your parents show little capacity for change in your relationship, if they go right back to "business as usual," you may decide that the healthiest thing for you to do is to stay in contact with them but on significantly less demanding terms. I've worked with many people who were unwilling to totally cut off their parents but were equally unwilling to return to the status quo. These people chose to pull back, establishing a cordial but somewhat superficial relationship with their parents. They stopped exposing their innermost feelings and vulnerabilities; instead, they limited their conversations to emotionally neutral topics. They established new ground rules about the nature of their contact with their parents. This middle position seems to work well for many of my clients and it might work well for you. It's okay to stay in contact with toxic parents as long as the relationship does not require you to sacrifice your mental health.

The third and final option is to give up your relationship with your parents altogether, for the sake of your well-being. Some parents are so relentlessly antagonistic after confrontation that they escalate their toxic behaviors. If this happens, you may be forced to choose between them and your emotional health. You've been shortchanging yourself all your life; now it's time for a new accounting system.

There is no way to face this third option without a considerable amount of pain, but there is a way to manage the pain: trial separation. Take a break from your parents. No contact for at least three months. That means no meetings, no phone calls, no letters. I call this "detox" time because it gives all involved a chance to get some of the poison out of their systems and to evaluate how much the relationship means to them. This moratorium on contact may be difficult, but it can be a time of enormous growth. Without the need to expend large amounts of energy on your conflicts with your parents, you'll have much more energy available for your own life. Once you have gained emotional distance, you and your parents might even rediscover some genuine positive feelings for one another.

When the moratorium is over, you need to assess whether your parents have softened their position. Ask them for a meeting to discuss it. If they have not changed, you can either try another moratorium or make the ultimate choice to break off from them completely.

If you decide that a final break is the only way you can preserve your well-being, I urge you to get professional counseling to help you through. During this time the frightened child inside you will need a lot of reassurance and calming. A sympathetic counselor can help you nurture that child while at the same time guiding the adult through the anxiety and pain of saying goodbye.

Joe's Decision

Joe's father, Alan, remained furious long after the confrontation. He continued to drink heavily. After several weeks, he had his wife, Joanne, deliver a message to Joe: if Joe wanted to see his father again, Joe needed to apologize. His mother called almost daily, pleading with Joe to acquiesce to his father's demand so that, in her words, "we can be a family again."

Joe sadly realized that the distortions of reality in his family would continue to impair his mental health. He wrote his parents a brief letter telling them that he was taking a ninety-day vacation from the relationship, during which time he hoped they might reconsider their positions. He offered to meet with them again after the ninety days to see if there was anything worth salvaging.

After delivering the letter, Joe told me he felt ready and willing to accept the possibility of a final and permanent goodbye:

> I had really hoped I'd be strong enough to keep up a relationship with them and not get so bent out of shape by their craziness. But right now I know that that's asking too much of myself. So, since it seems to be a choice between them or me, I choose me. This is probably the healthiest thing I've ever done, but understand what's going on: one minute I feel proud of myself and really strong, and the next minute I feel really empty inside. God, Susan, I don't know if I can handle being healthy—I mean, what's that going to feel like?

Though it was painful for Joe to break off from his parents, his demonstration of resolve gave him a new sense of inner strength. He began to feel more self-assured when he met women, and within six months had developed a love relationship that he told me was the most stable he had ever had. As his self-worth continued to improve, so did his life.

Whether you negotiate with your parents for a better relationship, pull back to a more superficial relationship, or sever your relationship altogether, you will have taken an enormous step toward disconnecting from the power of the past. Once you break the old, ritualistic patterns with toxic parents, you'll be much more open and available for a truly loving relationship with yourself and others.

Confrontation with Sick or Old Parents

Many of my clients find themselves in a painful dilemma about confrontation when their parents are very elderly, frail, or disabled. They are often caught up in powerfully conflicting feelings of pity and resentment. Some feel a strong sense of basic human obligation to care for their parents coupled with hypersensitivity to their demands. "What's the use," they say. "I wish I had done it years ago. They can't even remember." Or, "Mom would have another stroke if I confronted her. Why don't I let her go to the grave in peace?" And yet, without a confrontation, they know it will be harder to find peace for themselves.

I do not want to minimize the difficulties involved, but the fact that a parent is old or has a chronic illness does not necessarily mean that confrontation is out of the question. I do advise my clients to discuss the ramifications of emotional stress with their parent's physician to determine whether there is any significant medical risk. If so, there are alternatives to direct confrontation that still enable you to tell your truth, even if you have chosen not to tell it to your parent. You can write confrontation letters that you don't mail, you can read these letters to photographs of your parent, you can talk to siblings or other family members, or if you are in therapy, you can confront your parent in role-playing. I will discuss these techniques in more detail in the following section on "Confrontation with a Dead Parent."

These techniques have also proven effective for a handful of my clients who are full-time caretakers of one or both parents. If your parent is living with you and is dependent on you, your efforts to deal more openly with your relationship may diminish the tensions between you, making your caretaker role easier. But it's also possible that confrontation may create such discord that your living situation becomes intolerable. If your current living arrangements make it impossible for you to get some distance from your parents should your confrontation alienate them further, you may choose some of the alternatives to direct confrontation.

"I Can't Do It, She's Not Well Enough to Handle It"

Jonathan, whom we met in chapter 4, avoided involvement with a woman because he was still rebelling against his mother, who continually pressured him to marry. After a few months of therapy, he decided that there were many things he would like to say to his mother, who was eighty-two. Since her heart attack a few years earlier, she had been frail, but she nevertheless, continued her intrusive phone calls and letters. His visits with her were painful charades.

> I feel so sorry for her, yet I get really angry at the power she has over me. But I'm afraid that if I say anything now, it will kill her, and I'm not willing to have that on my conscience. So I just put on my good-boy act. Why couldn't I have spoken up fifteen or twenty years ago when she was a lot stronger? I could have saved myself a lot of pain.

At this point I reminded Jonathan that confrontation doesn't mean blasting the other person. If we could find a way for him to release some of his hurt and angry feelings in a controlled and gentle way, he would discover that there is always more peace to be found in truth than in avoidance. I didn't want to push him to do something that could have consequences he couldn't live with, but there was a very real chance that an honest interchange with his mother would enrich the quality of their relationship.

I told him about current work being done with ill and dying

parents and their adult children that indicates that an honest exploration of the relationship not only doesn't harm the parents, but often provides closure and comfort to all involved.

Jonathan's alternative was to ignore his feelings and pretend there was no problem. I told him I thought this would be a terrible waste of their remaining time together.

Jonathan struggled with this for several weeks. At my urging he talked to his mother's physician, who assured him that her medical condition was stable.

> I got the ball rolling by asking her if she had any idea how I felt about our relationship. She said she wondered why I always seemed so irritable around her. That opened the door for me to quietly talk to her about how her need to control me had affected my life. We talked for hours. I said things I never thought I'd be able to say. She got defensive . . . she got hurt . . . she denied a lot . . . but some of it got through. A couple of times her eyes filled with tears and she squeezed my hand. The relief was unbelievable. I used to dread seeing her, but she's just a frail little old lady. I can't believe how many years I was afraid of expressing myself to her.

Jonathan was able to be honest and real with his mother for the first time in his life and to effectively change the tone of their relationship. He felt as if he'd finally put down a heavy burden. He was also able to see his mother in the present, rather than being driven by memories and fears. He could now respond to her current reality, which was very different from the powerful, engulfing mother the little boy inside him remembered.

Jonathan's confrontation with his mother had some positive results, but this is not always the case. Age or illness doesn't necessarily make toxic parents more able to deal with the truth. Some may mellow in later years, and coming face-to-face with their own mortality may make them more receptive to taking some responsibility for their behavior. But others will become more entrenched in their denial, their abuse, and their anger as they feel their life slipping away. Their assaults on you may be the only way they know to fend off their depression and panic. These parents may go to their graves angry and vindictive without ever acknowledging you. It doesn't matter. What *does* matter is that you've said what must be said.

Confrontation with a Dead Parent

It's extremely frustrating when you've worked hard to get to the point of confrontation, but one or both of your parents are dead. Surprisingly, there are several ways to have a confrontation even though your parents may not be physically present.

One method I've devised, which has proved to be very powerful, is to write a confrontation letter and read it aloud at your parent's grave. This gives you a strong sense of actually talking to your parent and of finally being able to express the things you've been holding inside for so long. Through the years I've received very positive reports, from both clients and from members of my radio audience, as a result of these graveside confrontations.

If it is not practical for you to go to your parent's grave, read your letter to a photograph of the parent, to an empty chair, or to someone in your support system who is willing to stand in for your parent.

You have one more option: you can talk to a relative, preferably from the same generation as your dead parent(s). Tell that family member (preferably a close blood relative) about your experiences with your parents. You don't have to ask this relative to take responsibility for what your parents did but there is a tremendous release in being able to tell the truth to an aunt or an uncle.

You may get the same negative reaction you would have gotten from your parents if they were alive. The relative may react with denial, disbelief, anger, or hurt, in which case you should do exactly what you would have done with your parent: stay nonreactive and nondefensive. This is a wonderful opportunity to reinforce your understanding that the responsibility to change is yours, not theirs.

On the other hand, the family member may give you some surprising validation and even an apology on your parents' behalf. This happened to Kim—whose father controlled her with money and unpredictable moods. Even though her father had been dead for more than five years, she felt the need to confront some member of the family. She decided on her father's younger sister, Shirley, and invited her to lunch.

At the session following their meeting, I could see that Kim was clearly delighted with the results.

> You know, everybody was always in awe of my father. He was the superstar of the family and Shirley always acted like she adored him. So you can imagine how hard it was for me to tell her what a bastard he had been to me. But the damnedest thing happened when I did. She told me she had always been afraid of my father, that he was horrible to her when they were kids, and that she wasn't at all surprised by anything I was telling her. Then she told me—and this was the best—that about eight years ago she gave him a brown shirt for his birthday—you know, the kind the Nazis used to wear. She said she wanted to sew a swastika on it but that would have been going too far. We laughed, we cried, it was wonderful. The people at the restaurant must have thought we were nuts.

When Shirley opened up to Kim, she was saying, in essence, "I understand how you feel and I know that it's all real and true." Kim found that by taking the experience back to the generation from which it came, she was able to release a lot of her pent-up anxiety and guilt about the reality of what her father had done to her.

I realize that this technique may seem unkind, since in most cases these relatives are not responsible for your negative experiences. But you have to weigh the pros against the cons. If using a relative as a substitute parent helps you to heal self-defeating mental and emotional wounds, it certainly seems worth subjecting that relative to a possibly unpleasant conversation that may cause temporary upset.

There's No Such Thing as a Bad Confrontation

Confrontation is the climactic phase in the journey toward autonomy.

No matter what happens during or after any confrontation, you come out a winner because you had the courage to do it.

Even if you didn't come home with a trophy, even if you didn't get to say everything you'd planned to, even if you became defensive and ended up explaining yourself, and even if your parents got up and walked out on you . . . *you still did it.* You have told the truth about your life to yourself and your parents, and the fear that kept you trapped in your old role with them can no longer control you.

14 | Healing the Incest Wound

Professional help is a *must* for adults who were sexually abused as children. Nothing in my experience responds more dramatically and completely to therapy, despite the depth of the damage.

In this chapter I'm going to show you the treatment techniques that I have devised and refined in the process of working with more than a thousand incest victims. I am showing them to you because I want you to see how much hope there is for you and how extraordinary your recovery can be. I do *not*, however, want you to attempt this work on your own.

If you are currently in therapy, I suggest you encourage your therapist to do this work with you. This particular treatment process has a beginning, a middle, and an end. The roadmap is specific and clearly marked. If you follow it, you will reclaim your dignity and self-respect.

I know that some therapists and incest clients prefer the term *incest survivor* to the term *incest victim*, and that's fine. But for me, *incest victim* is a more accurate description of the individual's experience. I am certainly sympathetic to this semantic attempt to ease the pain, as long as the word *survivor* is not used to deny how much work needs to be done.

"Why Do I Need Therapy?"

If you were molested as a child, all or most of the statements on the following list will be true for you.

1. You have deep-seated feelings of unworthiness, guilt, and shame.
2. You are easily used and exploited by others.
3. You believe everybody else is more important than you are.
4. You believe the only way to get love is by catering to the needs of others at the expense of your own.
5. You have a very difficult time setting limits, expressing anger, or saying "no."
6. You draw cruel or abusive people into your life and are convinced that you can get them to love you or be nice to you.
7. You find it difficult to trust, and you expect people to betray you or hurt you.
8. You are uncomfortable with sex or your sexuality.
9. You have learned to act "as if" things are okay when they're not.
10. You don't believe you deserve success, happiness, or a good relationship.
11. You have a difficult time being playful or spontaneous.
12. You feel you never had a childhood.
13. You often feel angry at your own child or children and resent the fact that they have it better than you did.
14. You wonder what it would feel like to be normal.

These patterns of victimization started early. They are tenacious and difficult to break by yourself, but therapy can successfully end their hold on your life.

CHOOSING A THERAPIST

It is important to shop for a therapist specifically educated or experienced in working with incest victims. Many therapists are unqualified in this highly specialized area, and virtually no therapists learn anything about incest in graduate school. Question each prospective therapist about his or her special training and experience. If he or she has not worked with incest victims before or has not attended any workshops, seminars, conferences, or classes on incest treatment, I suggest you find someone else.

Those who are trained in family dynamics, and who use action-oriented techniques such as role playing, make the best therapists for incest victims. Freudian psychiatrists make the worst, because Freud significantly reversed his original (and accurate) positions on both the prevalence and the damage of incest; as a result, many Freudian psychiatrists and psychoanalysts meet their patients' accounts of childhood sexual abuse with skepticism or disbelief.

In the last decade many self-help groups for incest victims have been formed around the country. While these groups do provide some support and a sense of community to many incest victims, they lack the guidance of a therapist with the expertise to provide structure and direction for the work. A self-help group is better than no group at all, but it's far better to be in a group led by a professional.

INDIVIDUAL OR GROUP THERAPY

The best way to work through the incest experience is to join a group made up of victims like yourself led by a therapist who is experienced and comfortable with the issue.

One almost universal symptom of incest is a feeling of total isolation. But when you're surrounded by people talking about feelings and experiences that sound just like yours, the isolation begins to fade. Group members nurture and support you. In essence, they say: "We know how it feels, we believe you, we hurt for you, we care about you, we want you to be the best you can."

There are very few people who do not thrive in group, although most people are apprehensive about it at first. You may feel tense and self-conscious about talking about "it" in front of other people. Believe me, those feelings usually last no more than ten minutes.

A small number of incest victims are too emotionally fragile to handle the intensity of group. For them, one-to-one therapy is the alternative.

I always put male and female victims together in group. The gender may be different, but the feelings and traumas are the same.

The incest therapy groups at my treatment center are open-ended. This means that a new member can enter at any time. It also means that someone who is just beginning this work will be in group with people at different stages of progress. It's wonderfully encouraging for a new group member to see someone ready to graduate and leave the incest experience behind.

The First Time in Group

When a new client comes into group, we begin the session with an initiation exercise in which every group member tells about his or her incest experience: who it was with, what it involved, when it began, how long it went on, and who else knows about it. The new member goes last.

This initiation helps break the ice so that you can join the group in an active way. You will find yourself talking about your experience in detail for perhaps the first time. You will see that you are not alone, that other people have experienced similar traumas.

Your initiation will also continue the vital process of desensitization to the trauma for the other group members. Every time a new member is initiated, group members must repeat what has long been unspoken. The more often this happens, the more everyone in the group is desensitized to the shame and the guilt. The first time through is very difficult for any new member. There is a great deal of weeping and embarrassment. By the third or fourth time the experiences become easier to talk about, and the embarrassment subsides noticeably. By the time someone has told his or her story ten or twelve times, it is not much more difficult than talking about any other unhappy life event.

Stages of Treatment

I take incest victims through three basic stages: outrage, grief, and release.

Outrage is the deep anger that arises from feelings of violation and betrayal of the very core of one's being. It is the first essential part of this work and the most difficult.

Most adults who were molested as children have had plenty of practice at feeling sad, lonely, and bad. Grief is familiar to them, but outrage is not. As a result, they often try to skip over their outrage and move on to grief as quickly as possible. This is a mistake. Outrage *must* precede grief. Of course, it is impossible to keep intense feelings totally separate—there is grief in outrage and outrage in grief. But for the purpose of this work, they are distinct stages.

The Victim's Outrage

In order to put the responsibility firmly where it belongs, you must acknowledge your outrage and learn, in the safety of therapy, to let it out.

For many of you, this is easier said than done. You've spent years keeping the lid on. You may have repressed your outrage so effectively that you've become a submissive, self-sacrificing perfectionist. It's as if you've been saying, "I'm not damaged and I can prove it by being perfect. I sacrifice everything for others, I don't get angry, and I do as I'm told." Releasing your outrage is like uncapping a volcano. The resulting eruption may feel overwhelming.

If you've pushed your rage totally out of conscious awareness, you are also especially vulnerable to physical or emotional symptoms such as headaches or depression.

For others, the problem isn't how to get in touch with their outrage, it's how to control it. You may seethe with outrage at everyone around you except those at whom you're really angry—your parents. You may have a perpetual chip on your shoulder, displacing your outrage from your parents to whomever happens to come along. You may act so tough and belligerent that you scare people away.

The techniques I'll show you later in this chapter will allow you to externalize your outrage in *manageable* ways, to prevent you from losing control, and to allow you to open the pressure valve and let your outrage go.

The Victim's Grief

During the healing process, you're going to actively grieve over many losses—the loss of the "good family" fantasy, of innocence, of love, of childhood, of years that might otherwise have been happy and productive. This grief may overwhelm you. Your therapist must have the courage and the experience to lead you through it and bring you out the other end. As with any grief, there are no easy ways around it, no shortcuts.

Release and Empowerment

In the last stage of treatment, when you have exhausted your outrage and your grief, you will learn to take the energy they were consuming and use it to rebuild your life and your self-image. By this time, many of your symptoms will have either diminished significantly or become manageable. You'll have a new dignity and a new sense of yourself as a valuable and lovable person. You will be faced with a new option for the first time in your life—that of no longer feeling or behaving like a victim.

Treatment Techniques

The two primary techniques I use for treating clients are letter writing and role playing. I have also designed a number of group exercises that have proved especially helpful for incest victims and other adult children of toxic parents. These techniques can be used in both individual and group therapy. Since only a small percentage of the incest therapy at my treatment centers is done on an individual basis, I've selected my examples from group sessions.

Letters

I ask every group member to write one letter a week, especially in the beginning. They write these letters at home, then read them aloud to the group. Although no one is *required* to mail their letters, many group members *choose* to, especially when they begin to feel stronger. I ask my clients to write their letters in the following order:

1. to the aggressor(s)
2. to the other parent (assuming that one parent was the aggressor; adults who were molested by a family member other than a parent need to write first to the aggressor and then to each parent)
3. to the damaged child from your adult self
4. a "fairy tale" about your life
5. to your partner or lover (if you have one)
6. to each of your children

After this series of letters is completed, I ask my group members to begin the series again. In this way the letters become not only powerful tools for healing but clear barometers of progress. A letter written during the first few weeks of therapy will be very different, in both tone and content, from a letter written three or four months later.

Letter to the Aggressor

In the first letter—to the aggressor—I want you to let it all out, to get as outraged as you can. Use phrases like "how dare you . . ." and "how could you . . ." as often as possible. These phrases will make it easier for you to contact your outrage.

When I first met Janine, a gentle, petite, blond 36-year-old, she rarely spoke above a whisper. Her father had molested her from the time she was 7 until she was 11—but Janine was still clinging to the hope that she could somehow win his love. She was especially reluctant to acknowledge her inner rage at him. She wept through her initiation and was noticeably uncomfortable when I asked her to write her father a letter. I encouraged her to use her letter to get outraged at how her father had hurt and betrayed her. I reminded her that her father didn't ever have to see this letter.

From our work together, I expected her first letter to be tentative, full of yearning and wishful thinking. Was *I* in for a surprise:

> Dear Dad,
>
> You're not really "dear" and you only got to be my dad because you shot your sperm into Mom one night. I hate you and I pity you. How dare you violate your own little girl?
>
> Where's my apology, Dad? Where's my virginity? Where's my self-respect?
>
> I didn't do anything to make you hate me. I didn't try to turn you on. Are little girls tighter, is that it? Do small new breasts make you hard, you bastard? I should have spit on you. I hate myself for not having the courage to fight you. How dare you use your power as my daddy to rape me? How dare you make me hurt? How dare you not talk to me?

When I was really little you'd take me in the ocean and hold my hand and we would go through the waves, remember? I had your blue eyes, I trusted you. I wanted you to respect me so bad. I wanted you to be proud of me. You were more to me than just a child molester, but you didn't care, did you? I won't stand for pretending it didn't happen anymore. It did happen, Dad, and it's still alive in me.

Janine

Janine's letter brought more feelings to the surface than hours of talking ever could have. She was frightened by the intensity of her feelings, but comforted by the knowledge that she had a safe place to explore and express them for the first time.

Connie—the redheaded loan officer whose father had molested her from an early age and who later acted out her self-loathing by sleeping with hundreds of men—had entered this same group several months before Janine. Connie displayed a quick temper and had an aggressive, angry way about her. I called her my "tough guy," but I knew how small and vulnerable she really felt. In her first letter to her father, Connie's feelings spilled haphazardly across the page, without boundaries, without form. But when Connie read her second letter to her father, it was clear that both her feelings and her perceptions had become much more organized and focused:

Dear Daddy,

A lifetime has passed since I wrote my first letter for Susan's group—so much has changed. When I started you were still a terrifying ogre and in some ways I had become like you. Incest was bad enough, but I also had to live with your violence and threats of violence all the time. You were a bully and a tyrant. How dare you steal my childhood from me? How dare you ruin my life?

I'm finally beginning to put the pieces together. You are a very sick, disturbed man. You used me in every way that a man can use a person. You made me love you in ways that no father should make a daughter love him and I was powerless to stop you. I don't feel normal, I feel dirty. Things have been so bad and I have behaved in such self-destructive ways that anything, ANYTHING that changes has to be an improvement.

I can't solve your problems or Mother's problems but I can solve mine. And in the process, if either or both of you are hurt, there is nothing I can do. I didn't ask to be molested.

Connie

As Connie expressed her outrage she was able to leave behind much of her self-hatred and self-disgust. The more this happened, the more she strengthened her commitment to personal growth and healing.

Letter to the Silent Partner

After you've written your letter to your aggressor, you'll write to your other parent, in most cases your mother. If you think your mother didn't know about the incest, this letter may be the first time you've put these experiences into words for her.

If you think your mother *did* know about the incest, or if you actually told her while it was going on, there is an enormous amount of outrage that you need to express to her: outrage for the lack of protection, for being disbelieved or blamed, for having been used as a sacrificial lamb to keep a destructive marriage and a destructive family intact, and outrage at having been less important to your mother than her need for financial security or maintaining the status quo.

Connie's letter to her mother offers a poignant example of the tremendous ambivalence most incest victims feel toward their mothers. The letter began with a recounting of the sexual abuses she had suffered from her father. She moved on to express her view of her mother's role in this family drama:

> . . . I feel that you betrayed me, too. Mothers are supposed to protect little girls, but you didn't do that. You didn't take care of me and because of that he hurt me.
>
> Didn't you want to see? Or didn't you care enough to see? I'm so angry at you for all the lonely scared years I had. You abandoned me. Peace with him was so damned important to you that you sacrificed me to him. It hurt so much to know that I wasn't important enough to protect. It hurt so much that I shut my pain away. I can't even feel things like a normal person. My parents not only stole my childhood, they stole my emotions, too. I hate and love you so much that I'm really confused. Why didn't you take care of me, Mommy? Why didn't you just love me? What was wrong with me? Will I ever get any answers?

Connie's eloquent expression of her confusion echoes the confusion felt by all incest victims about why their mothers failed to protect them. As Connie put it, "Even animals protect their cubs."

LETTER TO THE DAMAGED CHILD

In many ways the letter to the damaged child within you may be the most difficult letter for you to write, but it may also be the most important. This letter begins the process of "reparenting" yourself.

Reparenting means to dig deep within yourself to find a loving, validating parent for the hurting child you still carry inside. This is the parent who, through this letter, comforts, reassures, and protects that part of you that is still vulnerable and frightened.

Many of you who were sexually abused as children have become alienated from your inner child. Your shame translates into contempt and loathing for that "tainted," helpless child. To defend against some of these extremely painful feelings, you may have tried to disown this child, but the child within you can only be hidden, not abandoned.

In this letter I want you to embrace that child and reintegrate him or her into your personality. Be a loving parent. Give the child the nurturing and support you never had. Make the child feel loved and worthwhile for the first time. Dan—the engineer who was sexually abused by his father during his entire childhood and adolescence—had long felt loathing for the little boy he once was, the little boy who was too weak to resist his father. This portion of his letter to that little boy shows how dramatically those feelings had changed after only a few group sessions:

> Dear Little Dan,
>
> You were a beautiful child, an innocent. You were pure love. I'm going to take care of you from now on. You were talented and creative. I'm going to express you. You're safe now. You can love and you can let love in. You won't be hurt. You can discern now. I'll take care of us. I'll pull us together. We were always apart, playing different roles, learning to cope. You're not crazy. You were afraid. He can't hurt you anymore. I've stopped taking the alcohol and drugs that were concealing your anger, your rage, your sadness, your depression, your guilt, and your anxiety. You can let go of those feelings now. I've stopped punishing us, like he did. I've surrendered to God. We are worthwhile. I am worthwhile. The world we made up is over now. We are waking up. It still hurts, but not as much. And it's finally real.
>
> Dan

Dan used this letter not only to communicate with the child within but to reassure himself that his decision to renounce drugs and alcohol was a self-affirming step. He understood for the first time, as he wrote this letter, the connection between his self-defeating behavior and his childhood pain.

The Fairy Tale

After you have written these three letters, I want you to write a story describing your life in fairy-tale language and images. You'll write about yourself as the little princess or the gentle young prince who lived with evil kings or ugly monsters or dragons in dark forests or crumbling castles. You'll write about the incest as the Black Plague or the thunderstorm or the end of joy or whatever your imagination creates.

This fairy tale is the first assignment you'll write in the third person; instead of using the point of view of "I," you'll write about "he" or "she." This will help you see your inner world from a new, more objective perspective, putting some emotional distance between you and your childhood traumas. By referring to the little girl as "her" instead of "me," the sharp pain of your experiences will begin to fade. When you bring your feelings to life through symbols, you will be able to deal with them on a level you've never approached before, and you will come away with a new, clearer understanding of what happened to you.

The only limitation I set is that your fairy tale, despite its sad beginning, have a hopeful ending. After all, the fairy tale is an allegory for your life, and there *is* hope. You may not really believe that when you begin this work, but by writing optimistically about your future, you will start to draw more positive pictures in your mind. This is especially important for people who cannot imagine a happy future for themselves. By imagining a better life, you can begin to develop concrete, attainable goals, and once you have goals, you have something to inspire you.

I'll never forget the day Tracy—who was molested by her insurance-salesman father—read her fairy tale. It was very long, so I've included only parts of it here, but the truth and the hope she was able to find through this exercise forever changed her perspective on her situation:

> Once upon a time lived a little plant in a rather isolated valley surrounded by mountains. The little plant, whose name was "Ivy," [an acronym for "incest victim"] was quite miserable, so she would often gaze over the river, secretly wishing to escape to the other side.

Ivy's little corner of the world was ruled by the notorious King Morris Lester, known to most everyone as Moe. You'll notice that when you put the nickname and the surname together, you come out with Moe Lester, and what you hear is actually what you get.

Moe had a passion for tender young plants. When Ivy was just beginning to bloom, Moe spied her and was taken by the fact that she was ripe yet as green as could be. Moe performed one ill deed after another with Ivy, but even so, she held him in reverence and treated him like a king.

Moe had no shame at all, but what he lacked, Ivy made up for. Poor Ivy withdrew from the world almost completely, and in her terrible aloneness she had only one companion: Gil Trip.

Gil was a lowly creature who slithered all over Ivy, nibbling at her leaves, her stem, and her roots. It was Gil, as much as anyone else, who kept Ivy sick and shackled in that valley.

A day did come, however, when Ivy was astounded to meet an emancipator. "Who are you?" asked Ivy in wonder. "I am your Fairy Godmother, otherwise known as Susan of the North. Pack your bags and make it snappy. You are about to be uprooted." Ivy panicked. "But there's no way over the river," she cried. "Yes there is," cooed Susan victoriously. "You may ride on my outrage. It has carried me far, and it will carry you too."

Clinging to the outrage that no one had ever held for her before, Ivy allowed herself to be jet propelled—swept up and out of the valley of her discontent.

In addition to her insights, Tracy's wonderful use of imagination and humor allowed her to recapture some of the playfulness that was so badly trampled in her childhood.

Some of my clients protest when I assign the fairy tale, claiming that they can't write or that the assignment is frivolous. But the fairy tale always turns out to be one of our most moving and healing exercises.

LETTER TO YOUR PARTNER

Your next letter should be to your partner. If you have no spouse, lover, or live-in companion, a former lover or ex-husband will do (remember, you do not have to mail this letter). Explain to him or her how your childhood trauma is affecting your relationship. You don't have to take responsibility for every problem the two of you have, but your inability to trust, your need to be compliant, and your experience of sexuality may be taking their toll. The most important thing about this letter is that you talk openly and honestly about what happened to you. This is an important part of letting go of your shame.

LETTER TO YOUR CHILDREN

Your series of letters ends with a letter to each of your children. If you have no children, you may write to the child you plan to have, or to the child you never had. Use this letter to reaffirm your ability to love and to understand that by experiencing your pain and coming through it, you are gaining the inner strength to be a better parent.

The Power of Role Playing

In group, after all the letters are read, we set up brief improvised scenes to deal with issues brought up in the letters. I have found these psychodrama or role-playing scenes to be a wonderfully insightful and effective means of working through the incest trauma and dealing with the other concerns in my clients' lives.

Role playing cuts through the intellectualizing and denial that you may be using as a defense against your feelings. It offers you a chance to express the full range of your emotions toward family members before you are ready to face them. It provides a safe atmosphere for you to try out new behaviors. All of these factors are essential for successful treatment.

Three months into group, Connie was feeling strong enough to mail her letters to her father and mother. But she realized that once her letters arrived, she would need a lot of support. I asked her whether her husband, Wayne, could provide it, and she sheepishly admitted that she still hadn't told him about her father's sexual abuse.

Like most incest victims, Connie was convinced that he would lose his attraction to her, that it would make her disgusting and repellent to him. Even though she had many years of evidence that Wayne was a loving, supportive man, her anxiety still prevented her from revealing her painful secret. But now she needed him to know.

To help ease Connie's fears, I asked her to use role playing in group to rehearse telling Wayne before she ventured to attempt the real thing. We played out a number of scenes with myself or another group member playing Wayne and reacting in a variety of ways, ranging from total acceptance to total rejection.

In one particularly dramatic scene, Connie herself played Wayne so that she could try to experience some of his feelings. I played Connie. After telling "Wayne" about what my father had done to me, I told him what I needed from him.

SUSAN (as Connie): I really need your love and support right now. I need to know that none of this makes any difference to you and that you don't hate me or think I'm dirty.

CONNIE (as Wayne): Of course I don't hate you. I just wish you had told me sooner so I could have been there for you. If anything, knowing this makes you even more precious to me. I've always known that there was something painful inside you that made you so suspicious and angry all the time, and now that I know what it is, it all starts to make sense. I wish I could do something to make the hurt go away, and I wish you had trusted me enough to have told me sooner. . . .

At this point Connie stopped the role playing.

CONNIE: I could really feel his love for me when I was being him. It's going to be all right. I know it is. And if it isn't [she smiled], I'll just punch him out.

You can use role playing to embolden yourself to break the silence. When Connie actually told Wayne about her childhood, she found that the rehearsals in group had eased her anxiety considerably. Wayne was indeed as understanding as she had sensed he would be, and his support throughout the remainder of her therapy was enormously helpful to her.

Exercises for Healing the Inner Child

In addition to the letter writing and the role playing, there are a number of extremely potent group exercises for healing. Following are two of the most powerful.

REWRITING HISTORY—THE "NO" EXERCISE

If you're like the great majority of incest victims, you don't know how to say "no." You may believe you are powerless, that you have to do whatever anyone asks. These beliefs have their genesis in your expereince of having been coerced, intimidated, and humiliated by a powerful parent.

To give yourself a rebirth of power, close your eyes and visualize the first time you remember being molested, but this time, change what happened. See the room where it took place. See your aggressor. Put your hands out and push your aggressor away, saying, "No!

You can't! I won't let you! Go away! I'll tell! I'll scream!" Visualize the aggressor obeying you. Watch him turn around and leave the room, becoming smaller and smaller as he walks out the door.

Even though you may feel considerable pain over the fact that you couldn't do this at the time, this rewriting of history is an exciting and empowering exercise. As Dan said:

> God, I would have given anything in the world to have been able to really do that. But even doing it now really put me in touch with strengths I didn't even know I had. None of us was able to protect ourselves then, but we can sure as hell learn to do it now!

Choosing to Be a Child, Choosing to Be an Adult

One of the most poignant group exercises we do involves members playing themselves at whatever age their molestations began.

In this exercise, it's important to recapture the feelings of being a child. To help you do this, try sitting on the floor—chairs and sofas are for grown-ups. Remember that little kids don't speak like adults—they have their own vocabulary and their own ways of perceiving the world. Once you've formed your group of abused children, tell your group leader about the "weird stuff" that's going on in your house. The other "children" can ask questions as well as comfort you. In the following excerpt from a recent group session, Connie had a major breakthrough.

Susan: Hi, sweetie, how old are you?

Little Connie (in a childlike voice): Seven.

Susan: I understand that your daddy is doing some really yucky stuff to you. It can help if you tell us all about it.

Little Connie: Well . . . it's real hard to talk about. I feel real ashamed, but my daddy . . . he comes into my room and he . . . he pulls my panties down and he touches me and he licks me . . . you know, down there, on my pee-pee. Then he rubs his pee-pee on my leg and he breathes real hard and after a while this gooey white stuff comes out and then he tells me to get a towel and clean it up and he tells me if I ever tell anybody he'll beat me up.

Susan: How do you feel when your daddy does those things to you?

Little Connie: I feel really scared and sick in my tummy. I guess I must be a really bad girl for my daddy to do this to me. Sometimes I just wish I could die 'cause then he would know how icky I feel and if I was dead he'd have to stop doing that to me.

At this point Connie's "tough guy" defenses crumbled. The other members of the group formed a circle around her and cradled her as she wept for several minutes.

Between sobs, Connie told us that she hadn't cried for years and that she was frightened by how defenseless it made her feel. I assured her that freeing up her soft, vulnerable side would be a great source of strength, not weakness. The frightened, hurting child inside her wouldn't have to hide anymore.

After your "child" has had a chance to express herself, and has been comforted and validated, you need to make a conscious choice to return to your adult self. Stand up and experience the size of your body. Feel your adult power. The ability to return to your adult self is a source of great strength that you can summon whenever you feel like a helpless child.

These are just a few of the many group exercises that your therapist may draw from. Along with letter writing and role playing, the group exercises are major steps along the road to devictimization.

Confronting Your Parents

As I write this I feel a deep sadness at having to warn you that the people who were supposed to nurture, love, and protect you will, in all likelihood, assault you emotionally when you dare to tell the truth. Everything I've told you about confrontation goes double when you confront the incest aggressor.

- You must have a strong support system.
- You must rehearse, rehearse, and rehearse.
- You must have shifted your beliefs about who is responsible.
- You must be prepared to significantly change your relationship with your parents, or even to sacrifice it.

If your parents are still together you can confront them at the same time or separately. However, I have found that in incest cases, it is usually less explosive to confront parents separately. Confronted together, parents of incest victims often close ranks to defend their marriage against what they perceive as an all-out attack. In that case, it will be two against one, and it becomes especially important for you to have a support person with you.

While there is no way to predict how any aggressor will react, confronting him by himself does seem to take some of the heat out. Your aggressor may deny that the incest ever happened, may become enraged and leave the session, may attack your therapist for encouraging you to hurt the family, may try to minimize his crimes, or may even acknowledge what he did. You must be prepared for anything. If he *does* acknowledge his crimes, beware of excuses. Aggressors often try to manipulate their victims into feeling sorry for them.

Though the steps of confrontation are the same as with other toxic parents, there are some very specific things you need to include in "this is what I want from you now." Your aggressor's response to these requests will be your only accurate indicator of your future relationship with him.

Here's what you want:

1. Full acknowledgement of what happened. If the aggressor claims not to remember, ask him to acknowledge that even

though *he* doesn't remember, it must be true because *you* remember.

2. An apology.
3. Full acceptance of responsibility and explicit removal of any responsibility from you.
4. Willingness to make reparations. For example, he can go into therapy, pay for your therapy, apologize to other people in your life for the pain he's caused, and be available to talk about this with you when you need to.

A word of warning: apologies can be very seductive and can create false hope that things will change significantly in your relationship. If apologies are not followed by behavioral changes in the aggressor, however, nothing will change. He must be willing to *do* something about the problem. Otherwise, apologies are empty words that will only set you up for further hurt and disappointment.

Obviously, few victims get a positive response to all or even most of these requests, but it is essential for your growth that you make them. You need to define the ground rules for any future relationship. You must show clearly that you will no longer live with lies, half-truths, secrecy, and denial. Most important, you must make it clear that you will no longer accept the responsibility for the violence committed against you—that you are no longer willing to be a victim.

"It's Time for Us to Stop Pretending"

Tracy decided to confront her father and mother separately. Tracy told her father that she was in therapy but didn't specify what kind. She said it would be very helpful if he would come in for a joint session with her. He agreed but canceled several appointments before he finally showed up.

Tracy's father, Harold, was a slightly built, balding man in his late fifties. He was impeccably groomed and looked every inch the executive that he now was. When I asked him if he knew why Tracy wanted him to come in to see me, he said he had "a pretty good idea." I began by asking Tracy to tell her father what kind of therapy she was in:

> I'm in a group for victims of incest, Dad. People who have fathers and sometimes mothers who did to them what you did to me.

Harold flushed visibly and averted his eyes. He started to say something, but Tracy stopped him and got him to agree to hear her out. She continued to tell him what he had done to her and how sick, frightened, confused, and dirty it had made her feel. Then she told him how the incest had affected her life.

> I never felt it was okay for me to like another man. I always felt I was betraying you or cheating on you. I felt like a possession, like I had no life outside you. I believed you when you said I was a slut—after all, I had this dirty secret inside of me. I thought it was my fault. I've been depressed most of my life but I learned to act like everything's okay. Well, everything's not okay, Dad, and it's time for all of us to stop acting. My marriage almost fell apart because I hated sex, I hated my body, I hated me! That's all changing now, thank God. But you've been getting off scot-free while I've been carrying the whole load. You betrayed me, you used me, you did the worst thing that a father can do to his little girl.

Then Tracy told her father what she wanted from him—an apology and a full acknowledgment of his responsibility. She also gave him a chance to tell her mother before she did.

Tracy's father was stunned. He accused her of blackmailing him. He made no attempt to deny the incest, but tried to minimize it by reminding Tracy that he had never "hurt her physically." He did apologize, but his primary concern was about the effects on his marriage and his professional status if all this became "public knowledge." He denied that he needed any therapy because he had led a "useful and productive life."

The following week Tracy pressured her father into "confessing" to her mother. Tracy then came to group and reported on the aftermath:

> My mother was pretty devastated but in the next breath she asked me to forgive him and not to tell anyone else in the family. When I told her I wouldn't agree to do that she asked me why *I* needed to hurt *them* so much. Do you love it—all of a sudden I'm the bad guy in all of this.

Everyone in group was eager to know how Tracy was feeling since she had taken this huge step. I will never forget her answer:

> I feel like this thirty-ton weight has been lifted off my shoulders. You know, what I realize now is that I have a right to tell the truth and I'm not responsible if other people can't deal with it.

We all were thrilled to see how Tracy had taken back her power and come a long way toward devictimizing herself. Ultimately, Tracy decided to maintain a relationship with her parents but to have only limited contact with them.

Running into a Stone Wall

Tracy needed very little help from me in her confrontation with her father. On the other hand, Liz—whose stepfather, the powerful local minister, not only abused her but almost strangled her when she found the courage to tell him to stop—needed a great deal, especially since her mother and stepfather insisted on coming in together. When Liz told her parents that she wanted them to come to a therapy session, they told her they would "do anything to help her with her mental problems."

When Liz was 13 she had told her mother about her stepfather's abuse in a desperate effort to stop it. Her mother hadn't believed her, and Liz had never brought it up again.

Liz's stepfather, Burt, was a courtly, ruddy-faced man now in his early sixties. It was significant that he wore his black clerical suit and white collar to the session. Liz's mother, Rhoda, was a tall, thin, stern-faced woman with black hair heavily streaked with gray. Both were full of righteous indignation from the moment they walked in the door.

Liz did and said everything she had practiced, but every time she attempted to talk about the molestations she was met with a stone wall of angry denial and accusation. According to her parents, she was insane, she was making it all up, and she was a wicked, vengeful girl, trying to get back at Burt for having been a "stern disciplinarian." Liz was holding her own but getting nowhere. She looked at me helplessly. I stepped in:

> You've both betrayed her enough—I'm not going to permit it anymore. I'm sorry that neither of you has the courage to admit the truth. Burt, you know everything Liz is saying is true. No one makes up these humiliating and painful things. And no one makes up years of depression and shame. The statute of limitations has run out on your crime, but I want you to know that because you're in a position of trust and authority with other children, Liz and I have reported you to Child Protective Services. If you ever hurt another child, that report will weigh heavily against you. I don't see how you can minister to other people when your whole life is built on a lie. You're a fraud and a child molester, Reverend! You know it and God knows it.

Burt's face turned to stone. He said nothing, but his rage was obvious. I turned to Liz's mother in one last attempt to get her to face the truth, but all my words fell on deaf ears.

Burt and Rhoda's defenses were impenetrable, and I saw no reason to prolong Liz's pain. She had all the information she needed, so I asked Burt and Rhoda to leave.

Liz knew that she had to make a choice between her parents and her emotional well-being. It was not possible for her to have both. Her decision didn't take long:

> I've got to cut them out of my life. They're just too crazy. The only way I could have a relationship with them is for me to be crazy too. Now that I'm so much stronger, it's like they're from another planet. God, Susan, that woman was supposed to be my mother!

She started to cry. I held her for several minutes as she sobbed. Finally, she said:

> I guess what hurts the most is realizing that they simply don't care about me and never have. I mean, by any normal definition of love, they don't love me.

With that last statement Liz showed a willingness to face the terrible truth that many adults who were abused as children have to face—in the final analysis, her parents were simply incapable of love. It was their failure and their character flaws that created this painful reality, not hers.

Confronting the Silent Partner

Connie's parents lived in another state, so she decided to confront with separate letters to her father and mother. During the exercise in which she played herself as a child, Connie had remembered that when her father molested her the first time, she had told her mother. It was especially important to Connie to find out why her mother had failed to take steps to protect her.

Connie was climbing the walls with anxiety after she mailed her letters. After three weeks she bemoaned the fact that she hadn't gotten an answer from her father.

"But you have," I said. "His answer is that he's not willing to deal with this."

Connie did, however, get a letter from her mother. She read part of it to the group:

> No matter what I say, it will always be inadequate for all the harm that has been done to you. At the time I thought I was protecting you the best I knew how. I did talk to him about it, but he apologized and swore he wouldn't do it again. He seemed so sincere. He begged for another chance and told me he loved me. No one will ever know my fear, my uncertainty. I didn't know what to do, I thought the problem was over. Now I realize to my own disgust how he tricked me so easily. I wanted a happy family so badly that I resorted to the big cover-up. I was so intent on keeping peace in our lives. My mind is going around in circles and I can't say any more about this right now. Maybe, as always, I've been no help to you, Connie, but please accept that I do love you and want the very best for you.
>
> Love,
> Mom

The letter stirred up some hope for Connie that the two of them could initiate a more honest relationship. At my suggestion, Connie set up a conference call between her mother, herself, and me. During the call, Connie's mother, Margaret, again expressed her sorrow over what had happened and again acknowledged her weakness and complicity. I too began to have hopes that these two women could build something of value between them . . . until Connie asked for the one thing she really wanted.

CONNIE: I don't expect you to leave him after all these years, but there is one thing that's really important to me. I want you to go to him and tell him how horrible what he did to me was. I don't want anything from him—he's a sick, crazy man and I've had to accept that. But I do want him to hear this from you.

Margaret was silent for a long moment.

Margaret: I can't do that. I just can't do that. Please don't ask me to do that.

Connie: So you're going to protect him over me, just like you always have. When I got your letter, I thought maybe, finally, I was going to have a mother. I thought maybe you could be on my team this once. Just being sorry isn't enough, Mom. You need to *do* something for me. You need to show you love me, not just say it.

Margaret: Connie, it was a long time ago. You have your own life, your own family now. He's all I've got.

Connie was bitterly disappointed when her mother refused to do the one thing she asked. But she recognized that her mother had made her choice a long time ago. It was unrealistic for Connie to expect anything different at this time in their lives.

Connie decided that for her well-being she would maintain minimal mail and phone contact with her mother and accept her mother's limitations. She decided to cut off all contact with her father.

"We Go On from Here"

Dan's mother, Evelyn, a retired high school principal, responded quite differently when he broke the silence. Dan's parents had been divorced for about ten years when Dan finally felt strong enough to tell his mother about the years of sexual abuse his father had inflicted on him.

Evelyn wept as she heard the details of what had happened to her son and went over and took him in her arms.

> Oh, God, honey, I'm so sorry. Why didn't you tell me? I could have done something about it. I had no idea. I knew there was something terribly wrong with him. We had an awful sexual relationship, and I knew he was always masturbating in the bathroom, but I never dreamed he would do anything to you. Oh, my baby, I'm so sorry, I'm so sorry.

Dan was concerned about loading too much on his mother's shoulders; he had underestimated her capacity to empathize. But she assured him that she would rather share the awful truth with him than live a lie:

> I feel like I've been hit by a truck, but I'm so glad you told me. So many things are starting to make sense now. So many things are starting to fall into place . . . like your drinking and your depression and so many things about my marriage. You know, for years I'd blame myself because he seemed to have so little interest in me sexually. And I'd blame myself for his temper. Now I know he was sick, really sick, and neither of us was to blame. So we go on from here.

Dan had not only given himself a gift by telling the truth, he had given his mother one as well. By telling her about the incest, Dan had answered for her many of the painful, bewildering questions she had about her marriage. Dan's mother responded as all incest victims yearn for their mothers to respond—with compassion, anger at the aggressor, and genuine support.

As Dan and his mother left my office arm-in-arm, I couldn't help but reflect on how wonderful it would be if all mothers responded this way.

Graduation

There comes a time in the treatment process when you will have written and rewritten all the letters, gone through the role playing, the exercises, and the confrontations, and made the decisions about your future relationship with your parents. You will see ever-increasing evidence of your strength and well-being. The changes in your beliefs, your feelings, and your behavior will be integrated into your personality. In short, you will be ready for "graduation."

This will be a sad but exciting time for you, for the other members of your group, and for your therapist. You will have to say goodbye to the only good family you have ever known, though many of my group members maintain close friendships long after they have left group. These friendships from group, based on having shared powerful emotional experiences, tend to be extremely strong and provide ongoing affection and support to help alleviate the sense of loss when you leave therapy.

The timing of your graduation will be guided by your needs. Most of the incest victims in my groups take a year to a year and a half to work through the treatment cycle. If your parents are unusually supportive, as Dan's mother was, that time may be shorter. If you elect to cut off your relationship, as Connie did with her father, you may need to stay in group somewhat longer to avoid piling one loss (of your group) on top of another (of your parent). I never cease to be amazed at the dramatic changes that occur in this relatively short period of time, especially when you consider how extensive the original damage was.

A New Person

From time to time clients who have graduated contact me to let me know how they are doing in their lives. I was especially delighted and touched by a letter I received recently from one of my first graduates, a young woman named Patty.

Patty was in one of the first incest victims' groups I conducted. She was then 16 years old. I mentioned Patty briefly in chapter 7; she was the little girl whose father threatened to put her up for adoption if she didn't submit to him. I had not heard from her for many years, but I remembered that she had been unable to confront her father because he had disappeared several years before she started treatment. Here's what she wrote:

> Dear Susan,
>
> I wanted to write and thank you again for helping me become a new person. Thanks to you and to the group, I am really okay.
>
> I am married to a great guy, we have three kids, and I have learned to trust again. I think because of what I went through I am a better mom. My kids know not to let people touch them in the wrong places and they know if it happened they could tell me and I'd be on their side.
>
> I finally did confront my dad. It took some doing, but I tracked him down and told him how I felt about him. His only answer was, "I am a sick person." Never once did he say he was sorry. But you were right, it didn't matter. I just needed to put the blame where it belonged and I felt better. Thank you for your love. I owe my life to you.
>
> Love always,
> Patty

Patty is not unusual. Though life may look grim from the perspective of an incest victim, therapy *does* work. No matter how low you feel, there is a better life for you, a life of self-respect and freedom from guilt, fear, and shame. All the people you've met in this chapter have moved from despair to health. You can too.

15 | Breaking the Cycle

Shortly after the publication of *Men Who Hate Women & the Women Who Love Them*, a woman named Janet wrote to say that she had just read my book:

> I recognized my husband and myself on every page, and what I realized was that not only was my husband abusive but that I had come from several generations of victimized women and abusive men. Your book gave me both the courage and the conviction to make it stop here. I'm not sure my husband is willing to change and I'm not sure whether I will stay with him. But I *am* sure that from now on, my children will see a mother who will no longer accept abuse of any kind and who will not allow them to be verbally abused either. My sons will not grow up believing that it's okay to be abusive to women and my daughter will not be programmed to be a victim. Thank you for leading the way.

Even though the cast of characters may change, the repetitive cycle of toxic behavior can remain for generations on end. The family drama may look and sound different from generation to generation, but all toxic patterns are remarkably similar in their outcome: pain and suffering.

Janet was bravely confronting the long-established patterns of abuse and passivity in her family. By changing her behavior and setting limits on her husband's emotional abuse, Janet had taken a giant step to ensure that her children would be freed from the power of the family legacy. She was breaking the cycle.

The phrase "breaking the cycle" was originally coined in relation to child abuse—preventing a battered child from growing up to beat his own children. But I've expanded the term to include *all* forms of abuse.

For me, breaking the cycle means to stop acting like a victim, or to stop acting like your abusive or inadequate parent. You no longer play the helpless, dependent child with your partners, children, friends, colleagues, authority figures, and parents. And you get help if you find yourself striking out at your spouse or children in ways that make you ashamed. Though the changes you make begin with yourself, you will find the effects to be much broader-reaching. By breaking the cycle, you are protecting your children from the toxic beliefs, rules, and experiences that colored so much of your childhood. You may be changing the nature of your family interactions for generations to come.

"I Can Be There for My Children"

One of the most effective ways of breaking the cycle is to make the commitment to be more emotionally available to your children than your parents were to you.

Melanie realized that just because she didn't get love and nurturing from her parents didn't mean she couldn't give it to her children. Even though it was a struggle for her to remain vigilant against old habits, her commitment was firm:

> I was so scared to have children. I just didn't know what kind of mother I was going to be. It's been really hard. There were a lot of times I screamed at them and told them to go to their rooms and leave me alone. I mean how dare they be so damned needy and demanding. But since I've been in therapy, I realize that's exactly how my mother treated me. So when I'm feeling low, I really make an effort not to shut them out. I have to reach way deep inside myself, but I do it. I'm not perfect, but at least I'm doing something to be better. Dammit, the buck's got to stop here!

Melanie took specific steps to heal herself. After she confronted her mother, the two women were able to talk much more openly about their feelings and experiences. Melanie learned that she was the product of several generations of distant, helpless mothers. It was exciting to see her take personal responsibility for not repeating those patterns with her own children.

In addition to her work in therapy, Melanie enrolled in a parents' support group. She had made a commitment to be a better parent, but because her only role models—her parents—were so inadequate, she wasn't sure what being a good parent entailed. She had never seen how a good parent acts. The parents' group helped ease many of her understandable fears and helped her deal with everyday domestic crises without either withdrawing or becoming panicked by her children's neediness.

Melanie also found new ways of taking better care of herself and of combating her inner emptiness. She made new friends, both from her parenting group and in a folk-dancing class that I suggested she join. She became much less vulnerable to her old pattern of attaching to troubled men and becoming their self-sacrificing caretaker.

"I Swore I Wouldn't Be Like My Father"

We began this book with Gordon, the physician whose father had beaten him with a belt. After six months of therapy, he had fully accepted the fact that he had been an abused child. He had done his letter writing, his role playing, and his confrontation with his parents. As he gradually released much of the pain from his past, he began to see how he had perpetuated the cycle of abuse in his own marriage.

Gordon: I swore a hundred times over that I wouldn't be like my father, but when I look back, I guess I treated my wife just like he treated me. I had the same training and got the same results.

Susan: Love and abuse were linked for you as a child. Your father represented both, sometimes at the same time. It makes sense that you should get them mixed up.

Gordon: I really thought I was different because I didn't physically abuse my wife. But I abused her with words and I punished her with my moods. It's like I left home but I took my father with me.

Throughout Gordon's life, he had denied the fact that his father had been abusive; throughout Gordon's marriage, he had denied the fact that he himself was abusive. But in fact, Gordon had merely substituted one kind of abuse for another. Gordon's father had controlled him through physical violence and pain; Gordon had controlled his wife through verbal violence and emotional pain. Gordon had become a rationalizer, a victimizer, and a tyrant just like his father.

As long as Gordon denied that he was, in a way, repeating his father's abusive behavior, he was not aware that he had a choice to make. If you don't see the cycle, you can't choose to break it. It took Gordon's wife's departure to make him face the truth.

Gordon was fortunate in that his hard work paid off. His wife, seeing the difference in him, recently agreed to a trial reconciliation. He has stopped intimidating and belittling her. He has dealt with his anger at the source instead of displacing it onto his wife. He is able to talk openly to her about his fears and abusive childhood. The cycle has been broken.

"My Kids Won't Have to Grow Up with an Alcoholic"

Glenn—who made the mistake of taking his alcoholic father into business with him—swore that he would never have anything to do with another alcoholic. Nonetheless, he found the cycle of alcoholism continuing in his own family. He had married an alcoholic, and his teenage children were in danger of becoming alcohol and drug abusers.

> I didn't think my kids were going to have the same problems I did, because I don't drink. But their mother drinks a lot and she refuses to get help. It really scared the hell out of me when I came home from work one night and found Denise sharing a case of beer with our two teenage boys. The three of them were loaded. I found out this wasn't the first time. My God, Susan, I don't drink and I still can't get alcohol out of my life. This has got to stop!

Glenn was no longer the timid, nervous man I had first met. He was willing to be far more confrontive with his wife, Denise, than he had ever been before. He knew he had to take forceful action if he was to break the cycle of alcoholism before it ensnared his children. He finally threatened to leave his wife—a threat he was prepared to carry out—unless she agreed to get help. As a result, Denise enrolled in Alcoholics Anonymous and their two children enrolled in Alateen, the Twelve Step program for young people.

If you are the adult child of an alcoholic, you are at significant risk to perpetuate the cycle of alcoholism in your own family. Even if, as in Glenn's case, you don't abuse alcohol yourself, you may very well gravitate toward a partner who does. When this happens, your children will grow up with the same alcoholic/enabler role models as you did. Unless you break the cycle, there is a strong likelihood that they in turn will become either alcoholics or enablers.

"I Don't Want to Hurt My Child"

In chapter 6 I introduced Holly, who was referred to me by the courts after having been reported for physically abusing her young son. I knew that to truly break the cycle, Holly would have to work on two tracks: the past and the present. But in her first few sessions I focused almost exclusively on techniques that would enable her to achieve the impulse control she so desperately needed. She had to regain control of her day-to-day life, which meant gaining control of her anger, before she'd be ready to begin the lengthier process of dealing with the pain of her childhood.

I insisted that Holly attend weekly meetings of Parents Anonymous, an extremely supportive self-help group for abusive parents. At P.A., Holly found a "sponsor"—someone to call if she felt she was in danger of hurting her son. The sponsor could then intervene by calming Holly, by offering advice, or even by coming over to help defuse the situation.

As Holly worked with P.A. on controlling her tendency to strike out under stress, we took a different but parallel approach in her therapy sessions. The first thing I wanted Holly to learn was to identify those physical sensations that preceded her angry or abusive outbursts. Anger has a lot of physiological components. I told Holly that her body was a barometer that would tell her what was going on if only she'd pay attention. As Holly began to tune in to the body sensations that she typically experienced before she became violent, she was surprised to discover how many she could identify:

> I didn't believe you when you told me, Susan, but it's true! When I get mad, I can feel my neck and shoulders getting real tight. A lot of grinding and gurgling goes on in my stomach. My jaw clenches up. I breathe real fast. My heart pounds like a sledgehammer. And I get hot tears behind my eyes.

These physical sensations were Holly's storm warnings. I told her that it was her responsibility to heed the warnings and avoid the storm. In the past, she would either yell or hit her son to release the enormous tension inside her. She had to find alternatives to these automatic reactions if she was going to break her family cycle of abuse.

Once Holly learned to recognize the physical signs of her rising anger, it was time to come up with specific alternative *responses* to those feelings. We talked a lot about the difference between response and reaction, but Holly had been on automatic pilot for so long that she had a very tough time thinking up new behaviors. To help get her started, I asked her what she wished her parents would have done instead of acting out their violence against her. She replied:

> I wished they had just walked away until they were calm. Walked around the block or something.

I suggested she could do just that the next time she got angry. Then I asked her what other things she wished her parents had done that she could apply to herself.

> I could count to ten . . . knowing me, I'd better make that fifty. I could tell my son I don't want to hurt him and tell him to go to another room for a while. Or I could call my sponsor and talk to her until I got it together.

I congratulated Holly on coming up with some excellent behavioral strategies. Over the next several months she was very excited about the changes she was making in managing her feelings and impulsive behavior. Once she saw that she could control herself, that she wasn't doomed to behave like her mother, she was ready to tackle the difficult task of dealing with her own pain as an abused child.

"I Won't Leave My Kids Alone with My Father"

Janine—who was molested by her father and spent the next twenty years trying to recapture his love—came out of her confrontation with a new sense of confidence. One of the members of her group asked her how she was handling her parents' relationship with her eight-year-old daughter, Rachel. Janine told the group that she had set very strict ground rules for how her parents could spend time with their granddaughter.

> I told them that there was no way I would leave Rachel alone with them. I said, "You know, Dad, nothing's changed. You haven't gotten any therapy. You're still the same person who abused me. Why should I trust you with my daughter?" Then I told my mother I had no faith in her ability to guarantee Rachel's safety. After all, she was in the house when he molested *me*.

Janine recognized what many incest victims do not—that breaking the cycle also means protecting other children from the abuser. Incest is a mysterious compulsion. The aggressor who molests his own daughter often goes on to molest his grandchildren or any other children who are available to him. Janine had no way of predicting whether her father would repeat his incestuous behavior, so she wisely chose to be cautious.

Janine also went to her local bookstore and bought her daughter a number of books written to help children learn the difference between healthy affection and inappropriate sexual behavior. There are also videotapes available on this subject. The object of these materials is not to scare the child but to calmly teach him or her about a subject that most parents find uncomfortable but that all children need to be aware of.

At my insistence, Janine took one more brave and healing step:

> I'm telling everybody in the family. You convinced me that I'm not only responsible for protecting Rachel, but all the other kids in the family, too. I mean, my father has access to all of them. Not everybody's thrilled with my decision, especially my parents. But they're going to have to deal with that. For years I kept my mouth shut because I thought I was protecting the family when I was really protecting my father. But by not telling, I was endangering the kids in the family.

Even though Janine acted responsibly and courageously, not everyone was grateful for the information. In a typical incest family, some of your relatives will thank you for telling, others flat-out won't believe you, while others may become enraged and accuse you of lying or of betraying your parents. As with confrontation, the response of other family members determines to a large extent the nature of your future relationship with them. Some of your family relationships may suffer, but sometimes that's the price you have to pay to protect children. Incest can exist only in a conspiracy of silence. Breaking that silence is a vital part of breaking the cycle.

"I'm Sorry I Hurt You"

One of the hallmarks of toxic parents is that they rarely, if ever, apologize for their destructive behavior. That's why apologizing to the people you may have hurt—especially your own children—is an important part of breaking the cycle. You may find this embarrassing or may see it as a sign of weakness. You may even be afraid that apologies will diminish your authority, but I've found that children will respect you all the more for it. Even a child can sense that a volunteered apology is a sign of character and courage. A heartfelt apology is one of the most healing, cycle-breaking actions you will ever take.

As Holly worked through the pain of her abusive childhood, she realized that she wanted to apologize to her son. But she was afraid to. She couldn't figure out what to say. I used role playing to help her. In our next session, I moved my chair close to hers and took both her hands in mine. I asked her to imagine that she was her son, Stuart. I would play the role of Holly. I asked "Stuart" to tell me how the abuse made him feel.

> **HOLLY (as Stuart):** Mom, I really love you, but I'm really scared of you, too. When you get crazy and start hitting me, I feel like you must really hate me. Half the time I don't even know what I did. I try to be good, but . . . Mom, please don't hit me anymore. . . .

Holly stopped, fighting off tears. She was experiencing her son's pain as well as her own. She would have liked to have said to her mother the things she imagined her son saying to her. She determined to go home and apologize to Stuart that night.

The following week, she came in glowing. Apologizing to Stuart hadn't been nearly as hard as she had expected. She just thought of the things she had always longed to hear from her own parents. She explained:

> I told him: "Baby, I've done some things that hurt you a lot and I'm really ashamed. I had no right to hit you. I had no right to call you bad names. You didn't do anything to deserve that. You are a terrific kid. It was me, honey, all me, but I'm finally getting the help I should have gotten a long time ago. See, my parents beat up on me real bad and I never knew how much anger I had inside of me. I've learned a lot of new ways to behave when I get mad and you've probably noticed that I don't lose it so bad anymore. So I honestly don't think I'm going to hit you anymore. But if I do, I want you to go next door and get help. I don't ever want to hurt you again. It's bad for both of us. I really love you, honey. I'm really sorry."

When you apologize to your children, you are teaching them to trust their feelings and perceptions. You are saying, "The things I did that you thought were unfair *were* unfair. You were right to feel that way." You also show them that even you can make mistakes, but that you are willing to take responsibility for them. The message there is that it's okay for your children to make mistakes, too, as long as they take responsibility as well. By apologizing, you are truly modeling loving behavior.

You have within you the power to change your children's destiny. When you free yourself from the legacy of guilt, self-hatred, and anger, you also free your children. When you interrupt family patterns and break the cycle, you give a priceless gift to your children, and to their children, and to the children who will follow. You are molding the future.

Epilogue

Letting Go of the Struggle

In the movie *War Games*, a U.S. government computer was programmed to start a global nuclear war. All attempts to alter the computer's program were futile. However, at the last second, the computer stopped itself, saying: "Interesting game. The only way to win is not to play."

The same could be said of the game that so many of *us* continue to play: trying to get toxic parents to change. We struggle to do whatever it takes to get them to become loving and accepting of us. This struggle can drain our energy and fill our days with turmoil and pain. Yet, it's futile. The only way to win is to not play.

It's time to stop playing, to let go of the struggle. This does not mean you have to let go of your parents; it *does* mean you have to let go of:

- trying to get your parents to change so you can feel better

- trying to figure out what you are supposed to do to get their love
- being so emotionally reactive to them
- the fantasy that one day they are going to give you the caring support you deserve

Like many adult children of toxic parents, you may know, on an intellectual level, that if you haven't gotten emotional nurturing from your parents by now, chances are you're not going to get it. But this understanding rarely filters down to the feeling level. The striving child within you probably still clings to the hope that someday your parents—no matter how limited they are—will see how wonderful you are and will give you their love. You may have a heartbreaking determination to make up for your crimes even if you're not sure of the charges, but when you go back to your toxic parents for the nourishment and validation that you missed as a child, it's a lot like going back to an empty well for water. Your bucket is going to come up dry.

Letting Go and Moving On

For many years, Sandy—whose religious parents relentlessly harangued her about her abortion—had been locked in the typical determined struggle to get her parents to change. It took great courage for her to recognize the hopelessness of her hope that she might somehow unlock her parents' love and acceptance.

> All these years, I believed that I had really wonderful parents and that I was the problem. It was really hard for me to admit that my parents don't know how to love me. They know how to control me, they know how to criticize me, they know how to make me feel guilty and bad, but they don't know how to let me be me, how to respect me. They give or take back their love depending on whether or not they think I'm a good girl.

> I know that that's not going to change. They are who they are, and I have better things to do than to keep trying to get them to be different.

Sandy had come a long way from her need to deify her parents. She had confronted them about their reaction to her abortion and had received some minimal acknowledgment from her mother that they were not as supportive as they might have been. However, they continued to make excessive demands on her time and her life.

Sandy asked me to help her work out some things to say that would allow her to set limits on her parents' visits, her availability to them, and their attempts to control her with guilt and criticism. Here are a few of the statements that Sandy and I came up with:

- Mom and Dad, I know that it means a lot to you to spend time with me. But I have my own life now and I'm not willing to make myself available to you whenever you want.
- I'm not going to let you attack me anymore. You have a right to your opinions, but you don't have a right to be cruel or belittling to me. If you start, I'm going to stop you.
- I can appreciate that this will upset you, but I'm going to be saying "no" to you a lot more than I have in the past. I'm not going to spend every Sunday with you. And I'm no longer willing to have you come over without calling first.
- I know that all this means there are going to be a lot of changes, and I know changes are scary. But I believe that they're healthy changes. I know we can come out of this with a better relationship.

Sandy was truly transforming the destructive interaction between herself and her parents. She set reasonable limits on their intrusive, controlling behavior while at the same time making no attempt to change their attitudes and beliefs.

One of the most difficult parts of letting go of the struggle is letting your parents be who they are. You don't have to lie still while they ride roughshod over you, but when they try, you do have to learn to tolerate your anxiety and control your reactions.

As Sandy expected, her parents were very upset with her new behavior. They didn't acknowledge that they had been intruding in her life and treating her like a child, but Sandy didn't need their acknowledgment. She had taken control of her life. Over time, her parents grudgingly accepted her new ground rules.

Sandy had been expending a lot of energy on her struggle with her parents. Now that she had let go of the struggle, she could redirect that energy toward her marriage and her personal goals. She and her husband actively set aside time to talk, to make plans, to make love, and to give their relationship the attention it needed. She also started to work toward her goal of someday owning a florist shop. About two years after she left therapy I was delighted to receive a flyer announcing the opening of Bouquets by Sandy.

You may continue to behave as if you were little or helpless because you are waiting for your parents to give you permission to be an adult. But the permission is within *you*, not them. When you truly let go of the struggle, you will find that you no longer have a need to sabotage your life.

Redefining Love

Love involves more than just feelings. It is also a way of behaving. When Sandy said, "My parents don't know how to love me," she was saying that they don't know how to behave in loving ways. If you were to ask Sandy's parents, or almost any other toxic parents, if they love their children, most of them would answer emphatically that they do. Yet, sadly, most of their children have always felt unloved. What toxic parents call "love" rarely translates into nourishing, comforting behavior.

Most adult children of toxic parents grow up feeling tremendous confusion about what love means and how it's supposed to feel. Their parents did extremely unloving things to them in the name of love. They came to understand love as something chaotic, dramatic, confusing, and often painful—something they had to give up their own dreams and desires for. Obviously, that's *not* what love is all about.

Loving behavior doesn't grind you down, keep you off balance, or create feelings of self-hatred. Love doesn't hurt, it feels good. Loving behavior nourishes your emotional well-being. When someone is being loving to you, you feel accepted, cared for, valued, and respected. Genuine love creates feelings of warmth, pleasure, safety, stability, and inner peace.

Once you understand what love is, you may come to the realization that your parents couldn't or didn't know how to be loving. This is one of the saddest truths you will ever have to accept. But when you clearly define and acknowledge your parents' limitations, and the losses you suffered because of them, you open a door in your life for people who will love you the way you deserve to be loved—the real way.

Trusting Yourself

When you were young, like all children, you used your parents' approval or disapproval as a gauge to determine whether you were good or bad. Because the approval of your toxic parents was so distorted, that gauge often required you to sacrifice your own version of reality in order to believe in something that didn't seem right to you. As an adult, you may still be making that sacrifice.

However, through the exercises in this book, you are shifting the source of your gauge from within your parents to within yourself. You are learning to trust your own perception of reality. You will discover that even when your parents don't agree with you or don't approve of what you're doing, you will be able to tolerate the anxiety because you don't need their validation anymore. You are becoming self-defined.

The more self-defined and independent you become, the less

your parents are going to like it. Remember, it is the nature of toxic parents to be threatened by change. Toxic parents are often the last people in the world to accept your new, healthier behavior. That's why it is so important that you trust your own feelings and perceptions. In time, your parents may accept the new you. You may even develop something resembling an adult-to-adult relationship with them. But they also may dig in even deeper and fight to maintain the status quo. Either way, it's up to you to free yourself from the destructive rituals of your family behavior patterns.

Becoming a true adult is not a linear process. It will take you upward, downward, forward, backward, and inside out. Expect to falter; expect to make mistakes. You will never be totally free of anxiety, fear, guilt, and confusion. No one is. But these demons will no longer control you. That is the key.

As you gain more control over your past and present relationship with your parents, you will discover that your other relationships, especially your relationship with yourself, will improve dramatically. You will have the freedom, perhaps for the first time, to enjoy your own life.

Suggested Reading

Beattie, Melody. *Codependent No More*. New York: Harper/Hazeldon, 1987.

Black, Claudia. *It Will Never Happen to Me*. Denver: M.A.C. Publishers, 1982.

Bowen, Murray. *Family Therapy in Clinical Practice*. New York: Jason Aronson, 1978.

Bradshaw, John. *Healing the Shame That Binds You*. Pompano Beach: Health Communications Inc. 1988.

Clarke, Jean Illsley. *Self-esteem: A Family Affair*. Minneapolis: Winston Press, 1978.

Forward, Susan, and Craig Buck. *Betrayal of Innocence: Incest and Its Devastation* (revised edition). New York: Viking Penguin, 1988.

Fossum, Merle A., and Marilyn J. Mason. *Facing Shame: Families in Recovery*. New York: W. W. Norton & Co., 1986.

Halpern, Howard M. *Cutting Loose: An Adult Guide to Coming to Terms with Your Parents*. New York: Bantam Books, 1978.

Herman, Judith. *Father-Daughter Incest*. Cambridge: Harvard University Press, 1982.

Kempee, C. H. *The Battered Child.* Chicago: University of Chicago Press, 1980.

Miller, Alice. *For Your Own Good: Hidden Cruelty in Child Rearing and the Roots of Violence.* New York: Farrar Straus Giroux, 1983.

Miller, Alice. *Prisoners of Childhood.* New York: Basic Books, 1981.

Weissberg, Michael, M.D. *Dangerous Secrets: Maladaptive Responses to Stress.* New York: W. W. Norton & Co., 1983.

Whitfield, Charles L. *Healing the Child Within.* Pompano Beach: Health Communications Inc., 1987.

Woititz, Janet Geringer. *Adult Children of Alcoholics.* Pompano Beach: Health Communications Inc., 1983.

About The Authors

SUSAN FORWARD, PH.D., is an internationally renowned therapist, lecturer, and author of the number-one *New York Times* bestsellers *Toxic Parents* and *Men Who Hate Women and the Women Who Love Them*, as well as *Obsessive Love; Betrayal of Innocence: Incest and Its Devastation; Money Demons; Emotional Blackmail; When Your Lover Is a Liar;* and *Toxic In-Laws*. In addition to her private practice, for five years she hosted a daily ABC talk radio program. She has also served widely as a group therapist, instructor, and consultant in many Southern California medical and psychiatric facilities, and she formed the first private sexual abuse treatment center in California. She lives in Los Angeles and has two grown children.

Susan Forward maintains offices in Sherman Oaks, California. For further information, call (818) 986-1161.

CRAIG BUCK, a film and television writer and producer, has also written extensively on human behavior for many national magazines and newspapers. He is the co-author, with Susan Forward, of *Toxic Parents, Obsessive Love, Betrayal of Innocence*, and *Money Demons*. He lives in Los Angeles with his wife and daughter.

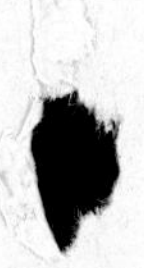